CANALS & CROSSROADS

An Illustrated History
of the Albany, New York
Roman Catholic Diocese

Written on the Occasion
of its Sesquicentennial
1847-1997

By Sally Light

For reprint permission and other information, write:

The Evangelist Newspaper
40 N. Main Ave.
Albany, 12203

Library of Congress Catalog Card Number: 97-73489

ISBN: 0-9658982-0-2

Edited by:
James Breig

Book Design by:
Carol Raabe
Donna Wait Lesson

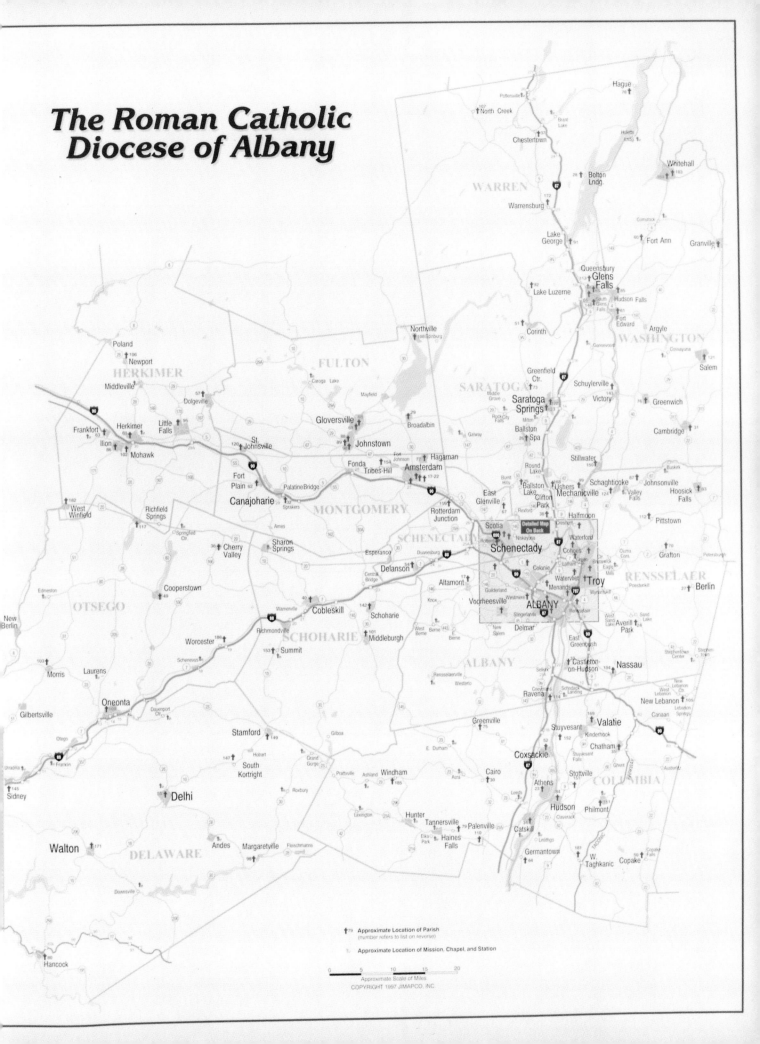

The Roman Catholic Diocese of Albany

Approximate Location of Parish
(number refers to list on reverse)

Approximate Location of Mission, Chapel, and Station

0   5   10   15   20
Approximate Scale of Miles
COPYRIGHT 1997 JIMAPCO, INC.

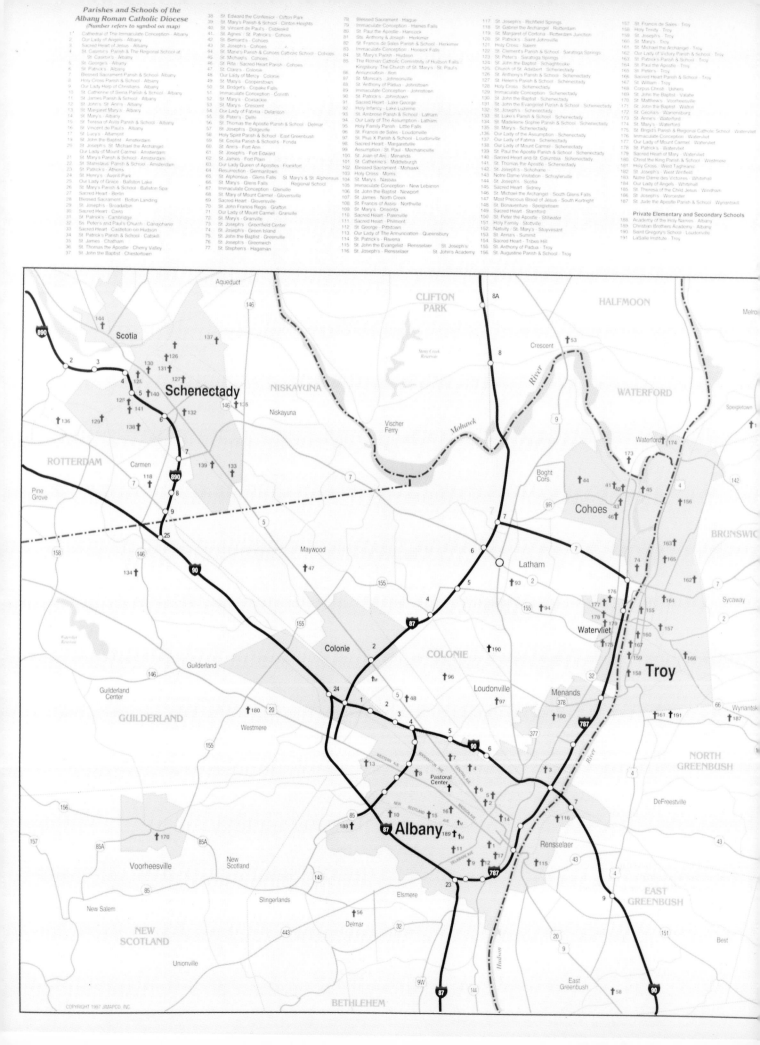

Parishes and Schools of the Albany Roman Catholic Diocese
(Number refers to symbol on map)

1. Cathedral of The Immaculate Conception - Albany
2. Our Lady of Angels - Albany
3. Sacred Heart of Jesus - Albany
4. St. Casimir's Parish & The Regional School at St. Casimir's - Albany
5. St. George's - Albany
6. St. Patrick's - Albany
7. Blessed Sacrament Parish & School - Albany
8. Holy Cross Parish & School - Albany
9. Our Lady Help of Christians - Albany
10. St. Catherine of Siena Parish & School - Albany
11. St. James Parish & School - Albany
12. St. John's St. Ann's - Albany
13. St. Margaret Mary's - Albany
14. St. Mary's - Albany
15. St. Teresa of Avila Parish & School - Albany
16. St. Vincent de Paul's - Albany
17. St. Lucy's - Altamont
18. St. John the Baptist - Amsterdam
19. St. Joseph's - St. Michael the Archangel - Amsterdam
    Our Lady of Mount Carmel - Amsterdam
20. St. Mary's Parish & School - Amsterdam
21. St. Stanislaus' Parish & School - Amsterdam
22. St. Patrick's - Athens
23. St. Henry's - Averill Park
24. Our Lady of Grace - Ballston Lake
25. St. Mary's Parish & School - Ballston Spa
26. Sacred Heart - Berlin
27. Blessed Sacrament - Bolton Landing
28. St. Joseph's - Broadalbin
29. Sacred Heart - Cairo
30. St. Patrick's - Cambridge
31. St. Peters and Paul's Church - Canajoharie
32. Sacred Heart - Castleton on Hudson
33. St. Patrick's Parish & School - Catskill
34. St. James - Chatham
35. St. Thomas the Apostle - Cherry Valley
36. St. John the Baptist - Chestertown
37. St. Edward the Confessor - Clifton Park
38. St. Mary's Parish & School - Clifton Heights
39. St. Vincent de Paul's - Cobleskill
40. St. Agnes - St. Patrick's - Cohoes
41. St. Bernard's - Cohoes
42. St. Joseph's - Cohoes
43. St. Marie's Parish & Cohoes Catholic - Cohoes
44. St. Michael's - Cohoes
45. St. Rita - Sacred Heart Parish - Cohoes
46. St. Clare's - Colonie
47. Our Lady of Mercy - Colonie
48. St. Mary's - Coopers town
49. St. Anthony of Padua - Corinth
50. Immaculate Conception - Corinth
51. Sacred Heart - Coxsackie
52. St. Mary's - Crescent
53. St. Peter's - Delhi
54. Our Lady of Fatima - Delanson
55. St. Thomas the Apostle Parish & School - Delmar
56. Holy Spirit Parish & School - East Greenbush
57. St. Cecilia Parish & Schools - Fonda
58. St. Ann's - Fort Ann
59. St. Joseph's - Fort Edward
60. St. James - Fort Plain
61. Our Lady Queen of Apostles - Frankfort
62. Resurrection - Germantown
63. St. Alphonsus - Glens Falls   St. Mary's & St. Alphonsus Regional School
64. St. Joseph's - Dolgeville
65. Immaculate Conception - Glenville
66. St. Mary of Mount Carmel - Glenville
67. Sacred Heart - Gloversville
68. St. John Francis Regis - Grafton
69. Our Lady of Mount Carmel - Granville
70. St. Mary's - Granville
71. St. George - Pittstown
72. St. Joseph's - Greenfield Center
73. St. Joseph's - Green Island
74. St. John the Baptist - Greenville
75. St. Joseph's - Greenwich
76. St. Stephen's - Hagaman
77. Blessed Sacrament - Hague
78. Immaculate Conception - Harries Falls
79. St. Paul the Apostle - Hancock
80. Sts. Anthony & Joseph - Herkimer
81. St. Francis St. Sales Parish & School - Herkimer
82. Immaculate Conception - Hoosick Falls
83. St. Mary's Parish - Hudson
84. The Roman Catholic Community of Hudson Falls - Kingsbury: The Church of St. Mary's - St. Paul's
85. Annunciation - Ilion
86. St. Monica's - Johnsonville
87. St. Anthony of Padua - Johnstown
88. Immaculate Conception - Johnstown
89. St. Patrick's - Johnstown
90. Sacred Heart - Lake George
91. Holy Infancy - Lake Luzerne
92. St. Ambrose Parish & School - Latham
93. Our Lady of The Assumption - Latham
94. Holy Family Parish - Little Falls
95. St. Francis de Sales - Loudonville
96. St. Pius X Parish & School - Loudonville
97. Sacred Heart - Margaretville
98. Assumption - St. Paul - Mechanicville
99. St. Joan of Arc - Menands
100. St. Catherine's - Middleburgh
101. Blessed Sacrament - Mohawk
102. Holy Cross - Morris
103. St. Mary's - Nassau
104. Immaculate Conception - New Lebanon
105. St. John the Baptist - Newport
106. St. James - North Creek
107. St. Francis of Assisi - Northville
108. St. Mary's - Oneonta
109. Sacred Heart - Stamford
110. Sacred Heart - Philmont
111. Our Lady of The Annunciation - Queensbury
112. St. Patrick's - Ravena
113. St. John the Evangelist - Rensselaer   St. Joseph's - Rensselaer   St. John's Academy
114. Immaculate Conception - Hague

115. St. Joseph's - Richfield Springs
116. St. Gabriel the Archangel - Rotterdam
117. St. Margaret of Cortona - Rotterdam Junction
118. St. Patrick's - Saint Johnsville
119. Holy Cross - Salem
120. St. Clement's Parish & School - Saratoga Springs
121. St. Peter's - Saratoga Springs
122. St. John the Baptist - Schaghticoke
123. Church of St. Adalbert - Schenectady
124. St. Anthony's Parish & School - Schenectady
125. St. Helen's Parish & School - Schenectady
126. Holy Cross - Schenectady
127. Immaculate Conception - Schenectady
128. St. John the Baptist - Schenectady
129. St. John the Evangelist Parish & School - Schenectady
130. St. Josephs - Schenectady
131. St. Luke's Parish & School - Schenectady
132. St. Madeleine Sophie Parish & School - Schenectady
133. St. Mary's - Schenectady
134. Our Lady of the Assumption - Schenectady
135. Our Lady of Fatima - Schenectady
136. Our Lady of Mount Carmel - Schenectady
137. St. Paul the Apostle Parish & School - Schenectady
138. Sacred Heart and St. Columbia - Schenectady
139. St. Thomas the Apostle - Schenectady
140. St. Joseph's - Schohane
141. Notre Dame Visitation - Schuylerville
142. St. Joseph's - Scotia
143. St. Michael the Archangel - South Glens Falls
144. Most Precious Blood of Jesus - South Kortright
145. St. Bonaventure - Speigletown
146. Sacred Heart - Stamford
147. St. Peter the Apostle - Stillwater
148. Holy Family - Stuttville
149. Nativity - St. Mary's - Stuyvesant
150. St. Anna's - Summit
151. Sacred Heart - Tribes Hill
152. St. Anthony of Padua - Troy
153. St. Augustine Parish & School - Troy

154. St. Francis de Sales - Troy
155. Holy Trinity - Troy
156. St. Joseph's - Troy
157. St. Mary's - Troy
158. St. Michael the Archangel - Troy
159. Our Lady of Victory Parish & School - Troy
160. St. Patrick's Parish & School - Troy
161. St. Paul the Apostle - Troy
162. St. Peter's - Troy
163. St. William - Troy
164. Corpus Christi - Ushers
165. St. John the Baptist - Valatie
166. St. Matthew's - Voorheesville
167. St. John the Baptist - Waltor
168. St. Mary's - Waterford
169. St. Brigid's Parish & Regional Catholic School - Watervliet
170. Immaculate Conception - Watervliet
171. Our Lady of Mount Carmel - Watervliet
172. St. Patrick's - Watervliet
173. Sacred Heart of Mary - Watervliet
174. Christ the King Parish & School - Westmere
175. Holy Cross - West Taghkanic
176. St. Joseph's - West Winfield
177. Notre Dame des Victories - Whitehall
178. Our Lady of Angels - Whitehall
179. St. Theresa of the Child Jesus - Windham
180. St. Joseph's - Worcester
181. St. Jude the Apostle Parish & School - Wynanskill

Private Elementary and Secondary Schools
188. Academy of the Holy Names - Albany
189. Christian Brothers Academy - Albany
190. Saint Gregory's School - Loudonville
191. LaSalle Institute - Troy

PARISH CLUSTER GROUPS

ALBANY CITY DEANERY:
Rev. Robert Hohenstein, Dean

Center City:
St. Patrick's
Our Lady of Angels
St. Casimir's
Sacred Heart/St. Joseph's
Black Apostolate
Spanish Apostolate
Vietnamese Apostolate

Middle:
St. Vincent De Paul
Holy Cross
Blessed Sacrament
St. Mary's
St. Margaret Mary's

South End:
Cathedral of the
  Immac. Conception
St. John's/St. Ann's
Our Lady Help of
  Christians
St. Thomas, Delmar
St. Patrick's, Ravena

West:
St. Catherine of Siena
St. Teresa of Avila
St. James

SUBURBAN ALBANY DEANERY:
Rev. James Daley, Dean

Cluster 1:
St. Ambrose, Latham
O. L. of the Assumption,
  Latham

Cluster 2:
St. Lucy's, Altamont
Christ the King,
  Westmere
St. Matthew's,
  Voorheesville

Cluster 3:
St. Clare's, Colonie
Our Lady of Mercy,
  Colonie
St. Francis de Sales,
  Loudonville

Cluster 4:
St. Pius X, Loudonville
St. Joan of Arc,
  Menands

NORTHERN ALBANY COUNTY DEANERY:
Rev. Lawrence McTavey, Dean

Cohoes:
St. Marie's
St. Agnes/St. Patrick's
St. Bernard's
St. Rita/Sacred Heart
St. Joseph's
St. Michael's

Waterford:
St. Mary's
St. Ann's
St. Augustine's, Troy

Watervliet:
St. Patrick's
Sacred Heart of Mary
Our Lady of Mt. Carmel
Immaculate Conception
St. Brigid's
St. Joseph's, Green Island

COLUMBIA COUNTY DEANERY:
Rev. Thomas Powers, Dean

Northern sector:
St. Mary's, Stuyvesant Falls/Nativity, Stuyvesant
St. John the Baptist, Valatie
Holy Family, Stottville
Southern sector
Hudson River communities:
Resurrection, Germantown
Holy Cross, West Taghkanic
St. Mary's, Hudson
Lake country communities:
St. Bridget's, Copake Falls
Sacred Heart, Philmont
St. James, Chatham

DELAWARE COUNTY DEANERY:
Rev. Robert Purcell, Dean

Cluster 1:
Sacred Heart, Margaretville
St. John the Baptist, Walton
St. Peter's, Delhi
St. Paul the Apostle,
  Hancock

Cluster 2:
Sacred Heart, Stamford
Most Precious Blood of
  Jesus, So. Kortright

FULTON COUNTY DEANERY:
Rev. Joseph Barker, Dean

Cluster 1:
St. Patrick's, Johnstown
St. Anthony's, Johnstown
Immaculate Conception,
  Johnstown

Cluster 2:
St. Mary of Mt. Carmel,
  Gloversville
Sacred Heart,
  Gloversville
St. Francis, Northville

Cluster 3:
St. Joseph, Broadalbin
St. Stephen's, Hagaman

GREENE COUNTY DEANERY:
Rev. Jeremiah Nunan, Dean

Cluster 1:
St. Patrick's, Catskill
St. Mary's Coxsackie,
St. Patrick's, Athens
St. Mary's, Smith's Landing

Cluster 2:
St. John the Baptist,
  Greenville
Sacred Heart,
  Palenville
Sacred Heart, Cairo
St. Theresa, Windham
Immac. Conception,
  Haines Falls

HERKIMER COUNTY DEANERY:
Rev. Joseph Benintende, Dean

Cluster 1:
Ss. Anthony/Joseph,
  Herkimer
St. Francis de Sales,
  Herkimer
Blessed Sacrament, Mohawk
Holy Family, Little Falls

Cluster 2:
St. Joseph's,
  W. Winfield
St. Joseph's,
  Richfield Springs
Annunciation, Ilion
Our Lady, Queen of
  Apostles, Frankfort

Cluster 3:
St. John the Baptist, Newport
St. Joseph's, Dolgeville

MONTGOMERY COUNTY DEANERY:
Rev. James Gulley, Dean

Cluster 1:
St. Patrick's, St. Johnsville
St. James, Fort Plain
Ss. Peter and Paul,
  Canojoharie

Amsterdam Cluster:
St. Casimir's
St. John the Baptist
St. Stanislaus
St. Joseph's, St.
  Michael's/OLMC
St. Mary's

Cluster 2:
St. Cecilia's, Fonda
Sacred Heart, Tribes Hill

PARISH CLUSTER GROUPS

OTSEGO COUNTY DEANERY:
Rev. Paul Roman, Dean

Cluster 1:
St. Mary's, Oneonta
Sacred Heart, Sidney
St. Joseph's, Worcester
Holy Cross, Morris

Cluster 2:
St. Mary's, Cooperstown
St. Thomas the Apostle,
  Cherry Valley

NO. RENSSELAER COUNTY DEANERY:
Rev. Donald Ophals, Dean

Cluster 1:
St. Anthony's, Troy
St. Mary's, Troy
St. Joseph's/Holy Trinity,
  Troy

Cluster 2:
Sacred Heart, Troy
St. William's, Troy
St. Francis de Sales, Troy
St. Paul's, Troy
Christ Sun of Justice, Troy

Cluster 3:
St. Henry's, Averill Park
St. Michael's, Troy
St. Jude's, Wynantskill

Cluster 4:
Immaculate Conception,
  Hoosick Falls
St. George's, Pittstown
St. Monica's, Johnsonville
St. Bonaventure's,
  Speigletown
St. John the Baptist,
  Schaghticoke
Our Lady of Victory, Troy

Cluster 5:
St. John Francis Regis, Grafton
Sacred Heart, Berlin
Immaculate Conception,
  New Lebanon

Cluster 6:
St. Patrick's, Troy
St. Peter's Troy

SO. RENSSELAER COUNTY DEANERY:
Rev. George St. John, Dean

Cluster 1:
St. John the Evangelist,
  Rensselaer
St. Joseph's, Rensselaer
St. Mary's, Clinton Heights

Cluster 2:
Holy Spirit,
  East Greenbush
St. Mary's, Nassau
Sacred Heart, Castleton

SARATOGA COUNTY DEANERY:
Rev. Edward Pratt, Dean

Cluster 1:
Assumption/St. Paul,
  Mechanicville
St. Peter's, Stillwater
Notre Dame/Visitation,
  Schuylerville

Cluster 2:
St. Edward's, Clifton Park
St. Mary's, Crescent
Corpus Christi, Ushers

Cluster 3:
Our Lady of Grace,
  Ballston Lake
Immaculate Conception,
  Glenville
St. Joseph's, Scotia

Cluster 4:
St. Peter's, Saratoga
St. Clements, Saratoga
St. Joseph's,
  Greenfield Center
St. Mary's, Ballston Spa

SCHENECTADY COUNTY DEANERY:
Rev. John Provost, Dean

Cluster 1:
Our Lady of the Assumption,
  Rotterdam
St. Margaret of Cortona,
  Rotterdam Junction
Immaculate Conception,
  Schenectady

Cluster 2:
St. John the Evangelist,
  Schenectady
St. Mary's, Schenectady
St. Joseph's, Schenectady
Holy Cross, Schenectady

Cluster 3:
St. Anthony's, Schenectady
St. John the Baptist,
  Schenectady

Cluster 4:
St. Helen's, Schenectady
Our Lady of Fatima,
  Schenectady

Cluster 5:
St. Paul the Apostle,
  Schenectady
St. Luke's, Schenectady
Sacred Heart/St. Columba,
  Schenectady

Cluster 6:
St. Gabriel the
  Archangel, Rotterdam
St. Madeleine Sophie,
  Guilderland

Cluster 7:
Our Lady of Mt. Carmel, Schenectady
St. Thomas the Apostle, Schenectady
St. Adalbert's, Schenectady

SCHOHARIE COUNTY DEANERY:
Rev. Thomas Berardi, Dean

St. Vincent de Paul, Cobleskill/St. Mary's,
  Sharon Springs
St. Anna's, Summit
St. Joseph's, Schoharie
St. Catherine's, Middleburgh
Our Lady of Fatima, Delanson

WARREN COUNTY DEANERY:
Rev. Joseph Anselment, Dean

Cluster 1:
Holy Infancy, Lake Luzerne
Imm. Conception, Corinth

Cluster 2:
Blessed Sacrament,
  Hague
St. John's, Chestertown
St. James, North Creek

Cluster 3:
Blessed Sacrament,
  Bolton Landing
St. Cecilia's, Warrensburg
Sacred Heart, Lake George

Cluster 4:
St. Alphonsus, Glens Falls
St. Mary's, Glens Falls
St. Michael's, Glens Falls
Our Lady of the Annun-
  ciation, Queensbury

WASHINGTON COUNTY DEANERY:
Rev. J. Barry Lonergan, Dean

Cluster 1:
Notre Dame, Whitehall
O.L. of Angels, Whitehall
St. Mary's, Granville

Cluster 2:
St. Ann's, Fort Ann
St. Mary's/St. Pauls,
  Hudson Falls
St. Joseph's, Fort Edward

Cluster 3:
St. Joseph's, Greenwich
St. Patrick's, Cambridge
Holy Cross, Salem

TABLE OF CONTENTS

A Message From Bishop Howard J. Hubbard

ALBANY HAS EXPERIENCED A 1997 SPRING TIDE OF ANNIVERSARIES: the Bicentenary of Albany as the capital of New York State, the 200th anniversary of St. Mary's Church in Albany, the Sesquicentennial observance of the Diocese of Albany and various other jubilees. A special anniversary rivets attention on the immediate celebration, and on the people, movements and events of the past that have contributed to the present reality.

"Canals and Crossroads: A Sesquicentennial History of the Albany Diocese" by Sally Light is an incisive and integral part of our celebration of the establishment of our Diocese of Albany on April 23, 1847 and merits our gratitude indeed. To reflect on that 150-year history is to discern the mysterious grace of God's providence, transforming for generation after generation even the most unpromising circumstances into opportunities for advancing the mission of Jesus the Risen Christ in this area.

A diocese encompasses a region that has its own unique story and that is shaped by its surface features and waterways, its indigenous people, its newcomers, its faith communities, its developing commerce, its political climate and its various cultures.

Sally Light's work points out that "the Albany area was still frontier in the 18th century."

The region had witnessed the earlier missionary efforts of the Jesuits, such as those of St. Isaac Jogues. The New York State legislative decision in 1817 to fund the building of the Erie Canal is especially linked with the growth of Catholicism in what became, 30 years later, the Diocese of Albany. The construction of "Clinton's Ditch" brought large numbers of immigrants to this region, many of whom were members of the Catholic Church. Expanding trade and commerce required construction of other waterways, highways, bridges and, later on, railroads for the transportation of products to trade centers.

Our history clearly connects the founding of our early churches not only with the pastoral needs of the people but also with the geographical features, and the trade and commerce of the region.

Two centuries ago, Catholics received ecumenical support in their efforts to establish St. Mary's, the first Roman Catholic church in Albany. That foreshadowed the ecumenical and interfaith cooperation that is part of our history. St. Mary's became the center for circuit-riding priests who ministered to Catholics for whom churches had not yet been built. Today, this historic church — with its unique sculpture of an angel that is part of the skyline — carries on its diverse ministries in downtown Albany.

The spires of our Cathedral of the Immaculate Conception, neighboring the massive Empire State Plaza structures, steadfastly proclaim the transcendence of the living God in the midst of everyday government and business. The command of Jesus our Savior to be "the light of the world" (Mt. 5:14) calls us in our Sesquicentennial Year to renew our mission as God's priestly people and to be such a light for our troubled and violence-torn world.

This superb history by Sally Light offers yet another way for us, during our Sesquicentennial anniversary, to "Honor Tradition and Discover Tomorrow" and will serve as an invaluable resource for years to come.

Bishop Howard J. Hubbard

Author's Note

IN AMERICAN ACADEMIA, HISTORICAL DISCUSSIONS rarely give much more than a fleeting mention to religious occurrences unless one of them is the focus of study. On the flip side, religious historical discussions rarely include the "secular" events that helped shape religious decisions. For example, the New York State trustee law under which all churches were placed was the result of the Protestant emphasis of the Revolutionary leaders, and the 18th-century Enlightenment (and its resulting Deism), which created a climate of tolerance toward Catholics among the intellectual leaders of the Revolution.

The time is ripe to meld history and religion in historical discussions, just as they naturally occurred in real life. At times, a religious particular characterized an event. At other times, war, economics, inventions, dances and photographs, did. Each should be accorded its due when relevant. Although it has a decidedly religious emphasis, this history has attempted to include historical events as they played a role in the development of Catholicism in the Albany Diocese. There are good reasons why anything happens; nothing occurs in a vacuum. Individuals — including Catholics — migrated to upstate New York because of jobs. Once they were here, other needs surfaced associated with eating, housing, counselling, marrying, baptizing, schooling, dying.

Furthermore, in spite of the theological differences, the early churches — Catholic and Protestant alike — shared more similarities than, perhaps, some would like to admit. Priests and ministers had similar educations in the classics. They usually were from the middle class. They had to deal with no funding from the government, and this untested idea of the separation of church and state took years to evolve. Because no religion was state-sanctioned, they were in competition with one another, and, therefore, were more open to what appealed to the general public. At the same time, ministers and priests could not let the laity's preferences run the churches. Much of the population was scattered in pockets without enough people of one religion to justify building a church. Yet churches were built and were sometimes used by more than óne denomination. In many cases, with no other choice, Catholics joined the only church in town if they wanted their children baptized. Many of them went back to the Catholic church as soon as one was built. In Dutch Albany, however, that was not possible for more than 100 years between the Glorious Revolution in 1688 and the building of St. Mary's in 1797.

One item cannot be overemphasized: The early Church in upstate New York was primarily Irish and French with some German. The French influence was localized to the Champlain Valley and the Adirondacks, and their churches operated out of Quebec. While many Irish came after the Famine in 1847, most of the churches established before the Diocese of Albany was born were predominantly Irish with a few German and French. These Irish had primarily

come in the mid-to-late 18th century, with many more arriving between 1818 and 1847.

Because after 1847 the Diocese covered a huge area and because this area was further sub-divided into the dioceses of Ogdensburg and Syracuse, and each of these has written a very complete history of its own, I have chosen to concentrate on the institutions confined to the area of what has been known as the Albany Diocese since 1886. I also have chosen not to dwell on priests who appeared in the early Church in a fleeting or questionable manner. Many of the men who appeared early in the New World were adventure-seekers. There were priests among them who left Europe under questionable circumstances or with questionable credentials.

In writing this document, I have been faithful to the facts as they were found. I have rarely embroidered on them, nor have I frequently imagined what might have happened as if it were the truth. I leave the fun of such flights of fancy up to you. Personally, I find the facts to be more fascinating when put in context.

In some cases, I have found errors in previously published works, often because the writers did not consult the primary sources which usually are hand-written with letters often formed differently from the current practice. It can be a chore to read them until one becomes accustomed to the variations. From reading these, I have found Bishop McNeirny's clearly-written signature, as well as Patrick Keely's. I think they knew how to spell their own names and were proud of their own particular variation. It became fashionable in the clergy-dominant

Above: The class of 1917 from St. Peter's School in Troy.

late 19th- and early 20th-century Church for them to regularize spellings, particularly of Irish surnames, which often exhibited a myriad of spellings for the same name. They were especially fond of adding an "e" before the final "y" in an effort to gentrify the name. That is unfortunate, because once an error is published, it persists and eventually becomes "God's truth" in the minds of many readers resistant to change even when they have the facts in front of them. I imagine poor Bishop McNeirny and Patrick Keely mentally correcting the spellings of their names.

Why the emphasis on such detail? Because inaccuracy in detail breeds inaccuracy in larger, more important items. In one sentence, there can for four or five different references that were brought together to produce the thought. A change in any one detail can distort the meaning of the thought.

When consulting various documents, it is my habit to copy the spelling used in the specific document quoted for two reasons: to give equal value to the different spellings (i.e. not to place a 20th-century value judgment on earlier words) and to show the cavalier attitude with which educated individuals in earlier times addressed spelling. One must recognize that often one person might use a tremendous variety of spellings. Within a document — sometimes one paragraph — the same word may be spelled a variety of ways. In addition to spelling, punctuation is also quoted with faithful adherence to the types of marks — or lack thereof — in the document. Thus, the reader may note unexpected irregularities.

Attention has also been paid to what the geographic areas were called at the time. References to the United States or Canada, for example, have been avoided until the appropriate time period. French and English spellings, sometimes for the same word, have similarly been employed when appropriate.

Finally, contrary to what most people believe, the Roman Catholic Church functions on a grassroots level. One illustration is how a church's name was chosen: It was the first pastor's name (St. Bernard's in Cohoes for Rev. Bernard Van Reith) or a later pastor's name (St.

Above: An early view of St. James Church in Chatham (The V. Whitbeck Studio, Hudson)

James in Chatham had been St. Patrick's), a bishop's sister's name (St. Anna's —originally named St. Anne's — in Summit, named for Bishop Gibbon's sister) or a primary donor's wife's name (St. Catherine's in Middleburgh for Thomas C. Smith's wife) or a real estate agent who had spent many years buying property for the Diocese (St. James in Albany for James Glavin, father of Msgr. Edward Glavin). As the text is read, other examples of grassroots functioning will surface.

In the history of the Roman Catholic Church of the Diocese of Albany, there have been glorious times, as well as sad ones and disappointments; yet prideful times and revitalizing times have always been expressed in the joy that is reflected in the faces of many priests, religious and laity in the Albany Diocese today.

Sally Light

Foreword

Travelling through time along canals and crossroads

ON THURSDAY, APRIL 22, 1847, Catholics in upstate New York enjoyed what an Albany newspaper called a "warm and beautiful" day, with temperatures in or near the 80s. In the afternoon, however, a "strong south wind" started blowing, "accompanied with thunder and lightning." As upstaters went to bed, a nor'easter charged in, and "a large quantity of rain fell."

Beginning the next morning, the temperature dropped 20 degrees in 12 hours and the Hudson River rose so high that the docks along Quay Street in Albany were covered with water, disrupting the markets there.

That portentous weather accompanied what might seem like a very strange event: Catholics who went to sleep in upstate New York on Thursday, April 22, 1847, woke up somewhere else on Friday, April 23. The "somewhere else" was the newborn Albany Diocese, severed overnight from the New York Diocese and sprawling over an area that encompassed everything above New York City to the Canadian border, from Massachusetts and Vermont on the east to beyond Syracuse in the west, and southwest to the Pennsylvania line.

Older Catholics now lived in their third diocese, having been members of the Baltimore Diocese that covered the entire nation when it separated from Great Britain and of the New York Diocese since 1808. That Diocese had grown too large to administer from downstate; hence, the creation of the Albany Diocese (and, at the same time, the Diocese of Buffalo).

However, neither the Albany Argus nor the Albany Evening Journal noted the overnight change. Their news columns focused instead on the war against Mexico, including General Zachary Taylor's victory in Vera Cruz, Admiral Matthew Perry's naval successes in the Gulf, and General Santa Anna's attempts to recapture what had been lost in previous skirmishes and battles. Just eleven years earlier, Santa Anna had been on the winning side — at the Alamo.

In Albany on the 23rd, the Broadway Odeon was hosting a performance by Miss C. Chapman in "French Spy; or the Fall of Algiers." Her acting had rendered her "so deservedly popular" that newspapers declared "the bare announcement" of her appearance "should be sufficient to fill the house." Tickets in the dress circle, the best seats, were 50 cents. Elsewhere that evening, Mr. Fleming was performing "Hamlet." Those not interested in plays could visit the Albany Gallery of Fine Arts on Broadway to view a painting titled "Battle of Lake Erie" for 25 cents. The same quarter of a dollar, spent near the corner of Lydius and South Pearl, would get Albanians into Spalding's North American Circus, which featured clowns, an equestrian troupe and a brass band. Friday was Albany's last chance to see such delights; the circus moved on to Troy the next morning.

At the Boston Depot, about to board the morning train, Levi Otis of Batavia had his pocket picked of two $50 bills drawn from the Troy Bank. In Canajoharie, George W. Caldwell replaced Peter C. Anthony as postmaster. The Albany Evening Journal printed part seven of "Dombey & Son" by Charles Dickens. Schooners named the Andrew Brown and the Lexington, the latter bound for Richmond, were tied up at the Albany pier where five tons of dried apples could be purchased by food brokers. On South Pearl Street, family members and friends mourned 18-year-old Sarah Ann Yates, who had died of consumption at 5 p.m. on the previous day.

The Van Schaack Variety Store at 44 South Market Street offered "an extensive collection of House Keeping articles, Fancy Goods, Perfumery, Toys, &c., at wholesale and retail." The shelves were stocked with indelible ink, backgammon boards, battledores and shuttlecocks, pails, and tubs.

Elsewhere in the world in 1847, Liberia proclaimed itself an independent republic, Paul von Hindenburg was born and Felix Mendelssohn died. Evaporated milk was sold for the first time, and Parliament in England limited women and children to 10-hour work days. In America, Thomas Edison was born and Salt Lake City was founded by the Mormons.

While such great things were occurring around the world, Catholics in their new Diocese, like most people everywhere, faced what they faced the day before and what we face in our own times: ordinary life. Their day was filled with births and deaths, sunny days and thunderous nights, buying and selling, entertainment and news, war and peace, pickpockets and clowns. From its very beginning, the Albany Diocese was part of that daily life, offering solace to widows, building institutions for orphans, sending chaplains to the military, staffing schools for children, founding hospitals for the physically sick and offering prayers for the spiritually ailing.

Of course, the story of upstate Catholics goes back farther than the creation of the Albany Diocese in 1847. It reaches back to a French missionary and an Indian maiden; it includes an Irish land-owner and a Flemish merchant; it encompasses Canadian voyageurs and German immigrants. Their stories are told in this book, "Canals and Crossroads" by Sally Light. The title is drawn from the modes of transportation that criss-crossed the early Diocese and drew people, including Catholics, into the area. Along those canals and beside those crossroads, churches, schools, hospitals and orphanages sprang up. But there is another kind of canal and crossroad: the interior ones each of us takes in our journey of faith. On them, we float and raft, walk and drive, moving through time toward our eternal destination. How our predecessors in faith took their journeys is the story to be found in the following pages.

James Breig

PART I
Before There Was A Diocese

Chapter 1
NEW WORLD, ANCIENT FAITH

*'We have here Papists, Mennonites and Lutherans
among the Dutch; also many Puritans or
Independents and many atheists.'*

When Father Isaac Jogues escaped his Mohawk captors and took refuge in Fort Orange (which would later become Albany), he was treated kindly by Domine Johannes Megapolensis, the Dutch Reformed minister. The Domine visited the French Jesuit often when he was in hiding, and, in fact, probably saved his life.

Why was Pastor Megapolensis so protective of a man who was a rival for native converts and who represented the religion that

Calvinists detested? Part of the answer is simple: Johannes Megapolensis was born Johannes Grootstadt of Catholic parents. Brought up Catholic while the Reformation was blooming around him, he felt at least an empathy for Father Jogues.

That display of ecumenism revealed an early manifestation of what has come to be associated with Americans and American Catholicism: a taste for pragmatic compromise and consensus in order to succeed. Even at such an early date, the province of Nieuw Nederland hosted many different ethnic and religious groups that had to get along for survival. That cooperation is a characteristic that echoes throughout the history of the Roman Catholic Diocese of Albany.

Catholicism came to the vast area north of New Amsterdam more than two centuries before the Albany Diocese was formally established in 1847. Samuel de Champlain brought Recollets to Quebec in 1615; in 1632, Jesuits were established to minister to the spiritual needs of both the settlers and the native nations; and in 1642, Father Isaac Jogues first appeared in what became New York State when he was captured by the Mohawks while being accompanied by his Huron escort to pick up supplies for the missions in Huronia. The captives were brought to the Mohawk Valley to a village near Auri-

Preceding page: Jean LaLande, Isaac Jogues and Rene Goupil.

Left: Father Jogues (CNS photo)

Next page: An Iroquois Indian ("The Empire State")

esville called Ossernenon.

While most of the Hurons were killed, Father Jogues and his donne, Rene Goupil, suffered various classical tortures. (A donne was a layman associated with the Jesuits and often assigned to accompany a specific individual because he could bear arms, which a Jesuit was forbidden to do.) Ironically, Goupil was a surgeon, which might have helped Father Jogues in his physical sufferings, had Goupil lived. However, the donne was killed, and Father Jogues suffered the painful maiming of some of his fingers, as well as much scarring.

That Father Jogues was an extraordinary man is apparent in his writings. Completely aware of the possible dire consequences, he nonetheless felt a strong calling to minister to the native nations. He discussed the various and sometimes horrible outcomes of his actions in a dispassionate, logical manner; yet it is obvious from his often accurate perceptions of the Mohawk psyche that the French priest was a loving, ethical man who fully expected — and welcomed — martyrdom as a result of his decisions. He knew what he was doing and chose to follow his convictions regardless of the consequences.

Isaac Jogues recognized the complexities of the interrelationships among the various native nations, the French and the Dutch. He was more concerned that he make a correct moral decision based on promoting those mutual relationships than on the practicality and common sense of his decisions. That characteristic frustrated those who tried to help him. In short, he was a political man without the politics. He had a higher calling.

During his ordeal among the Iroquois, Father Jogues was claimed by a clan which, although it treated him as a slave, attempted to mitigate some of his suffering. About a year later, while on a Mohawk trading trip to Fort Orange and a fishing trip south of Fort Orange, he heard that the Iroquois had taken four Hurons captive and had already killed two others at Ossernenon. Wanting to go back to the village to baptize the remaining Hurons, he fabricated an excuse to leave the fishing party. He was accompanied — as a slave always was — by a small group of Iroquois. They went to Fort Orange where he learned that the Mohawks left at the village were awaiting his return to burn him, a favorite way to torture and kill. Apparently, a Mohawk group had gone to Montreal to ambush the French, but it had not gone well; one of their group had been killed and two wounded, and Father Jogues was to be the scapegoat for what he would call "these adverse encounters."

Some of the native peoples literally believed in an eye for an eye. When they lost a warrior in battle, they expected another body to replace the one they had lost, so prisoners were taken whenever possible to use as objects of future vengeance, if for no other reason. That is why Father Jogues had been kept a slave for a year: Because he was associated with the enemy, he could be used to replace the dead warrior. Whether or not the replacement was tortured and spared, or killed appeared to depend on the immediate whims and impulses of those taking their revenge.

A warning

Also hearing that a band of Iroquois intended to spy on the French and Hurons at Fort Richelieu, north of Lake Champlain, Father Jogues decided to warn the French via a letter carried by a friendly Huron. When the French received the letter, they fired their cannon on the Mohawks who had accompanied the letter-bearer and frightened them so badly that they abandoned their arquebuses, powder, lead and other baggage, and fled. The priest was blamed for both of these occurrences, thus the death warrant. (An arquebus was one of the first portable guns, an early type of rather large handgun that rested on a fork or a hooked staff when fired. This "stick-that-shot-fire" and killed with one puff terrified the Mohawks.)

Arendt Van Curler, the Dutch commander at Fort Orange, was well-respected by the Mohawks. When Father Jogues, Goupil and the other Frenchmen had been captured the previous year, he had gone to the Mohawks in a futile attempt to effect their release. Furthermore, Van Curler was aware that the French governor of Quebec had successfully prevented an attack by the northern Indians on the Dutch, for which he was grateful. He expressed his appreciation by suggesting to the French Jesuit that he escape via a ship that was set to sail in a few days. He was astonished when the priest wanted to think it over to weigh the moral implications.

When he did decide to escape, Jogues found it difficult. The ship's officers said they would take him back to France and ensure his safety only if he would get onto their ship and not disembark until arriving in France. Van Curler promised to hide a small boat at the river's edge so that Father Jogues could paddle out to the ship at night. To do that, he had to slip out of the barn where he and the Mohawks were staying and hike to the river about a mile away. (It is believed that St. Mary's Church in Albany now lies on the site where the barn was located.)

Because Father Jogues' Mohawk guards slept right next to him and the Dutch farmer's dogs were untied at night — a particularly large one had already bitten the priest deeply on the thigh — it took him a couple of sleepless nights before the opportunity to escape presented itself in the figure of a servant boy who somehow prevented the dogs from yelping in the predawn hours. After running about a mile on his injured leg to the Hudson, the priest found that the boat was wedged aground in the mud at low tide. After shouting at the sleeping shipmates for several minutes as the sun rose and getting no response, Father Jogues realized his lack of prudence and his solitary state. He would have to rely solely on his own strength. He mustered all he had, and with a burst of adrenalin, freed the boat from the muck.

Once on the ship, he was secreted in the hold with a large chest placed over the hatchway. Two days later, Domine Megapolensis boarded to tell the priest that the Iroquois had threatened to burn Dutch houses and kill cattle unless he was returned. Father Jogues decided to leave the ship at night — to the disgust of the sailors, who pointed out that they could no longer protect him. He went to Van Curler's house and then was moved to the garret in the home of a tight-wad old man where he was rather poorly concealed while Van Curler convinced the angry Mohawks that the priest was worth the substantial ransom of 100 pieces of gold that the Dutch provided.

The Mohawks — in fact, all native peoples — by this time had grown quite accustomed to using European goods, and they needed money to buy them. If the Mohawks had not taken the coins, Father Jogues would have been martyred at this earlier date. These negotiations took time, so the ship sailed without him. He was obliged to hide for six more weeks until another ship arrived, and he was then invited by Governor Willem Kieft of New Amsterdam (later named Manhat-

tan) to stay there while awaiting passage to France.

While Father Jogues was staying at the house of the stingy man (who kept for himself most of the provisions sent to feed the priest), Domine Megapolensis visited fairly often and called a surgeon to Jogues' aid. As Father Jogues pointed out: "To increase my blessings — that is to say, my crosses — the wound which a dog had inflicted upon me...caused me so great a pain that, if the surgeon of that settlement had not put his hand to it, I should have lost not only the leg but life; for gangrene was already setting in."

A helping hand

"Megapolensis" is a combined Latin-and-Greek version of the pastor's original surname, Grootstadt — meaning "big" or "major city." It was common practice among the well-educated Dutch Calvinists to alter their names in that manner. He was influenced by his uncle, who had become a Dutch Reformed minister. A telltale clue that may explain his decision to become a Calvinist is that he married a stepdaughter of the same uncle.

Johannes felt a sincere compunction to help Father Jogues, partially out of a sense of responsibility. The Dutch had taught the Iroquois that making the sign of the cross was "of no account," which the natives interpreted minimally as being a hex or, worse, as causing death. Because the Jesuits baptized not only children but also adults who were near death, their subsequent demise was connected to the sign of the cross. Father Jogues found out considerably after the fact that Goupil had been killed because he had made the sign of the cross over a man's grandson.

Once in France, Father Jogues sent back to Van Curler the 100 pieces of gold used to ransom him, as well as money to pay for the clothing and support provided while he had awaited the ship in New Amsterdam. Throughout the history of the Church, both men and women religious have worn a variety of clothing. During some eras, they reserved their habits for use only at religious ceremonies and wore the daily clothing of the time for ordinary use. At other times, they wore their religious habits in public and donned lay clothing in private. In the mid-1600s, the Jesuits were known as the Black Robes for their distinctive habit. Domine Megapolensis recommended to Father Jogues that he wear lay clothing for his own safety among the predominantly Protestant people of New Amsterdam, as well as among the natives. Once in New Amsterdam, Governor Kieft gave him a Dutch-style cloak and hat, and had a black coat made for him.

While there, Father Jogues commented on some individuals that he met, including other Catholics. He also pointed out that there were 18 different languages spoken in Nieuw Nederland, and that although the Dutch Reformed church was the only one legally permitted, the Dutch were lax in enforcement. Catholics, Puritans, Lutherans and Anabaptists (Mennonites) also attempted to maintain their faiths.

At a later date, when Domine Megapolen-

At the same time . . .

1640: Rembrandt paints "Self-Portrait"

1643: Louis XIII of France dies; succeeded by his five-year-old son, Louis XIV

1645: Capuchin monks explore the Congo River

sis became the minister serving New Amsterdam, he complained that "we have here Papists, Mennonites and Lutherans among the Dutch; also many Puritans or Independents and many atheists." The thrust of his comment was to object to the Dutch West India Company's relatively new policy of sending Jews. Thus by the mid-1600s, a host of religions were represented in the New World.

In addition to Father Jogues, Megapolensis also talked about Father Francesco Giuseppe Bressani (anglicized by 19th-century writers to Francis Joseph Bressani), a Jesuit from what would become Italy. Father Bressani also was captured by the Mohawks and, like Jogues, mistreated by mutilation of his fingers in 1644. Father Bressani, too, was brought to the Dutch; ransomed from the Mohawks; fed, clothed and healed by their surgeon; and returned to France — all at the expense of Fort Orange. Again like Jogues, he returned from France to New France and wrote Megapolensis a letter of gratitude.

Megapolensis commented on a letter from Bressani that attempted to reconvert him to Catholicism by stating coolly: "I returned such a reply that a second letter was never sent me." However, his positive attitude toward Bressani — and earlier Jogues — shows that a bond had been forged between men of similar background. Governor Kieft also responded generously to both men, unlike his treatment of Quakers and some shipwrecked Puritan ministers. In addition, Van Curler at Fort Orange and an unnamed minister on the ship that took Father Jogues down river behaved favorably toward him.

Father Jogues expressed amusement over that shipmate: "They made me embark in company with a minister who showed me much kindness. He was supplied with a number of bottles, which he dealt out lavishly, especially on coming to an island, to which he wished that my name should be given with the noise of the cannon and of the bottles; each one manifests his love in his own fashion."

Furthermore, there is a story of a Lutheran Pole who greatly admired Father Jogues, in addition to other residents of New Amsterdam who were sympathetic to his plight. While many of the Dutch who settled Nieuw Nederland were Calvinists, they came from an area in which there were many Catholics. Furthermore, in Holland, they had been noted for their tolerance of the Independents (Puritans), many of whom had left in the first half of the 1600s for the New World.

In 1644, Father Jogues returned to New France (Canada). The next year, the Mohawks and the governor of New France concluded a peace treaty. The governor wanted to send an embassy to the Mohawk Valley,

and Father Jogues volunteered. He was well-received by the Mohawks and subsequently returned north. Because of this success, he wanted to return to the valley to resume his missionary efforts. By the time he did, however, the temper had changed, and a significant number of Mohawks wanted to renew war with the French. Father Jogues was killed with a hatchet on October 18, 1646, at the village of Ossernenon near Auriesville. Donne Jean de la Lande, who had accompanied Father Jogues, was killed the next day.

According to Domine Megapolensis, Father Jogues' missal, breviary and clothing were taken to the minister by the Mohawks. Father Jogues died as he had anticipated: with the grace of martyrdom.

Early Contact

In 1609, when Henry Hudson sailed up the North River — which later would be named after him — Mohicans appeared in their canoes with gifts of fur, food and tobacco. The explorer reciprocated with gifts of "knives and trifles," the latter apparently beads. Although it is widely believed that this particular native community had not yet had previous contact with Europeans, their immediate neighbors to the west, the Mohawks, had. A few weeks earlier that same year, Samuel de Champlain — accompanied by Hurons and Algonquins — used his arquebuses to defeat a group of Mohawks on Lake Champlain.

The Mohawks were already using French axes obtained in warfare with the Algonquins found along the St. Lawrence. They used the axes to cut down trees in the enemy's path to hinder pursuit. In addition to such spoils of war, by the early 1600s, the Iroquois had gone north to the St. Lawrence to trade directly with the French. Even if the Hudson River natives had not yet seen Europeans, at least they had heard about them because they all traveled distances on hunting trips and for their intertribal warfare.

More than a century earlier, along the eastern shore, French, Portuguese, English and Spanish fishermen were setting up huts and scaffolds, which were raised frameworks to dry fish for easy transport back to Europe. Broken shards and small metal bits left at the sites were picked up by the Indians and used as decorative trinkets. As early as 1511,

on a map showing a section of the northeast coast of North America, Bernardo Silvano, a Portuguese, delineated the Gulf of St. Lawrence, indicating that the fishermen knew about the St. Lawrence River to the west.

In spite of various attempts in the 1500s, it was not until 1600-1603, just a few years before Hudson, that two Frenchmen made successful trading voyages to the St. Lawrence. Champlain was a member of the 1603 voyage; in 1609, he established a permanent post in Quebec. Between those dates, he befriended the Hurons, an Algonquian nation related to, yet generally at war with, the Iroquois, and had traveled to Ticonderoga in today's New York State. Those moves in combination with the Mohawk defeat on Lake Champlain successfully estranged the Iroquois, who normally traveled freely for hunting purposes on the North American continent. They went in all directions hindered only by their lack of beasts of burden — except for dogs — and of the means for wide-water travel.

Native peoples

In those early years, North America was all one huge territory being explored by various rival European groups. There was no Canada and no United States, and there were only small outposts of ethnic groups, whether European or native. Movement was determined by kinship, friendship, territorial protection or the lack thereof. By all accounts, the Iroquois — and more particularly the easternmost group, the Mohawks — were the most aggressive native group in

North America in the 17th and 18th centuries. Earlier, in the late 1500s, the Hurons had soundly whipped the Iroquois and had reduced their numbers so greatly that the Iroquois had vowed revenge. It was a tactical mistake on Champlain's part to alienate such a determined group as the Iroquois by choosing to befriend their chief enemy.

Almost immediately in 1609, the Hurons and Iroquois established a great rivalry for acquiring the pelts that the Europeans wanted. The best skins were found north and west of the Hudson River, primarily around the Great Lakes and particularly north of them into Huron territory. In the ensuing years, the Iroquois were successful in fighting the Hurons for the right to take skins from what was called Huronia. By 1649, the Huron numbers were drastically reduced and their populations scattered, some to Iroquois territory as prisoners of war. When there were sufficient numbers, these prisoners, after having served their term as slaves to their captors, formed Huron villages that sprang up separate from, yet often adjacent to, Iroquois villages.

There also was intermarriage between native nations by individuals captured during raids. Kateri Tekakwitha's mother, for example, was a Catholic Algonquin from the Quebec area; she was adopted by a French farmer when her parents died. At 12, she was captured by Mohawks in a raid and brought to the Mohawk valley to become a slave.

Since the Jesuits had lived with the Hurons, the destruction of that nation effectively wiped out the Jesuit mission. In 1660, a sachem or chief from the Cayugas (the Iroquois west of the Onondagas) requested and received a Jesuit priest from New France to serve the converts. Thus, it was natural that because Champlain was the one who had brought over the religious groups, the Hurons would be more receptive to conversion, and the Mohawks — if for no other reason than the hostility felt toward the Hurons — would reject the French religious overtures. Territorial protection was — and remains — one of the basic motivating factors in life.

Kateri Tekakwitha, Lily of the Mohawk

During this time of Iroquois raids, Kateri Tekakwitha was born in 1656 in the Mohawk valley. Her father was a Mohawk chief. When Kateri was four, her parents and baby brother died of smallpox. She, too, caught the disease, which left her pockmarked and nearly blind. Her uncle adopted her and also acquired the chieftain position of his brother. He gave her the name "Tekakwitha" after watching her move around the house using her hands to find things. The name has been given various translations, but all of them basically mean "she who gropes," or "she pushes with her hands," or "she who cuts the way before her."

She was a quiet child who early on spent a great deal of time by herself. As she matured, she refused to get married, an unusual situation by native standards.

By 1665, New France, tired of the torment

of the continual Iroquois raids in the St. Lawrence valley, sued for peace. All of the Iroquois except the Mohawks accepted, so that the French felt justified in isolating that nation by burning their villages in the Mohawk valley the following year. In 1667, after the burning of Ossernenon near Auriesville by marquis de Tracy, a new village was built near Fonda on the north side of the Mohawk River, and Jesuit Father John Pierron was sent to minister to it.

Because of persecution by the non-Catholic natives, 40 converts (out of 300 living in the village) petitioned Tekakwitha's uncle in 1673 to move to a Catholic settlement near Montreal. Other Iroquois villages also were experiencing a depletion in their populations due to this migration to New France. That movement upset the balance of power even more rapidly within their groups, as well as among native nations, and between them and the Europeans.

At right: Kateri Tekakwitha (CNS photo)

The Iroquois saw the departures as a form of treason. Their men were joining their former enemy — the Hurons and French — in Huron territory. In addition to wars and migration, the native populations had declined significantly because they were not resistant to various European diseases.

Tekakwitha was among those who wished to convert. On Easter Sunday 1676, when she was 20, she was baptized and given the name Kateri (Mohawk for Catherine) by Father Jacques de Lamberville. It was common for many native women converts to be named for St. Catherine of Siena. By the next year, Kateri had escaped to Caughnawaga (south of Montreal), accompanied by native converts, one a relative of her mother's. There, she lived an exemplary life, making her first Holy Communion on Christmas Day 1677. Upon meeting the nuns who had founded the hospital, Hotel-Dieu, in Montreal, she learned of their vows and wanted to establish a religious community for native women. When she could not do so, she made a vow of perpetual virginity and chastity on March 25, 1679.

Kateri died in 1680 at 24 of a strange fever that lingered for months, perhaps precipitated by the self-inflicted penances which she practiced and which dismayed her confessor. Immediately after her death, her skin — which had been badly scarred by smallpox and darkened by the fever — smoothed and lightened. Because of this transformation and her reputed saintliness, people came from all over New France to her grave, and many were healed. Eventually, she was called the "Protectoress of Canada." Known as a quiet, retiring, prayerful woman, the Lily of the Mohawks was believed by some to have been a mystic who lacked the means to reveal her thoughts except verbally to a select few.

While Kateri represented the good that can come from a life branded by her circumstances, she remained an oasis in the French Jesuit efforts to win converts among the Mohawks. It has been universally recognized that the number of native converts was low in the 17th century.

English Ascendancy

In 1664, the English seized power from the Dutch in the New World. New Amsterdam was renamed New York, and Fort Orange was rechristened Albany to honor James, the Catholic brother of King Charles II. James, the Duke of Albany and York, would later become the ill-fated James II.

Although the British maintained Dutch laws and culture, inevitable changes developed. In 1670, the English formed Hudson's Bay Company, based on Henry Hudson's ex-

> # At the same time . . .
>
> **1670: Pope Clement X elected**
>
> **1672: Peter the Great of Russia dies**
>
> **1673: Marquette and Joliet reach headwaters of Mississippi**
>
> **1676: Kara Mustafa becomes Grand Vizier of Turkey**

plorations. That allowed the English a foothold in what was already being called Canada. However, it took almost a century until after the Seven Years War — also called the French and Indian War — in 1763 that the French were expelled and New France was reduced to Québec, now a part of an English colony. Throughout that period — from about 1690 and during much of the first half of the 18th century — the French and English would battle, using the native nations on both sides.

In spite of their waning influence, the French Jesuits stayed in the Mohawk valley until 1687. There is evidence that they returned on occasion in the early 18th century, primarily staying in the central part of the province in the Finger Lakes area. Since most of the Mohawks who converted had moved out of the area, there was less of a need for the Jesuits to serve Catholics in eastern New York.

Gov. Thomas Dongan

From 1682-1688, Colonel Thomas Dongan, an Irish Catholic, was the fourth English governor of New York. He had served under

Louis XIV as colonel of an Irish regiment in the service of France and often corresponded in French with the governor of Canada. In his letters, Dongan established for the first time his understanding of the boundaries of New York as being south of the Great Lakes and north to the St. Lawrence River, although specific latitudes were not given. It was apparent from the French governor's reply that he disagreed with Dongan's perception, setting the stage for further conflict.

Above: Court Street in Albany in 1686 (Leonard Tantillo drawing)

Opposite page: Thomas Dongan

The reason for the dichotomy was based on a difference of opinion over how the boundary should be drawn, the one ageless, universal reason for war. Governments either traditionally seek natural boundaries, such as rivers or lakes, to bound property claimed, or declare artificial boundaries, dictated by parallels, such as latitude lines or county or provincial boundaries.

In the real world of ordinary people, boundaries are created more naturally by focusing on sound universal principles based in geography. One of the most decisive natural occurrences is the watershed. Natives followed the streams, creeks, rivers and lakes in canoes. The easiest path is downstream. The Europeans learned the easiest routes from them and used their method of quick and easy boat-building. The watershed in the North Country goes both north and south, and not in a convenient latitudinal line.

The Hudson starts at Lake Tear of the Cloud on Mount Marcy and flows south through the Flowed Lands to Calamity Brook. Nearby Marcy Brook flows north to the Ausable River, ending in Lake Champlain and eventually from the Richelieu River to the St. Lawrence. As the names illustrate, Ausable, Champlain and Richelieu are French, while Hudson, Flowed Lands and Calamity are English. While this appears to be an oversimplification, it is representative of what actually happened: The French claimed the northerly flowing watershed and the English, the southerly. That occurred until hostilities erupted toward the end of the century. At that time, Dongan was attempting to follow the natural boundary of the St. Lawrence River on the north.

Dongan convened the first representative assembly in the province. It adopted a "Charter of Liberties," which defined the organization of the assembly, the protection of property and the right to assent to taxation, as well as many individual rights, such as habeas corpus, trial by jury, limitations on excessive bail and the exemption of private homes from having to quarter troops during peace time.

Those laws and rights were considered the requisite expectations of Englishmen and formed the basis of the future New York State Constitution. This charter also included a clause on religious freedom for all who "profess faith in God by Jesus Christ," a phrase specified by the assembly. Originally, Dongan had included Jews and Indians in his desire for universal protection of religious freedom, so he accorded those groups gubernatorial protection. While the assembly was disallowed in 1683, and the charter declared null and void in 1691, both laid the seeds of representative power and individual rights that came in the next century.

In order to define land grants that would be legally valid, Dongan established a city charter in Albany in 1686 as a law of the assembly. (Albany still operates under it, the oldest city charter still in use in the United States.)

Dongan was highly esteemed by the natives. Partly to avoid the Iroquois convert exodus to New France and partly to maintain the native population in the New York colony, the governor appeased the Iroquois sachems by asking in 1685 for English Jesuits to come to work among them. He was also motivated by the slackening beaver trade in the colony. Since the trade depended on the natives to supply the skins from the west, it was imperative to retain the numbers of Iroquois along the east-west New York transportation route. Fewer Iroquois meant less income for the English and Dutch. Dongan repeated his request in 1687, but there is no record of the Jesuits coming.

Early priests

Between 1683 and 1690, one to three English Jesuit priests were, however, in New York City. They started a Latin school, but it had few students. A chapel was built in the fort for them, as was one for the Anglican clergy. (The Dutch Reformed already had a church.) One of the Jesuits was born in Antwerp and one in Flanders, so two of them spoke French and Dutch, as well as English, three of the main languages spoken in Albany.

All three priests were in Albany in 1686 or 1687 for about a four-month period. Domine Godfridus Dellius, the Dutch Reformed minister, railed against Catholicism during that span, because he wanted "to arm the people against the seductions of three English Jesuits, Smith, Gage and Harrison, who could speak both French and Dutch,...and resided at Albany during that period." Ironically, by the end of the 17th century, Domine Dellius would be accused by Governor Bellomont of being a papist traitor.

Domine Dellius was the first Dutch Reformed minister to spend the time and find the money — from the English government — to convert the Mohawks. By 1693, he was able to claim 200 converts. In the process of doing so, he had become friendly with the Jesuit missionaries, an association that earned him the papist label. ("Papist," a derogatory term for Catholics, referred to their allegiance to the pope.)

Father Henry Harrison revisited Albany with Dongan in August 1687 for a conference with the Iroquois. He did not return to New York with the governor, choosing instead to stay throughout the winter. It is presumed he ministered to the Dutch and French Catholics who are recorded in the courts as living in Albany at that time.

In Dongan's 1687 report on the "Province of New-York," he informed the Committee of Trade in England on the various religions, listing ministers for the Church of England, Dutch Calvinist, French Calvinist, Dutch Lutheran, "few Roman Catholicks; abundance of Quakers preachers men & women especially; Singing Quakers, Ranting Quakers; Sabbatarians; Antisabbatarians; Some Anabaptists; some Independents; some Jews; in short of all sorts of opinions there are some." Dongan, who operated out of New York City, was describing the entire New York province. New York City was then the main center; Albany was the second largest city.

In February 1688, Father Harrison, still in Albany, acted as an interpreter with the French agents for Dongan, who had returned. The French ambassadors were both Jesuits, one of whom could speak English; Dongan did not speak Dutch. It was probably at this time that the priest left some items in a house Jan Van Loon owned, items which would later cause Van Loon some difficulty.

Glorious Revolution

After James II had a son by his second wife, thus assuring a Catholic heir to the English throne, the Protestant leaders in Parliament asked Mary — his Protestant daughter by his first wife and now married to a Dutch ruler — to take the throne. After the "Glorious Revolution" of 1688 and the ascendancy of the Dutch Protestant William of Orange with his English wife Mary, Catholicism was out of favor — and Governor Dongan was out of a job.

In 1689, Jacob Leisler, an adamant German Calvinist, seized control of New York and proclaimed himself lieutenant governor. Among his many papers, he published a deposition of two men who were told that "all Images erected by Col. Thomas Dongan in the fort should be broken down & taken away, but when we were working in the fort with others, it was commanded...to help the priest John Smith to remove [them], [which] was soon done, because said removal was not far off [i.e. at a distance] but in a better room in the fort." They were "ordered to make all things for Said Priest, according to his will."

In spite of the general anti-Catholic tenor of the English government, the courtesy shown the priest and the objects from the chapel in the fort show respect. The statues could have been maliciously destroyed.

Because of his attempts — none of which panned out as planned — to establish an assembly, legalize a charter of rights and win the native nations to the English side, Dongan was considered "a man of integrity, moderation, and gentle manners, and, though a professed Papist, may be ranked among the best of our governors." (The truth of this statement lies in its author, a later historian who was vehemently anti-Catholic.) Although Dongan lost power in 1688, he did not return to England until 1691, earlier having fled to New England to avoid Leisler's posses.

The previous year, the Catholic French and Iroquois living near Montreal were ordered "to commence hostilities against New England and New York, which had declared for the Prince of Orange." Leisler threatened invasion of Canada amid rumors of an incursion from Montreal. The result was the Schenectady Massacre, which the French called the "taking of Corlear [sic]." (After his fame in the 1640s trying to ransom Fathers Jogues and Bressani, Arendt Van Curler moved west in 1661 to found Schenectady with a small group of settlers from Fort Orange. Van Curler's name was associated with the town and the river. At that time, it was spelled Arent Van Corlaer.)

With this massacre, the rivalry between the French and the British escalated into more than a trade war. The French were demonstrating their desire to control British

North America, and almost 75 years of inter-mittent wars would ensue before the dispute was resolved in 1763 by the Treaty of Paris following the French and Indian War.

Besides aggression, an additional means the French used to establish their presence in northern New York was to populate the area. Three or four village forts were estab-lished by the French near what became the Canadian border along Lake Champlain and the St. Lawrence. Although all of these forts and villages would eventually end up in the Diocese of Ogdensburg, they were a part of the Albany Diocese until 1872. Prior to the Revolution and the establishment of the New York-Canadian border, they were supplied by priests out of Montreal and Québec, pri-marily Récollets, Jesuits and Sulpicians, who considered their villages part of the Québec Diocese.

Farther south, there were French traders at Saratoga, many of whom traveled to or

Above: Jan Van Loon's house as it appears today, with its historical marker (James Breig photos)

lived in Albany in the late 1600s. After the Schenectady Massacre, it is assumed — based on the disappearance of their names from the census — that the French returned to Saratoga, if not to the North Country.

Jan Van Loon

In spite of his Dutch-sounding name, Jan Van Loon (or Loan) spoke French and came from Luyck in what is now Belgium. On the 1697 Albany County census, he is listed as a papist. His Catholicism was well-docu-mented in at least one court case in which he was cited for blasphemy when he accused an-other Catholic man of being "like a renegade in Turkey" for joining the Dutch Reformed church.

Van Loon, a smith, made enough money to acquire sizeable real estate holdings in Al-bany and the Athens-Coxsackie area (his home can still be seen in Athens). He had lived in Albany until around 1695 when he and his wife moved to Athens. They were still there in 1725.

In 1690, a man renting a house of Van

Loon's, as well as another man who would be the primary witness against Van Loon at the blasphemy trial, presented Leisler's commission with an inventory of items found in the house, including: an old chest with "12 little Patrenoster Chains (Rosaries), 1 priest's white surplice," and a small basket with a 16-pound bell, carpenter's tools and "some other pieces of old Iron."

The next year, after Leisler had been hanged and the regular government restored, Van Loon applied to the Albany mayor's court for the return of the goods, identified as belonging to "Mr. Harrison the priest": "a chest with sundrey goods, a basket of yron worke and a bell." Historians have speculated on what Van Loon was doing with Father Harrison's property and what it was for in the first place; one theory is that the priest intended to build a church in Albany.

Catholicism Underground

As a result of the Protestant ascendancy to the British throne and due to French aggression, Catholicism (except for the French in the North Country) went underground. In 1698, excluding Iroquois and Mohicans, there were less than 1,500 people in Albany County; about 800 were children, 270 women, 380 men and 23 "Negros." At this time, Albany County included all of upstate New York north of Dutchess County.

The number of Catholics was probably a handful. The 1697 census of Albany County lists only Jan Van Loon and someone named Hillebrant, both living south of Albany. How-

At the same time . . .

1700: Unmarried women taxed in Berlin

1703: Delaware separates from Pennsylvania to become own colony

1705: Edmund Halley predicts return of his comet

ever, judging from the number of Catholics who have searched for ancestors in the records of Albany's First Church (Dutch Reformed) and found them, there were probably more than believed. In addition, if a search were made of surnames and their place of origin, it would not be surprising if a significant percentage of the early Dutch were originally Catholic. If Catholic parents had a choice of a Calvinist baptism or no baptism at all, some chose the former. In the Dutch Reformed church, which stipulated that one parent of the child must be a member of the church, Catholics were accommodated by letting them choose members of the church as baptismal sponsors in lieu of their own membership. If the parents were not the sponsors, they did not have to belong to the Dutch Reformed Church.

The only other church in the Albany area was Lutheran; it had acquired its first pastor in 1669 after the English takeover. Although there are no records extant from the early colonial period, the General Church Orders of 1686 indicate that a Lutheran minister should baptize any unbaptized children when requested, regardless of church affiliation. For example, there are records of pastors baptizing Negro slaves whose parents presumably were not Lutheran. Jan Van Loon's children were apparently raised Lutheran. In 1727, they gave the land for the Lutheran church in Loonenburgh (present-day Athens) on property near their parents' home.

Anti-Catholic legislation

A new development would further complicate the lives of Catholics; in 1700, the new governor, the earl of Bellomont, drafted an anti-Catholic law which prohibited priests from remaining in or coming to the province. If caught, they were to suffer perpetual imprisonment. If they escaped and were captured, they were to be killed. Anyone harboring a priest had to pay a fine of two hundred pounds and stand for three days in the pillory.

Bellomont was so determined to have this law passed that when his council voted against it, he cast a ballot as a member of the council to produce a tie. He then voted again, this time as president, to get a majority and subsequently approved it as governor. Although the council did not agree with his actions, it did not have the power to overrule him.

That law was so little regarded that Abraham Schuyler openly invited Jesuit Father Pierre de Mareuil to Albany in 1709 just as hostilities between the French and English erupted again. When visiting the Onondagas, "he told the Rev. Father de Mareuil, who had remained, that his life was not safe, insinuated to him that the only means of extricating himself from certain danger to

which he was exposed was to accompany them to Orange, which this good Father complied with." When Father Mareuil "came to Albany...the government caused every attention to be paid to him."

The only example of compliance with the 1700 law involved an Anglican clergyman, John Vry, who was hanged in New York City in 1741, allegedly because he was a friend of Negroes who had been falsely accused of setting a fire, but really because he was suspected of being a Roman Catholic priest. The law's existence did, however, discourage Catholics from Maryland or Pennsylvania — or Europe — from settling in New York.

Suspicions

Because of his position as an Englishman owning confiscated Irish property, the anti-Catholic laws that Bellomont promoted were probably more anti-Irish than anti-pope. However, because of the historical confusion of politics and religion in all European governments, including the Papal States, the allegiance of Catholics was always suspect. It was believed that a Catholic under duress would choose the pope over his native country. Anti-Catholic laws resulted.

In 1701, another anti-Catholic New York law was passed, prohibiting "Papists and Popish recusants...from voting for members of assembly, or any office whatever, from thenceforth and for ever." (A recusant was a person who refused to attend the services of the Church of England or to recognize its authority.) This law would stay in effect until the American Revolution.

Keeping the Mohawks Friendly

Because the Albany area was still the frontier in the 18th century, much diplomatic, as well as religious, energy was consumed trying to proselytize the Iroquois in the hope of keeping them friendly to the English cause. The English, motivated primarily by fear of French expansion, needed their help to protect the Mohawk valley corridor in particular.

The English continued the Dutch policy of cultivating the Iroquois for economic gain;

but, beginning in 1700 with meetings of the Five Nations, they further attempted to persuade them to become political allies against the French. The Iroquois were not impressed with the unmaintained garrison at Albany, however, and doubted its security against an attack. It was not until the American Revolution that many of them aligned themselves with the English — to their detriment.

Since a 1628 war in which the Mohicans were vanquished, they had been paying an annual tribute to the Mohawks — a common practice — so the Mohicans felt obligated to consult with them whenever the English

Below: A 1765 treaty between Sir William Johnson and the Delaware Indians (National Portrait Gallery)

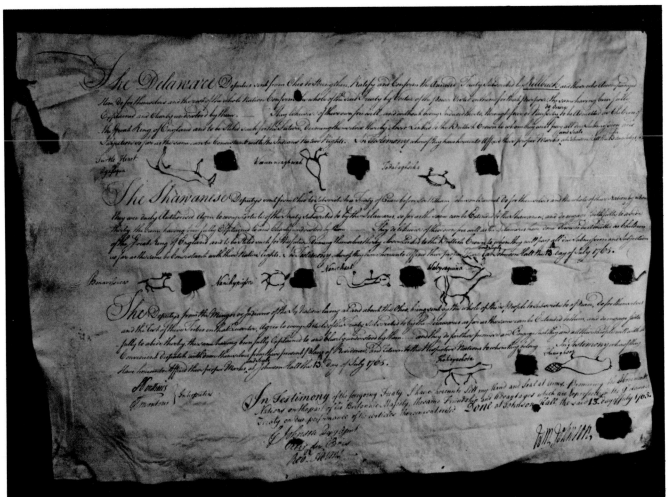

wanted their support in fighting the French. The Mohawks themselves had divided allegiances: There were French Mohawks and English Mohawks. As a result, at times they remained neutral. Although the Mohicans also were often neutral, they frequently sided with the Dutch and later the English.

In the 1600s, the Iroquois had blamed the French for introducing diseases and the new religion whose practices they associated with death and natural disasters. In the next century, they would hear the reasonings of their neighbors to the east, the Mohicans, who always had been friendly with the Dutch and English.

Fear and faith

By the mid-1700s, several Mohicans believed that they themselves were responsible for the bad things that had happened, such as their worsening economic plight, and that these misfortunes were a result of their own religious beliefs. They observed that the European God favored the Christians by increasing their numbers and making them prosperous, while the native population experienced the opposite. They believed, for example, that the Christian God gave them diseases because they did not believe in Him. For those reasons, many Mohicans converted to the Calvinism of their Dutch Reformed and Congregationalist neighbors. Such an economic interpretation of religious beliefs — the now famous American Protestant work ethic — was very different from the spiritual approach espoused by the Jesuits.

As the French grew stronger in the 1740s,

and especially after the burning of Schuylerville in 1745, the English fear of them became pronounced. A Mohican sachem could not resist goading a minister who had admitted fear of the French and their natives: "You must certainly not have the true faith nor ye right God, for if you had, He is strong and can help you. What can anyone do unto you, nothing can happen to you but what he wills. But I think you don't believe on him in your heart, and therefore you are so afraid."

Middle ground

In spite of the Mohican conversion, the Mohawks noted that the Mohicans did not prosper and increase under Calvinism. They also regretted the loss of fun and rejoicing that accompanied that religion. The Calvinists abolished their "customs, dances and rejoicings at marriages, etc." Furthermore, all of the native groups were more attracted to the ceremony, festiveness and joy of Catholicism, whose priests were officially still banned from the colony. In 1712, the arrival of an Anglican minister at the mouth of the Schoharie Creek would provide a middle-of-the-road religion.

At this time, a church for the Mohawks was established in Fort Hunter. (The stone parsonage still exists.) Before the clergyman went, the Mohawk sachem wanted to know if his real motive was to buy land. It was not. However, later in the century, Sir William Johnson thwarted moves to acquire large amounts of land by other ministers of other sects. The Jesuits, on the other hand, with their base of operations in Québec, did not concern themselves with land acquisition in New York. Perhaps it was because they were single, did not have families to support, had "a knowledge of the world," were "as distant from gloominess as from levity" and were singularly motivated to leave a legacy of conversion that their intentions were not suspect.

Palatine Settlement

In addition to proselytizing the Mohawks, the British used another means of locking the French out: settling the Mohawk and upper Hudson valleys with Europeans sympathetic to England. Thus, soon after the establishment of the Anglican church in 1712, Palatines appeared in the Mohawk valley near Canajoharie. Shortly thereafter, they were in German Flatts and ultimately as far west as what became Fort Stanwix (Rome). The Protestant German Palatines who were settled in Germantown and West Camp in 1710 and in Schoharie by 1715 were placed "where they may be usefull to this Kingdom particularly in the production of naval Stores and as a frontier against the ffrench and their Indians." These people from the Rhineland were invited because Queen Anne's consort was a Lutheran Danish prince.

In the Palatinate, however, there were also Catholics, Lutherans and other sects. It was recognized by one of their Lutheran ministers that there were some Catholics among the Palatines, since Germans frequently married across religious lines. In fact, in villages in what is present-day Germany and the Alsace region of France, there often was one church which served both the Lutherans and the Catholics, Mass and services being held at different times on the same day.

Queen Anne sent back to the Palatinate those families who were professed Catholics, eliminating them for possible emigration. But the officials did not send back mixed-church families if the one parent who was Catholic would say that he or she was non-practicing.

The minister would find out once the family was established here if the Catholic refused to support the Lutheran church. In Europe, it was a common practice for the government to support the church. In many cases, the connection was inseparable, a concept that Americans find hard to comprehend. Even today, Germans, including those who do not have a religion, must designate annually which church their taxes will support. In New Amsterdam in the mid-17th century, a Catholic Frenchman who lived in Brooklyn explained that he did not want to contribute to the support of the Reformed minister. That was deemed a "frivolous" excuse, and he was fined 12 guilders.

Merchants and farmers

To sustain themselves, the Palatines traded furs and farmed. By the Revolution, their grain crops, especially wheat — which came from both the Mohawk and Hudson valleys — helped feed the troops; New York became known as the breadbasket of the nation.

In addition to farming, the Palatines in the Mohawk valley provided transportation between Albany and newly established Fort

Oswego, which now became a fur-trading center in competition with Albany. They serviced a few portages — "Carrying Places" as the English called them — such as those around Little Falls and between the rivers, lakes and creeks that provided the main means of transportation.

Peter Kalm, a Swedish botanist who traveled extensively throughout the Northeast and Canada, wrote in 1749: "The merchants from Albany spend the whole summer at Oswego, and trade with many tribes of Indians who come with their goods." There was other trade at Albany. Merchants there, in collusion with French merchants in Canada, made Albany a center for smuggling along the Hudson/Champlain corridor. At this point, England's factories produced goods relatively cheaply that were coveted in the New World, while France was still largely an agricultural nation. English goods imported to Canada through France cost more than the same goods brought through the New York colony. Although it was illegal to send English goods from New York to Canada, it was very profitable to exchange the goods for furs — primarily beaver skins, according to Kalm.

The men who carried these products in their canoes were mainly French voyageurs, some of whom had settled earlier at Saratoga and points north. Thus, although the English and French were officially battling for control of the New York colony, clandestine trade, travel and the ensuing cultural exchanges between the different peoples continued unchecked.

Sir William Johnson

Sir William Johnson walked propitiously into this situation, using his considerable abilities to learn languages and to mingle with and work with peoples from a variety of economic and educational backgrounds. He was comfortable with a Palatine, Mohawk, French, Dutch or English farmer or landed gentleman. He deliberately created win-win economic situations. He appeared generous and judicious to all. In exchange, he expected loyalty. He also was, perhaps, the most outstanding historical example in New York of a Catholic who went underground.

His mother's English family, the Warrens, had an estate in Ireland and were Catholics who supported the unfortunate Catholic King James. His father, a Catholic tenant farmer on a neighboring estate, rented 199 acres and a grist mill. Catholics were forbidden to buy land, and the leases they had were renewable every 31 years. Any improvements made by a tenant were automatically considered part of the tenancy and were used by the landlord to charge more rent when the lease was up for renewal. As one of William's brothers observed of this catch-22: "No money, interest, nor friends. Consequently can't expect to rise."

Thus, when his uncle, a naval captain, asked William to develop property he had bought on the Mohawk near Fort Hunter, William welcomed the chance to emigrate. Sir William started the first major trading post on the Mohawk in 1738, shortly thereafter acquiring a large amount of land. His first consort was a Palatine woman from a prominent family. Following her death, Molly Brant, a Mohawk and an older sister of the famous Joseph Brant of Revolutionary War fame, took her place.

It was because of Johnson's desire to educate the children of the tenants and the Iroquois, including his own offspring, that he established free schools after he had been made the Commissioner of Indian Affairs in 1747. Prior to that, the commissioners had been officials of the Albany government with more interest in personal gain from trade. The schools and missions closed in 1756 after the French and Indian War broke out. By that time, Johnson was a major general and superintendent of the Six Iroquois Nations and their allies. He reopened them after the end of the war.

Church and State

Some of the schools were run by ministers. It was hoped that some of the pupils, including Mohawks, would continue beyond the ele-

At the same time . . .

1730: Emperor Yung Cheng of China reduces slavery

1733: Bach composes short version of Mass in B Minor

1738: American painters Benjamin West and John Singleton Copley born

mentary level to become teachers and ministers for their own group.

At this time, the purpose of higher education was to train priests and ministers. Once a child had basic literacy, in most of the trades and professions, he was educated by the apprentice method. Lawyers received young men to clerk, and thereby, learn law from them. Physicians, surgeons, chemists and apothecaries did the same, as did stone masons, carpenters and artists. In many cases, it was not necessary to be very literate, because learning did not occur from books.

To become a priest or minister, one studied philosophy, which required extensive reading; that is why all colleges and universities were started — even in Europe — under a specific denomination. At this time, the Puritans had Harvard; the Anglicans, William and Mary; and the Congregationalists, Yale. It was not until the mid-18th century that higher education added scientific disciplines as an expression of the Enlightenment, and the purposes of education changed to include theoretical mathematics and science. Those soon acquired practical applications in engineering and architecture, among others.

William Johnson established glebes for the Dutch Reformed and Lutheran parsonages already in the Mohawk valley. (A glebe is land belonging or yielding revenue to a church or ecclesiastical office.) He also appealed to the Anglican Society for the Propagation of the Gospel in Foreign Parts for ministers and teachers, and he permitted the settlement of Congregationalist ministers to start schools.

For political reasons, however, he did not permit the Scottish and Irish Catholics among his tenants to form a church. In this English territory, the 1700 anti-priest law was still on the books, and Catholics were associated with enemy France.

Early Irish

In the 1760 Provincial Army muster rolls for Albany County during the French and Indian War, 24 percent — a significant number — of the troops listed Ireland as their place of birth. These would have been first-generation arrivals. Other men with Irish names on the roll listed their places of origin as various locations in the New World. Thus, they were, at least, second-generation Irish.

Because the troops were composed of volunteers, many were poor men who were not recorded on tax lists — hence not property owners — and had joined for the 15-pound bounty, the clothing allotment and the daily allowance, which varied according to rank. Because these rolls represent a poorer class, that almost one-quarter of them are Irish does not necessarily mean that this repre-

sents the same percentage of Irish in the general population. It is presumed, however, that some of these Irish were Catholic and lived as tenants of Johnson, who had recorded their request to form a Catholic church.

When ministers or priests worked among the natives, their denomination usually gave a small stipend for their support. All of the priests in the New World were members of religious communities, which supplied the funds for their missions. In the Protestant denominations, the financing of stipends might come from the sale of property owned by the church or from the pockets of parishioners. The latter was a New World precedent for many denominations. They were accustomed to having the government pay for their ministers. The Dutch Reformed parishioners in 17th-century Fort Orange, for example, complained and, in some cases, were unable to contribute. At a later date, Catholics would also be rudely awakened to the necessity of the collection at Mass.

State payments

The New York government did supply the missionaries with the corporeal items used in daily life to give to the Mohawks. It was a form of early welfare that was exchanged for a pledge of allegiance, a hangover from feudalism. The following items illustrate what was commonly given: "The Com^{rs} Gave the following presents to the Mohawk Indians vizt 6 kegs powder 6 boxes of lead 12 Blankets 12 Shirts 2 duffel Blankets 5 pair Stockings 200 flints & 50 lb Shot."

Earlier, the Dutch and the French governments also provided items as needed. The French were known, in particular, for their lavish presents. In the late 17th century, Father Harrison was paid by the English government. The fact that part of the churches' budgets was financed by the state did not change in the colonies until after the Revolution with the separation of church and state in the U.S. Constitution, a unique contribution to western political philosophy.

Catholics from Scotland

In 1773, under the aegis of Sir William, Irish Father John McKenna appeared in the Mohawk valley with approximately 220 people. Although some were reputed to be Irish and German, the majority were Scottish Highlanders, reportedly from the MacDonald clan, who were sympathetic to King James. Johnson may have invited them to settle on his patent because he personally felt sympathetic to priests and the Catholicism he knew from his youth, in spite of his opting for the Church of England once he lived in the Mohawk valley. Father McKenna knew some of his flock, because he had been ordained in Scotland after being educated at Louvain in what is now Belgium.

It is intriguing that Johnson welcomed these arrivals when he had refused the formation of a Catholic church some years earlier. The anti-priest law had not yet been repealed, but the fear of the French had waned after the English vanquished them in the French and Indian War. Sir William was not even censored for his action; his peers probably looked aside because of his power-

ful position in the English government.

In 1774, just before he died and as the seeds of Revolution were being sown, Johnson thoroughly disapproved of separating from England. Had he lived, he would have been branded a Tory, as his family was. Father McKenna and many of his flock also were Loyalists and fled to Canada in 1775 and 1776. They became part of a British company under Sir William's nephew with Father McKenna as their chaplain, and took part in raids and battles in the Mohawk valley. After the Revolution, some of the Highlanders who had not left for Canada because they had remained loyal to King George were still in the Mohawk valley. The others had settled in Glengarry County in Ontario, across from Ogdensburg.

Although these Catholics and the French in the North Country were small in number, the Catholic presence was also felt indirectly in other ways. That governmental agents and officials felt obligated in almost every aspect of colonial life to comment about Papists — or the lack thereof — casts a significant light on the few Catholics extant. Their very existence must have been believed a significant threat to the overwhelmingly vast majority who were Protestants. As late as 1771, after the French and Indian War, an Anglican minister from New York City complained that no Protestant missionaries were being sent among the Iroquois: "The Iroquois themselves have often requested Missionaries might be sent to them, and are much dissatisfied at being neglected in matters of Religion by the government. They are surprised that when the present government supports two Popish Missionaries among Indians who are of another Religion, and fought against us during the last war. They proceed further to make a comparison between our conduct and that of the French in this respect; which is always to the advantage of the latter, who constantly paid the closest attention to the conversion of the Indians."

Ironically, in just five years, these officials would have to sing a different tune. France would come in as an ally to the colonies against England, and Catholic chaplains would appear with the French troops. They would also say Mass for the colonists. With the exception of Father McKenna for a couple of years and the French Jesuits, Sulpicians and Récollets who appeared on occasion or were present in northern New York, the regular practice of Catholicism in the 18th century was limited or nonexistent for a time period that spanned two generations before the Revolution.

In spite of the dearth of Catholicism in New York, yet the professed fear of it, there was a genuine appeal of Catholicism for Protestants, as well as for natives, which Johnson had already recognized. Kalm described Christmas Day, 1750, in Philadelphia this way:

"Nowhere was Christmas Day celebrated with more solemnity than in the Roman Church. Three sermons were preached there, and that which contributed most to the splendor of the ceremony was the beautiful music

At the same time . . .

1750: Thomas Gray writes "Elegy Written in a Country Church Yard"

1752: Great Britain adopts Gregorian calendar

1756: Aaron Burr born

1759: George Frederick Handel dies

heard to-day. It was this music which attracted so many people. An organ was to be heard only in the papal place of worship. The officiating priest was a Jesuit, who also played the violin, and he had collected a few others who played the same instrument. So there was good instrumental music, with singing from the [back] organ-gallery besides. People of all faiths gathered here, not only for the high mass but particularly for the vespers. Pews and altar were decorated with branches of mountain laurel. At the morning service the clergyman stood in front of the altar; but in the afternoon he was in the gallery, playing and singing."

People were starved for an opportunity to rejoice and be merry on such a joyous occasion. Only the Catholic Church provided an outlet for such expression in the pageantry of its celebration and in the mystery, solemnity and dignity of its rituals. Although Kalm was describing Philadelphia, the same characteristics would ingratiate the Church at the end of the 18th century to the many Protestants in Albany who welcomed the formation of St. Mary's parish.

Chapter Two
CATHOLICISM IN A NEW NATION

'With great pleasure we have noticed the success of the subscription, opened a few days since for erecting a Roman Catholic chapel in this city.'

The 1771 List of Inhabitants records that Albany was the largest county in the New York colony. Twice as large as New York County, it had a population of 42,706. (Dutchess County was the second largest and New York third.) The City of Albany lay at the crossroads of the main transportation routes, which at that time were the waterways in the New York colony: the Hudson River/Lake George/Lake Champlain corridor and the Mohawk River. The Saint Lawrence, Lake Ontario and the Niagara River were the other significant routes, but they lay on the perimeter of the colony.

Geographically, the population of Albany County represented most of the area of the colony north of Dutchess County. The settlement had spread only as far west as Fort Stanwix. There also were pockets at Niagara, Oswego, and north on Lake Champlain and the Saint Lawrence. Ranging south along the Hudson and east to the Massachusetts Bay, it had not been frontier for years. Even many of the higher ranges of the Taconic Mountains had been populated for at least ten years.

At the conclusion of the French and Indian War, Canada was added as the 14th colony in North America. It was treated differently, however, because of its high concentration of French and native Catholics. Under the terms of the treaty, the British were required to permit Canadians continued use of French civil law, possession of their property and freedom to practice their religion, all of which were expressed in the Quebec Act of 1774. Furthermore, they were not required to take the Oath of Supremacy; instead, they professed a simple oath of allegiance to King George.

The remainder of the colonies were incensed that Canada was singled out of all of the colonies, including Ireland, for special treatment. (That same year, the Irish Parliament passed a similar oath in which there was no reference to the pope.) The heavily Protestant lower 13 colonies were so angered over Canada's special status that they listed the Quebec Act as one of the "Intolerable Acts." Its passage unleashed an outburst of anti-Catholic feeling, vented, in part, by General Philip Schuyler's hounding of the Loyalist Scottish Highlanders, which resulted in the departure of some of them for Canada with Father McKenna in 1776.

Although it would not be until 1778 that the French Alliance would be signed, it became apparent that France would become the principal ally of the American colonists during the Revolution. As a result, the Continental Congress sent a delegation to Canada: Benjamin Franklin, Samuel Chase and two Catholic cousins: Charles Carroll, believed to be the richest man in the colonies (but who as a Catholic had no right to vote), and Father John Carroll. Both had been educated in France and made apt ambassadors to Canada. The delegation passed through Albany on their way north, with Father Carroll noting in a letter to his mother that "we were met by General Schuyler and entertained by him during our stay, with great politeness and very genteely."

The delegation's purpose was to try to mitigate the anti-Catholic outbursts. It was too late, however, and Canada was no fool. The men were coolly rejected, in particular by the very Bishop of Quebec who had brokered Canada for England. He threatened to excommunicate any Catholic who helped the Americans and to suspend any priest who allowed Father Carroll to say Mass. Ironically, French Canada was to remain forever British.

Revolution and Catholicism

The results of the French alliance were apparent as early as 1775, when George Washington banned the celebration of Guy Fawkes' Day — called "Pope's Day" in the colonies — in order to avoid offending the French. Guy Fawkes was one of several Catholic conspirators who planted gunpowder in the cellar under Westminster to blow up Parliament and King James I, his queen and his oldest son in 1605. One of the conspirators blew the whistle, and Fawkes was discovered in the cellar with the gunpowder.

What naturally resulted were more persecution of Catholics and a day of public thanksgiving in England, both of which were carried over to North America. It also sparked the enactment of the Oath of Allegiance to King James, which included a denial of papal authority. The oath was required of anyone suspected of recusancy — refusing to attend services in the Church of England or to recognize its authority. The oath acquired various permutations over the years until it became the Oath of Supremacy, which was outlawed by the Quebec Act

in Canada alone. Washington was attempting to moderate the effects of a hated law that served only to divide.

Ironically, colonial Catholics could ultimately thank the Enlightenment for providing a milieu open to accepting Catholicism in the New World. Deism was the widely held religious philosophy among the intellectuals and upper classes in England, Germany and France, as well as in the colonies. Deists believed that after creation, God withdrew, leaving the world to function according to a commonly held, rational, natural set of universally accepted religious and moral rules. Superficial differences in the dogma and ritual of all religions were insignificant and therefore tolerated.

In spite of the church affiliation of some of them, Benjamin Franklin, Thomas Paine, George Washington, John Adams and Thomas Jefferson, among others, were Deists. The combined influence of these unusually gifted political leaders, along with the mid-18th century evangelical schisms in Congregationalism and in Anglicanism, created a zeitgeist, or spirit of the times, in which religious liberty was included in the Constitution, and the laws written specifically against Catholics ultimately were repealed.

Meanwhile, in Philadelphia, many Protestant members of Congress attended a "Te Deum" arranged by the French Minister to celebrate the Declaration of Independence. They also were present at the funeral Mass of a diplomatic representative of the Spanish government. Thus, exposure to Catholicism was introduced to some Protestants, who were responding primarily for diplomatic reasons.

Further diplomatic reasons dictated that some laws had to be mitigated. Because the British held New York, the French fleet had to land at Newport; so Rhode Island hastily repealed a 1664 law which refused citizenship to Catholics. New York, on the other hand, due to John Jay's influence, worded its new Constitution of 1777 in such a way that Catholics were refused future citizenship.

After the Revolution, Alexander Hamilton spoke vehemently in the New York Assembly against imposing an oath on Catholics. He pointed out the difference between native sons and foreign born: "The foreigner...may with propriety be asked...[to] abjure his former sovereign. The man born amongst us, educated with us, possessing our manners, with an equally ardent love of his native country, to be required to take the same oath of abjuration — what has he to abjure? He owes no fealty to any other power upon earth. Why should we wound the tender conscience of any man? and why present oaths to those who are known to be good citizens?" In 1790, Congress assumed exclusive power over the naturalization laws, thus making the New York law inoperative. Nevertheless, it was not officially repealed until 16 years later.

Above: A Gilbert Stuart portrait of Archbishop John Carroll, whose diocese included the entire United States. His brother, Charles, signed the Declaration of Independence.

Priests still were not allowed to say Mass legally in New York, even though French chaplains accompanied their troops there. For the moment, Catholics had to content themselves with fighting the Revolution for "religious as well as civil liberty," as Charles Carroll wrote years later.

Alexis de Tocqueville, after his nine-month visit to the United States in 1831 and 1832, justified Catholic participation and support of the Revolution: "Catholicism seems to me...to be one of those [doctrines] most favorable to the equality of conditions. For Catholics religious society is composed of two elements: priest and people. The priest is raised above the faithful; all below him are equal."

Except for Father McKenna and some of his group, there were few Tories among

Catholics, including the French in the North Country. Two regiments designated as "Congress's Own" were recruited among the French-Canadians, some of whom had been evicted from their homes in the New York colony by General Burgoyne. After the war, the New York legislature set aside 130,000 acres on the western shore of Lake Champlain as bounty for them.

Within the French troops were a number of Catholic officers, such as Pulaski and Kosciuszko, both Polish; and DeGrasse, Rochambeau, d'Estaing and Lafayette, all who distinguished themselves throughout the Revolution and were recognized as heroes by Protestant America. There also were several colonial Catholics who held positions of responsibility under George Washington, although none from the Albany area.

Following the election of George Washington as President, Bishop John Carroll, Charles Carroll, Daniel Carroll, Dominick Lynch (of Fort Stanwix and New York City) and Thomas Fitzsimmons, as representatives of the American Catholic community, wrote a letter of congratulations. Washington's reply unofficially sanctioned the acceptance of Roman Catholicism:

"And I presume that your fellow-citizens will not forget the patriotic part which you took in the accomplishment of their Revolution, and the establishment of their Government, or the important assistance which they received from a nation in which the Roman Catholic faith is professed."

Early Priests, A Diverse Group

Following the treaty signed at Paris in 1783 to end the Revolutionary War and the repeal of the New York anti-priest law in 1784, some of the priests who had accompanied the French troops chose to stay. Others arrived, fueled by the excitement of conquering the wilderness and the noble savage, ideas popularized by Rousseau. Some of the latter were less than stable and had to deal with a very young, very Protestant country that was establishing laws vastly different from the European tradition of the priests' background. The early Church in the new nation had rocky beginnings for about 50 years.

There were exceptions, however. The Jesuits had been suppressed by Rome for political reasons in 1773. Those Jesuits already in Pennsylvania and Maryland, such as Father John Carroll, stayed pretty much in their own bailiwicks in low profile, quietly awaiting the lifting of the suppression. Before it occurred in 1814, Father Carroll was appointed prefect apostolic in 1784 and then bishop of the Diocese of Baltimore in 1789. His See was the entire United States, and he had few priests to serve the widely scattered Catholics.

In New York in the North Country, the Diocese of Quebec had been supplying surplus priests, beginning with the French Jesuits in the 17th century. After the Revolution, this lack of priests south of the border was compensated for by the supply of priests in Canada who were escaping the French Revolution and who were available for service in the United States, as well as in Canada. Because of the crazy pattern of the watershed, the rough geography in the North Country and the nebulous border, which caused sparks on and off with the British until 1818, the French were the primary group to populate the North Country as an extension of Canada. (The boundary was not established until the Webster-Ashburton Treaty in 1842.)

As a result, they also supplied priests out of Quebec, eventually with the tacit approval of Bishop Carroll and his successors. The same happened elsewhere in the United States. If a bishop visited an area which was not within his jurisdiction, and there was a sacramental necessity, such as a Confirmation, he performed it and then wrote the resident bishop about the action. With French priests operating out of the See of Quebec, the records were — and are — naturally kept in that diocese, not in Baltimore or New York or Albany. (Thus, if one is looking for ancestral sacramental records, such as a baptism in Whitehall, it is possible it might be found in Canada.)

In 1784, Father Charles Whelan, an Irish Capuchin and chaplain on one of DeGrasse's ships, decided to stay in New York City where he formed St. Peter's Church. However, he was not well-received by the Catholics there. Shortly thereafter, another priest arrived whose credentials were in question. Nevertheless, the people were so happy to see the new priest that they voted for him over Father Whelan, who went to Johnstown to live with his brother, Dr. Joseph Whelan. After spending a few months there, he went

At the same time . . .

1771: First edition of Encyclopedia Britannica published

1775: James Watt invents steam engine

1778: Rousseau and Voltaire die

1783: Famine devastates Japan

to Maryland and then Kentucky, arriving back in Johnstown in 1790.

We know when he returned to Johnstown because from there he ordered Carey's newly printed Bible that year, the first Catholic Bible published in the United States (in Philadelphia). Although there are no records, it is possible that he ministered in the Albany area, as well as Johnstown, during those few months he was here, thus continuing the sporadic benefit of sacraments upstate. From the 1790 census, we know that, in addition to the Whelans, there were some Catholics who remained in the Johnstown area after Father McKenna departed in 1776.

What is more significant than Father Whelan's inability to get along with people and, hence, his wanderings, is that he was voted out of his church in New York City. Father Carroll was not yet bishop when that occurred. Consequently, there was no official head of the Church in the United States. Moreover, individual states, beginning with New York in 1784, established a Protestant style of church governance in their laws. All church incorporations had to comply with this presbytery concept in which each church was independent of and relatively equal to each other.

That meant every church chose a board of trustees by a vote of all adult males. The trustees formed a parochial corporation with wide administrative powers especially designed to control the pursestrings. While the law stated its intention not to interfere in the "doctrine, discipline, or worship" of churches, priests were often not appointed to the board of their own church, so they had no control over ecclesiastical decisions that involved the physical plant.

What often resulted was a form of patronage whereby the largest contributors attempted to control not only the physical plant, but also the choice of priest or dismissal of him when he irritated them. Thus, the parishioners who voted Father Whelan out were acting as their Protestant counterparts did in similar situations when a minister was disliked. Trusteeism — because its design was contrary to the normal hierarchical procedure in the Roman Catholic Church — created legal, as well as ecclesiastical problems for priests, bishops and Rome that were not mitigated in New York State until 1863 — significantly during the Civil War when many Irish were distinguishing themselves and, hence, their religion — when the laws were changed favoring the Catholic position.

St. Mary's Formed

In 1783, Ireland gained legislative independence from England, although they were still subject to George III. While the numbers were not yet large, serious Irish emigra-

tion to the United States started at this time and included priests. Among these new Irish-Americans were Dr. Joseph Whelan and his family, including his brother, Charles, a priest.

In the 1790s, the Irish would form the basis of St. Mary's parish in Albany, the second Catholic church formed in New York State. (The first was St. Peter's in New York City.) On July 8, 1796, the Albany Gazette noted: "With great pleasure we have noticed the success of the subscription, opened a few days since for erecting a Roman Catholic chapel in this city. It bespeaks the tolerant and liberal disposition of the country, to find our citizens of every persuasion emulous in assisting their Roman Catholic brethren with the means of building here a temple to the God of Heaven, in which they can worship according to the dictates of their own consciences. The corporation unanimously resolved to present them with a piece of ground for the site of their church."

A subscription was a common means of funding the incorporation and construction of churches, academies and other sizeable buildings designed for people congregating in large numbers for educational, religious or entertainment purposes. Often the same building sufficed for audiences of all purposes — both private and governmental. In small towns, even the town council or party caucuses met in the meeting house. To fund its construction, people pledged a certain amount, often for a share or two, and signed their name.

As the Gazette points out, subscribers were not just Catholics; and the City of Albany — the "corporation" mentioned — gave the land for the church. Although there was precedent for the ecumenism evident in these universal donations to build St. Mary's church and the gift of land — the Dutch Reformed, Lutheran and Anglican, among others,

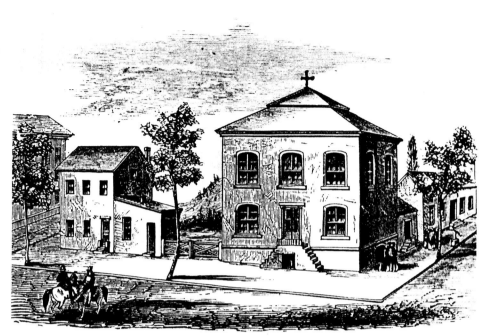

had all received free gifts of land — it was the first time that such generosity was extended to Roman Catholics north of New York City.

St. Mary's Church

By October 1796, St. Mary's was incorporated as "The Roman Catholic Church in the City of Albany." Those individuals interested in forming the church had met in James Robichaux's house. The trustees were Thomas Barry, Louis Le Couteulx, Daniel McEvers, Terence O'Donnell, Jeremiah Driskil, Michael Begley, James Robichaux, William Donovan and Philip Farrell. At least six of the nine trustees were Irish.

When the duke de La Rochefocault Liancourt visited Albany in 1775, he haughtily

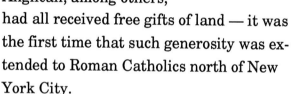

Above: St Mary's Church in Albany as it appeared in 1798.

Next page: The unusual cornerstone identifying founders and builder of St. Mary's (Kate Blain photo).

mentioned that "some French families reside in the town and its vicinity; that of M. Le Couteux...is the only one whose acquaintance I wished to obtain." Le Couteulx was in partnership with Mr. Quesnel, a merchant from St. Domingo. In 1820, he was listed as a "druggist and serj. at arms sen. [Senate]" at 61 Washington.

Information is known about some of those who formed St. Mary's:

• Several records mark the life of **Thomas Barry.** In 1756, he was a baker. Ten years later, he was on the tax list with a home. In 1771, Thomas was a merchant with a variety store near the Dutch church on lower State Street. Before he helped found St. Mary's, he was a member of the Anglican church, St. Peter's. He appears to have spent at least some of the Revolutionary War years in Philadelphia and knew Alexander Hamilton. On the 1790 census, there were 13 people living in Thomas' house. In 1805, he was wealthy enough to give Ezra Ames $20 for a portrait of himself and to spend $10 on a frame for it. (Ames was an influential painter from Massachusetts. While the location of this portrait is unknown, like other Ezra Ames' works, it probably still exists anonymously in someone's "instant ancestors" collection, and eventually will surface.)

• On the 1790 census, **Jeremiah Driskile** lived in the second ward and had four in his household.

• The same year, **Terence O'Donnald** married Sarah Hale, so had only two at his house.

• In 1813, **Philip Farrel** was a chandler on 50 Church Street; he had been listed as a candlemaker since 1798. On the 1799 tax list, he owned a house and lot in the first ward. On the 1800 census, there were four in his family.

• **Michael Begley** also was on the 1799 tax list in the first ward. His home was

worth more than Farrel's. In 1803, he was a witness for the marriage of Mary McWilliams to a stone-cutter, **William Hennigan,** also an early member of St. Mary's.

• **Daniel McEvers** also was in the first ward on the 1799 tax list, but he was only taxed for items of personal value, not real estate. He must have rented a room there.

• **James Robichaux,** who had lent his house for the organizational meeting, was one of the Revolutionary War refugees from Canada. He was a captain in the First Canadian Regiment in 1775, fighting against the British. He lost his house and stable to a conflagration that destroyed many homes in 1797; but he was still in Albany in the third ward on the 1800 census.

• **William Donovan** was the only trustee who could not be found in early sources outside of St. Mary's. As research continues, he may be found in an unexpected place.

Cornerstone laid

On September 13, 1797, the cornerstone of St. Mary's Church was laid by Thomas Barry on the lot designated by the city, located on Pine Street between Barrack (now Chapel) and Lodge streets. The cornerstone was an oval engraved with a skull and crossbones separated by the inscription "I.H.S." with a cross over the H. Underneath were the names Thomas Barry & Louis Lo Crouteulx, Founders and E.C. Quinn, Master Builder, with the date A.D. 1798.

Emanuel C. Quin owned three houses in the first ward for which he was taxed on the 1799 tax list. He rented two of them, one of which was a good size. The third one was substantial, valued at $1,470, but assessed for only 86.75+- percent of its value, or $1,274. While most other towns and cities assessed at full value, this appears to be one of the first instances in upstate New York of taxing on a partial or proportional assessment, a practice which was to become commonplace in the 20th century, yet not recognized by law until the 1970s.

On September 10, 1798, the Albany Gazette wrote: "We can inform our brethren of the Roman Catholic faith, that their church in this city is so near completed as to be under roof, glazed and floored (fire proof). To the citizens in general of this city and its vicinity, and several of the other cities of the United States and Canada, the sincere prayers of the members of this church are due for their liberality in aiding to erect it." Thomas Barry had appealed to Canada for funds. Many Albany Protestants also contributed.

The brick church was not large, only about 50 feet square with its front door facing south on Pine Street. Its hip-on-hip roof was crowned with a cross. The sanctuary was only about 12 feet square. Galleries ran along the south and west walls, the latter boasting a small organ donated by Mrs. Margaret Cassidy. Before the church was built, Mass had been offered in her home at 60 Barrick Street (now Chapel) near the church site, as well as in the home of William Duffy

(also spelled Duffey and Dufee, the latter indicating possible French origin) at the corner of Broadway and Maiden Lane. There was a small rectory west of St. Mary's, also facing Pine Street.

What St. Mary's did not have was a priest. It is believed that an Irish Capuchin Father named Thomas Flynn, referenced in a letter of Father Mantignon of Boston to Bishop Carroll in 1798, was the priest who occasionally said Mass at the Cassidys' and Duffys'. Apparently, he was at Fort Stanwix ministering to some 70 families there. Four hundred families living in the Mohawk valley were also mentioned in the letter, undoubtedly some of those Scots and Irish settled by Johnson on his lands earlier in the century.

Father Mantignon also mentions Comte de La Tour Du Pin and his wife, who had recently returned to France before St. Mary's was barely begun. For two to three years, they had lived in Watervliet (now Colonie) on property currently owned by the Sisters of St. Joseph of Carondelet. The de La Tours lived in a modest, wooden house which burned in the early 19th century. Shortly after, it was rebuilt as the more substantial brick house visible today.

The de La Tours were a titled family who came to America to escape certain death during the French Revolution in 1794. Henrietta-Lucy was a lady in waiting to Marie-Antoinette. Her father was executed, as were other family members. According to the memoirs of Madame de La Tour du Pin — which are delightfully written — after they arrived here, they became fairly successful farmers, actually doing the work themselves and deliberately avoiding putting on airs.

When their young daughter died in 1795, Henrietta-Lucy was devastated and particularly mourned the lack of a Catholic priest "in Albany or anywhere else in the neighborhood." She then poignantly portrayed how she returned to the faith: "I could not describe exactly the change which took place in me. It was as if a voice cried out to me to change my whole nature. Kneeling on my child's grave, I implored her to obtain forgiveness for me from God, Who had taken her back to be with Him, and to give me a little comfort in my distress. My prayer was heard. God granted me the grace of knowing Him and serving Him; He gave me the courage to bow very humbly beneath the blow I had received and to prepare myself to endure without complaint those future griefs which in his justice, he was to send to try me. Since that day, the divine will has found me submissive and resigned."

Other Early Priests

In addition to aristocrats like the de La Tours, in the 1790s, a number of French priests came to escape the purging and predictable death at the hands of the French revolutionary Jacobins. They formed a large corps of prominent priests and ultimately bishops, including one for the New York Diocese, which encompassed Albany at that time.

Some German priests also came. The earliest well-beloved priest to serve New York

At the same time . . .

1789: George Washington inaugurated as first President of the U.S.

1792: Denmark becomes first nation to abolish slave trade

1796: Edward Jenner discovers vaccine against smallpox

City on a part-time basis was Father Ferdinand Steenmeyer (or Steinmeyer), better known as Father Farmer, a Jesuit who ministered to all, but particularly to the German Catholics in Philadelphia beginning in 1758 until his death in 1786.

What was true in the 17th century, was also true in the 18th: Catholics spoke several languages; and although Catholicism was now sanctioned, finding priests to serve them was a continuing problem. Many French priests, and some of the German, never learned English well, which irritated the Irish, who by this time had been speaking English for at least 200 years. As often happened, if a German or French priest were the only one available for a generally Irish parish, the Irish trustees made life so difficult that the priest would want to leave. Most priests suffered — but not in silence.

Furthermore, the German and Irish parishioners did not always get along well in the same parish, leading Germans to form their own parishes with German-speaking priests. In particular, the language spoken — as well as cultural differences — was the deciding factor in choosing a church, true also among the Protestants. While it is possible to follow universal ceremonies in a different language, it is impossible to go to confession or discuss intimate problems in a foreign tongue.

As commonly occurred at this time, the trustees of early churches attempted to find their own priest. If one were found, they would petition Bishop Carroll to either appoint him or approve of him and "grant the necessary faculties" or permission.

St. Mary's did not have a language problem, but it did have other requirements. After Albany became the state capital in 1797, the custom arose of having various local clergy give the convocation opening the legislative sessions. In order for each sect to make a good impression, it became imperative that the chaplain be a good speaker. More than one priest was rejected by St. Mary's trustees because they feared that he would not represent the Catholic population favorably. They wanted a priest of distinction who would exude stature.

The first priest to serve St. Mary's was Father John Thayer, a former Congregationalist minister and chaplain to John Hancock's company during the Revolution. He was converted in Italy after witnessing a miraculous cure at the graveside of recently buried (and later canonized) Benedict Joseph Labre. Father Thayer was ordained in Paris in 1789, eventually returning to the United States where Bishop Carroll assigned him to St.

A priest celebrates an outdoor Mass in 18th-century America (CNS photo)

Mary's. He remained for a brief period.

Toward the end of 1798, Father Matthew O'Brien, recently arrived from Ireland, was assigned to Albany. In 1800, he was transferred to St. Peter's in New York City, to the consternation of the Albany parishioners. Father O'Brien, an excellent orator, alternated with the other local clergy in opening legislative sessions with a prayer. Because of his well-written and expertly delivered sermons, many Protestant statesmen attended St. Mary's when the legislature was in session and contributed generously to its support, thus showing the universal appeal of the pastor.

When George Washington died, the City of Albany planned an elaborate funeral ceremony on his next birthday in 1800, beginning with an oration at 9:00 a.m. delivered by Father O'Brien in St. Mary's. Lengthy excerpts of it were quoted in the Albany Gazette. After the funeral, everyone paraded on State Street, followed by a service in the Dutch church and a mass meeting and speech in City Hall. Four months later, Father O'Brien was reassigned to New York. It was he who welcomed the conversion of a future saint — Elizabeth Seton — in 1805, an event that would have repercussions in Albany a few years later.

Twenty-nine men signed a letter to Bishop Carroll praising Father O'Brien and regretting his departure. They included the trustees and "principal" parishioners: Richard Allanson, John Wm. Barry, Thomas Barry, John Bonor, Patrick Bryan, Patrick Campbell, James Cassidy, Henry Clarke, Edward Cody, Richard Cody, John Dougherty, William Duffy, Thomas Ennis, Philip Farrel, James Gallihar, William Hannagan, James Herring, John Jenkins, Louis LeCoulteaux, James Mahar, Dennis McMullen, David O'Barr, Alexander O'Brien, Patrick O'Callaghan, James Robichaux, Patrick Reed, Patrick J. Reilly, Patrick Walsh, and Dennis Wrian.

Priestly Problems

After Father O'Brien left, the Albany Catholics had many problems securing a priest. Father Stafford supplied for a short time in 1800. Then Father Fitzpatrick came. In 1801, the trustees wrote Bishop Carroll: "At present we have none qualified for the pulpit but Mr. Fitzpatrick, whose sermons are instructive and edifying and may be heard with satisfaction, but he is very defective in his delivery, and does not please the congregation after the many and able preachers we have been favored with." ("Mr." was the polite form of address to all men of education and stature in the 19th century.) Father Fitzpatrick left suddenly and went to Philadelphia to assist there.

Father Boutin ministered at St. Mary's briefly, but his knowledge of English was so lacking "that it was impossible for more than one or two to understand any part of it. We really pitied Mr. Boutin, but we are afraid his want of knowledge of the English language would be an insurmountable objection."

While in New York City, Mrs. Thomas

Barry discovered Father Cornelius Mahoney, whom Bishop Carroll would not appoint until he received an exeat from his bishop to formally transfer him. A year later, in 1802, Thomas Barry and the trustees were not pleased with their latest pastor. "Mr. Maloney our present priest came here last fall from New York, waited all winter at no small expense to me for his [illegible] without saying Mass or giving us a private prayer. I paid his passage from New York, paid ——dollars for his board then brought him to my own house and kept him most of the winter, free of cost, paid out 70 pounds for a house or a presbyter. We got him a new suit of broad cloth, thirty dollars in his pocket in order to go to Baltimore to see what he had to say for himself to your Lordship. Last spring he stopped at New York for good reason. He well knew that your Lordship would not place such an ignorant man at Albany when you had a trial of him."

Thomas penned more complaints. Finally, he moaned: "The trustees are ashamed to acquaint your Lordship of his behaviour being that they were so warm in his behalf not knowing he was so ignorant as he proved to be. They were like a drowning man grasping at a straw, glad to get any man after Fitzpatrick left, this or rather run away. He is no preacher, he can say Mass and the Rosary after a manner, for he is very short-sighted, cannot see well." Barry continues: "Ireland...could not send a more...avaricious man abroad. Old Father Whelan could say something to the purpose to what he can." Thomas concludes: "My Lord when the Legis-

lature meets this winter they call for all the different ministers to give a short prayer in, and are well paid for it, what a shame will it be for our priest cannot appear for want of ability, it was not so with Dr. O'Brien or Fitzpatrick."

In the same letter, Barry mentions: "This will be handed to you by Mr. Lecoutelx who was the best friend I had in founding the Catholic church in Albany and who has now brought a handsome print from Canada for the altar." (Shortly thereafter in 1804, Louis Le Couteulx went to Buffalo, where he was instrumental in building the first Catholic church there, fittingly named the Church of St. Louis.)

Litany of Priests

The struggle to obtain a priest for Albany continued. The trustees paid the passage from Ireland of Franciscan Father Michael Egan. To their surprise, he appeared in 1803 in Lancaster, Pennsylvania, ministering to a church that repaid the Albany group $142 for his travel expenses.

In 1804, Recollect Father Luke Fitzsimmons was in Albany but left for Canada at the end of the summer. He briefly was in Cornwallis, Charleston and Glengary, where the Loyalist Scots and Irish from Johnstown had fled before the Revolution.

Also in 1804, Thomas Barry mentioned Father Gallagher, who was supposed to go to Albany, yet nothing had been heard from him, and Father Kenny, whom "they speak well of" in Philadelphia. Again, nothing happened.

The litany of priests continued. Father James Byrne, assistant at St. Peter's in New York City, visited occasionally in 1806. In 1807, a spirited letter was sent Bishop Carroll. Father Michael Hurley, O.S.A., had been in Albany briefly and was enthusiastically received: "With pleasure we can inform your Lordship that we have had the Rev. Mr. Hurley here these last five Sundays and to our great satisfaction found our church crowded with all denominations of people every Sunday. The legislature in session, many of the members came to hear him. Such a man as him, my lord, would have a respectable congregation in less than a year in this place, for some Protestants declared that they would subscribe toward his support." Barry recounts how the church was packed and that one day the collection "was $95 towards finishing the church." (Normally it was $8 or $9.)

To entice him, Father Hurley was offered a salary of $800 for one year — an unusually generous amount — along with a furnished house and an offer to be in Schenectady every fifth Sunday to form another church — and, hence, receive another salary. He was not tempted.

Previously, in 1804, Father M. Carr of Philadelphia visited New York, Albany and "Balstown" [Balltown Road/Ballston Lake/Spa] and had written Bishop Carroll that in Schenectady and Troy, "there are some reputable Catholic families very much in want of Spiritual assistance," if only priests would come.

Father Carr also mentioned another common method of paying for the construction of large buildings for gatherings: the lottery. "I am requested by a friend to procure for him if possible, No. 16,696 in the Cathedral Church Lottery. He has deposited in my hands $10 for the payment thereof." (The cathedral mentioned probably was St. Patrick's in New York, which was built in 1809.) In addition to subscription, a variety of lotteries helped build many churches, particularly Catholic and Anglican.

Microcosm

While the details of this early struggle to shape St. Mary's appear repetitive, they are characteristic of the times, as well as of the pivotal role that trustees would play in the development of the Catholic Church in America. In deference to New York State law and the dearth of priests, lay trustees organized St. Mary's, not because of a desire to possess authority over priests, but because they desperately wanted a priest, the sacraments and spiritual guidance. Even well-meaning trustees, such as Thomas Barry, at times did not perceive their own heavy-handedness.

St. Mary's was the only church for about 20 years upstate, a very long time for one church to provide all of the sacraments for everyone needing them. Thus, its detailed development should be recognized as a representative microcosm of generally what some of the future churches also went through, particularly when they were an isolated church with a vast parish. (There is neither space nor time to provide such details about every parish formed in the Albany Diocese;

interested Catholics should contact their parish for its unique history.)

In 1807, after Father Hurley left, Father Michael James Bushe arrived, ministered — and died within a year. He was buried in St. Mary's cemetery in the old burial ground that was eventually moved to create Washington Park. Father Weddin, a German priest, was a temporary supply in 1810 for a year.

In 1813, Father Paul McQuade was in Albany and preached a sermon at the Catholic Cemetery for the burial of Thomas Barry, "a respected merchant and citizen." In 1814-15, Father McQuade was listed in the Albany City Directories as the pastor of St. Mary's. He was, perhaps, the first of the circuit-riding priests who used St. Mary's as a base for somewhat regular trips around a huge parish encompassing what would become the Roman Catholic Diocese of Albany.

Winning the Revolution had opened up the Mohawk valley west of Fort Stanwix by eliminating the Iroquois threat. They were pushed ultimately to Canada and Wisconsin. By 1810, settlers — among them, Catholics — were starting to flock to that part of the state. Father McQuade visited Utica and administered the last rites to Mrs. John C. Devereux, who had been Ellen Barry. She was brought back to Albany and buried in St. Mary's cemetery as Elenorn Devereux.

The Devereaux brothers, John and Nicholas, were born in Ireland of French and Irish stock. John spent a year in France learning to play the violin and to teach dancing, au

At the same time . . .

1802: Napoleon becomes president of Italian Republic

1804: Beethoven composes "Eroica," his third symphony

1807: Garibaldi and Longfellow born

1811: Paraguay becomes independent from Spain

courant in France at that time. As St. Mary's was being built, he was a dancing master in New England, where he "danced $1,000 out of the Yankees." Upon moving to Albany, he married Ellen Barry, probably related to Thomas. By 1802, John Devereux was in Utica with a dry goods store. Nicholas came at this time and eventually became even more prominent than his brother. In 1816, Bishop Connolly wrote that the Rev. Mr. McQuade insisted on leaving his flock at Albany, "notwithstanding all my entreaties to deter him from taking such a regrettable step."

Circuit-Riding Priests

The Church outside of New York City was primarily a mission area and was viewed as such. For several years, St. Mary's in Albany was the main church many priests used as a base for their circuits to outlying areas to baptize, marry, bury and catechize. Before the railroads simplified travel to some areas, the horse was their principal means of travel. Jesuit Father John Grassi, writing in the early 1800s, captured the flavor of the experience: "I shall say nothing of the services in city churches, because they are the same as in Europe, so far as the number of priests will permit: but it will not be without interest to say something of those which are held in the country churches situated at a distance from any dwelling house, which are by far most numerous. On Saturday, the missionary leaves his residence, and goes to take up his lodgings with some Catholic family near the church. Having arrived at the house, he puts the Blessed Sacrament in some decent place, and also the Holy Oils, without which he never sets out on a journey. On the following morning he rides to the church, and ties his horse to a bush. The whole morning is spent in hearing confessions: meanwhile the people from distances of four, six, ten miles, and even more, are coming in on horseback, so that often the church is entirely surrounded with horses. Mass begins towards noon; during the celebration, those who can read make use of prayerbooks and pious hymns, for the most part in English, are sung by a choir of men and women. The sermon comes after the Gospel, and it is preceded by the Gospel read in the vernacular. The preacher either reads or delivers his sermon, according to inclination and sometimes it is deferred until after Mass to enable the priest to take some refreshment, which the faithful never fail to supply....Vespers are not said, as the people live so far off and are so scattered; and so when Mass is over, the children recite the cathecism, infants are baptized, or the ceremonies are supplied in the case of those already baptized in danger, prayers for the dead are recited or the funeral services are performed over those who have been buried in the churchyard during the absence of the priest. Finally, one must attend to those who ask for instruction in order to join the Church, or who wish to be united in the bonds of holy Matrimony."

Because St. Mary's was a mission church with a circuit, its trustees included one for Schenectady, one for Lansingburgh and one for the out-missions. In 1823, the trustees were John Cassidy, John Reynolds, John Duffan (or Duffau), Richard Allanson, Patrick Murcphy, Philip Carroll and Thomas Gough for Albany; James O'Connor for Schenectady; and Keating Rosson for Lansingburgh.

Significant Case

In 1815, Father Anthony Kohlman, a German Jesuit in New York City, returned some goods stolen by a person who had confessed the crime to him. In the ensuing trial, he stated that he was not free to reveal what he had been told. DeWitt Clinton, mayor of New York and the presiding judge, ruled that the secrets of the confessional were inviolate, at that time a precedent and now a principle that has prevailed: "The witness in this case evidently believes that his answering in this case would expose him to punishment in a future state, and it must be conceded by all that it would expose him to privations and disgrace in this world. If he tells the truth, he violates his ecclesiastical oath; if he prevaricates, he violates his judicial oath. The only course is for the Court to declare that he shall not testify or act at all."

While this case did not occur in Albany, it manifested the ethics that Catholicism represented in the eyes of the Protestant majority. Due to the fairly constant travel the priests of New York and Albany would experience in the late teens and twenties of the 19th century, it had inevitable repercussions in Albany.

Narrowing the focus

In 1807, Robert Fulton, with the financial backing of the Livingstons, had developed a viable steamboat, revolutionizing Hudson River travel. Now Albany and New York were only a day apart, and soon would be less. As a result, the attitude regarding priestly assignments changed. Once assigned to St. Mary's in Albany, a priest no longer had to fear spending his remaining days "in the sticks."

The New York Diocese had been formed in 1808, although the first resident bishop, John Connolly, did not arrive until 1815. Albany — once a part of the single diocese that encompassed America — was now a part of a geographically smaller diocese. That meant Bishop Connolly could be more focused than Bishop Carroll ever could have been. Bishop Connolly sent Father Michael O'Gorman to St. Mary's in Albany for a couple of years. He traveled on his circuit west several times, celebrating Masses in homes, courthouses, meetinghouses and schoolhouses in Schenectady, Auburn, Salina, Canandaigua and Rochester.

In Utica in 1819, the Devereux brothers organized the western Catholic laymen as "the first Catholic Church of the western District of the State of New York," and a Mass was celebrated at the Utica Free Academy, a nonsectarian school started by the Devereux family and others. Nicholas Devereux's wife, a Protestant, wrote her mother: "I was very much surprised to find so many Catholics in this part of the country, Some came 50 miles, and some two days journey to partake of the sacrament. This will show you how much attached they are to their religion. The canal has brought many Catholics to this place." Although she assured her mother that she still attended her own church, 20 years later, she became a Catholic.

This was the beginning of St. John's, the second church in the Albany jurisdiction, which was dedicated in 1821 with the blessings of Father O'Gorman. In 1819, he supported Father John Farnam's appointment to build the church. Its land had been donated by a Protestant woman, and the Devereux brothers supplied much of the financial assistance.

Expansion

In 1820, three additional churches were launched in the western part of New York State: St. Patrick's in Rochester, Holy Family in Auburn and St. James in Carthage, east of Watertown. Of this group, St. James would be the only church located in the Albany Diocese when it was formed.

As with St. John's in Utica, these churches were founded after several years of being served by circuit-riding priests who used any available building large enough for the congregation. Thus, their founding dates reflect the first evidence of actual church formation, whether it be a record of land purchased, such as a deed, a New York State law passed recognizing the incorporation of a church, or a notice of such in a newspaper.

Almost all of the first churches formed in each separate city or town started as circuit-riding missions from an established church elsewhere. For example, St. Mary's was used as a base for priests who rode the circuit up and down the Hudson and along the Mohawk. There were predictable reasons a second church was started: The population of the first church was overflowing; the population base had moved; or a non-English-speaking ethnic group had appeared. These churches would not necessarily have been missions. Thus, their dates are easier to establish.

After the Americans won the Revolution, the British still maintained forts in the Upper Midwest and Northwest. In 1805, Napoleon's victory at Austerlitz assured French control over much of the European land mass, while Nelson's victory over the French at Trafalgar assured Britain's continued supremacy of the seas. Britain attacked ships bound for ports other than her own, while Napoleon indiscriminately seized any ships not clearly serving him.

Life as a sailor on a British ship was harsh, and there were many desertions in every port. American ships often were boarded and searched for these "deserters," who were impressed into service on the British ships. A high percentage of the sailors — now legally American citizens — had been born in the British Isles. The British took advantage of this to further negate the results of the Revolution. This harassment, which even occurred in American ports, resulted in the second war of American independence — the War of 1812.

The victory of the United States in that war combined with the abdication of Napoleon to open the seas to immigration. Europeans, particularly those from the British Isles, flocked first to Quebec, beginning in 1816, and then to New York, starting in 1822. At the same time, certified Irish paupers — Catholics had preference — were sent to both cities with their passage paid for by a government eager to rid Ireland of its overpopulation.

Canals

Meanwhile, in 1817, the New York State legislature authorized $7,000,000 to build the Erie Canal. Many of the newly arrived

Illustrations celebrate rail and canal transportation (New York State Bicentennial Souvenir Booklet, 1886).
Page 50: Henriette de La Tour du Pin

immigrants were put to work, primarily as laborers digging "Clinton's ditch," which was 40 feet wide by 4 feet deep and 363 miles long. Although most of the men were laborers, stone cutters were also employed to dress the stone used to line the ditch and the locks. While many of the workers were recruited from among the farmers who lived along the path, 3,000 Irishmen were working on the canal in 1818. A laborer made 37-and-a-half to 50 cents a day compared to a skilled mechanic's $1.25; he also got a quart of whiskey. A contingent of workers traveled west along the Mohawk River as the canal progressed, and shanty towns sprang up to house them.

The Erie Canal was not the first in New York State. In 1795, one was completed around Little Falls; in 1797, the canal around Rome was finished; and in 1798, the one around German Flatts opened to improve Mohawk River transportation from the Cohoes Falls west. When the Erie Canal was built 20 years later, these segments had to be improved and, in some cases, changed. The Champlain Canal began at the same

time as the Erie because it was connected to it, starting in Waterford and ending near Whitehall in the South Bay of Lake Champlain. Its purpose was to divert trade from Quebec to the Troy/Albany area, opening up local trade with the northeast corner of the state.

River freight

Across the Hudson from Troy, at West Troy (now Watervliet), the mouth of the south branch of the Mohawk River served as a basin for boats. The Champlain/Erie Canal entered the Hudson in at least four places via side-cut canals from Waterford to Albany, but the main terminus was in Albany, east of Colonie Street. Lock 2 in Waterford was the one farthest north, while two in West Troy were found at approximately 23rd Street and south of the arsenal, which had been built in 1812. Traffic was so heavy on the canal that these side canals proved a boon in keeping the shipping flowing. Troy was in a perfect location to take advantage of the raw materials and freight that was transferred from the smaller canal boats to the river sloops and later onto steamers.

The eastern side of the Hudson was primarily farming country until after the Revolution. A few ferries connected Troy to Albany and the west side of the Hudson River. There was no bridge until 1804 when one was built at Lansingburgh.

Although the ferries were kept busy, they were not always safe. Henriette Lucy de la Tour du Pin, the Catholic who had fled the French Revolution, described her frightening experience one night when she boarded the ferry between Troy and West Troy with her horse. Four oxen were boarded after her. Shortly after the ferry had launched into the river, all four oxen simultaneously leaned over the same side to drink, making the ferry heel to that side. A quick-thinking man jabbed his penknife in the rump of one ox, causing it to jump overboard. The other three followed suit, and the ferry returned to an even keel; the rest of the passengers and Henriette's mare arrived safely on the other side.

Ferries were used throughout most of the 19th century even after bridges were built across the Hudson. There was no bridge at Albany until 1866 because special interests protected Troy's industrial and rail advantage. Rail lines fed into the bridge at Waterford. In 1886, there were only two bridges between Troy and West Troy, one for trains and one for wagons. There were four ferries, in addition to more north and south of Troy.

In the winter, people eagerly awaited the three to four months when the Hudson would freeze over the two- or three-foot depth necessary for transportation to cross it. Henriette explained: "Before venturing on to the river, it was necessary to wait until the places where it was safe to cross the ice had been marked out with pine branches for, without this precaution, there was great danger. Every year there were accidents through lack of care. Indeed, since the tidal rise and fall at Albany, and as far up as the junction of the Mohawk, was some seven or eight feet, the ice was often unsupported by water."

In the 1790s, and the first decade of the 19th century, a variety of mills were built on the Wynant-skill and the Poesten-kill creeks. Although the Dutch started the mills, several were bought and developed by New Englanders in the early 19th century, including one by Erastus Corning, whose parents had settled in Chatham from Connecticut.

The opening of the Champlain Canal on September 10, 1823, and the Rochester-to-Albany section of the Erie Canal in October opposite Troy provided the transportation necessary to ship manufactured products north and west, and south on the Hudson

River. At the opening of the completed Erie Canal in 1825, a great celebration took place. Albany city Alderman John Cassidy, president of St Mary's parish trustees, ensured that the clergy, as well as St. Patrick's Society, marched in the parade.

Where jobs were, people came to take them, thus increasing Troy's and Albany's populations. In 1820, the population of Troy was 5,264. Five years later, it had increased by 2,595 to 7,859. By 1824, there was a large enough resident Catholic population to assemble for worship in an old schoolhouse on Ferry Street in Troy, giving birth to St. Peter's Church. The next year, Father Patrick McGilligan arrived to stay for two years, and the courthouse was used for services. Property was deeded to St. Peter's in 1826, and it was incorporated in 1827. Keating Rawson, Patrick Irwin, Edward Dawler, Patrick Mooney, Patrick Cole, George Donlevy, Philip Quin, Michael Agan and James Cantwell were elected trustees.

Rawson was a convert received into the Church, as the unverified story was told, along with a Miss Eldridge, also from Lansingburgh, by Bishop Connolly when he visited Albany shortly after his ordination in 1817. Previously, Rawson had served as the trustee from Lansingburgh for St. Mary's. That same year, a frame church, 40 by 60 feet, was built, and Father John Shannahan became its first official pastor. In 1834, a 40-foot brick addition was added with a basement to house a school. James Fitzpatrick, the sexton, was the schoolmaster.

Schools

St. Peter's was not the first Catholic school in upstate New York. In 1828, Mrs. Margaret Annesley, a Protestant, strongly recommended that a Sunday school be formed at St. Mary's in Albany. French-born Peter M. Morange, an upholsterer, church trustee, organist and poet, headed the school. In addition to Catholic women, Mrs. Annesley was invited — and consented — to be a teacher. This school was so successful that a grammar school was soon started, staffed, part-time, by lay women. Then Mrs. James Meline headed it full-time.

Soon, Bishop John Dubois, the third bishop of New York, was petitioned for nuns to run the school. Three Sisters of Charity from Emmitsburg, Maryland, arrived in Albany in the autumn of 1828 at his invitation. Thus within only a year, the fledgling Catholic school system developed from a weekly Sunday school to a five-day-a-week elementary school.

The Sisters of Charity had been founded in Baltimore not quite 20 years earlier by Elizabeth Ann Bayley Seton, a convert from the Episcopal Church received by Father Matthew O'Brien, the beloved priest at St. Mary's. (Pope Paul VI proclaimed her a saint in 1975.) In Albany, the sisters taught in a rented abandoned bakery until the larger second church for St. Mary's was finished in 1830; the school was moved to its basement. They also took a few orphans into their convent. In 1832, when the cholera epidemic was brought from Canada, the sisters opened an orphan asylum in a building adjoining the church.

John Olmsted, a 21-year-old native of Spencertown who worked as a clerk in New York City, wrote a letter to a friend in Green River (now Austerlitz): "The Cholera first visited this country in 1832. I remember it well because I was sent by my employers as a witness to Plattsburgh, in the spring of that year, and met the victims...as they fled southward from Canada to avoid it. I went by steamboat to Troy, from there to Whitehall by canal packet; thence to Plattsburgh by steamboat, returning by way of boat to Burlington, Vt., thence by stage through Vergennes, and Castelton [sic] to Troy. The whole country was frightened and so was I."

Olmsted was probably sent upstate to find out how widespread the epidemic was. Because farmers had stopped bringing in their produce to sell, supplies to cities became distressfully low and prices rose dramatically. Since he was employed by a wholesale grocery warehouse, the owners wanted to know when the goods would return to normal levels. In Albany, the price of a bushel of potatoes rose 300 percent, and many stores were closed. People burned tar in the belief that the oily smoke would abate the epidemic.

Amid such an atmosphere, the Sisters of Charity started a "select" school in a room of the asylum to provide quality education for girls whose parents could afford it. The fees supported the orphans and the sisters. The sisters also continued to teach the girls in the basement of the church in the free

At the same time . . .

1816: Rossini composes "The Barber of Seville"

1819: Simon Bolivar becomes president of Colombia

1821: Napoleon and John Keats die

1826: Russia declares war on Persia

school, while John Maloney and John Flinn taught the boys.

The arrival of the sisters gave a new dimension to Catholic life in Albany. The youngest — and hardiest — of them was Sister Mary DeSales Tyler. When her companions fell sick and returned to Baltimore, she stayed in Albany. She came from an outstanding family, all of whom were converts. Her cousin, Virgil Barber, was an Episcopalian minister and principal of the academy in Fairfield, north of Little Falls. He became enthralled with the message in a prayer book titled, "A Novena to St. Francis Xavier," which he had borrowed from his Irish servant-girl. In 1817, he and his family of five moved to New York City where he opened up a school with the help of a Catholic priest. He and his family then became Roman Catholics. Eventually, they moved to Baltimore, where he and a son, Samuel, joined the Jesuits, and his wife and one daughter became Visitation nuns. Two other daughters became Ursuline nuns.

Virgil's father, Daniel Barber of New Hampshire, also an Episcopalian minister, became a Catholic, too. After his wife's death, he took minor orders and became a sub-deacon before he died. His wife, daughter, sister (Mrs. Tyler), her husband and their children also converted. Three Tyler daughters, including Sister Mary DeSales, became Sisters of Charity; and a fourth transferred to the Visitation Order. A son, William, became the first Bishop of Hartford. That family of converts with ties to the Albany area enjoyed national attention in the 1820s; but in 20 years, there would be more prominent individuals, also with local ties, who converted under the influence of the Oxford Movement.

Railroads

When John Olmsted listed the variety of conveyances he used to discover the extent of the cholera epidemic, he revealed what was available to the traveler. The means he did not list were: sloop, packet, canoe, ark, ferry and related raft variants on water; and wagon, sleigh and, of course, foot, on land. His return trip via land shunned the regular water route, possibly to avoid cholera contamination but perhaps also because it was a quicker return route. Charles Dickens recorded on his 1842 trip to the United States that the coach run between Whitehall and Albany took from early morning until 5 p.m. Passengers often combined stage and water travel, especially when there were several canal locks, because it took so much longer waiting for the locks to fill. Passenger travel along the Hudson traditionally disembarked at Albany and took a stage to Schenectady to avoid the 27 locks in between on the Erie,

thus saving a day's travel.

Beginning in 1833, a new method, the railroad, provided an additional option between Albany and Schenectady. Train cars were drawn by horses to the junction of Madison and Western Avenues in Albany, where the engines took over for the rest of the trip to Schenectady. The first trains primarily followed the water route that was originally designed to complement the canals as short cuts around the tedious locks and the winding courses water routes necessitated. By 1836, trains could travel to Utica and in 1839, Syracuse. In 1841, the eastern side of the Hudson was connected to Boston. By 1842, there was a Buffalo-to-Albany run. By the 1850s, train tracks connected the state in all four directions, and products built in Troy and other small towns during the power revolution were distributed throughout the United States.

The Erie Canal was enlarged in the 1840s-'50s. The route was moved in some locations and locks improved, this time to compete with the railroads. The canal excelled in shipping bulky, high-tonnage items, including lumber, flour, wheat, wood, coal, stone, lime, clay, railroad iron and salt. Near the eastern terminus, logs were floated down the Hudson; lumber was also brought on the Champlain canal from Glens Falls to the Troy and Albany lumber districts.

In the 1830s, the Erie Canal carried many immigrants — primarily Irish and Germans — who had arrived from Europe at New York City. Many of them came with specific plans to travel west on the canal. They disembarked at locations where a relative, friend or neighbor had already settled and was expecting them. (In 1832, for example, the German great-great grandparents of the author paid for the passages of their mostly adult children to New York City with the intention of traveling west on the Erie to settle in St. Catharine's, Ontario. On the canal, great-great grandmother gambled successfully enough to set each son up in business and to have dowries for the daughters. When they got to Rochester, the hotels were so crowded that they were put up in the lobby of one. The next day, Anna Maria Begy, the great-great grandmother, announced that they were staying in Rochester. She had had it with traveling. By the time her husband died in the early 1840s, some of the children had already moved to St. Catharine's — note the German spelling — which is near Niagara Falls. Eventually, Anna Maria also ended up buried there.) In the Albany area, the ratio of Irish to Germans for much of the 19th century was nine to one; but the farther west one traveled, the higher the percentage of Germans became until the ratio was reversed in Buffalo.

The newly arrived immigrants settled where work was available. Throughout the 1830s and '40s, railroad construction provided some of those jobs. The canals and the rivers were another source of employment

Above: St. Peter's, first church in Troy, 1837.
Next page: 1837 baptismal records from St. Peter's.
(Parish anniversary book)

for sailors and stevedores, as well as for the teenage boys who walked the mules and the horse teams towing the boats between Albany and Buffalo until the waterways were closed by ice. In the 1840s, the Erie was so congested by traffic that it had to be enlarged, primarily by immigrants. Immigrants also found jobs in related industries, such as shipbuilding, carriage making, livery stables, lumber yards and the arsenal.

Mills and tanneries

The Hudson/Mohawk corridors with their multiple streams cascading down hills provided places for mills to be established utilizing water-power and, later, steam. Everyone needed grist and saw mills for survival. Fulling mills to prepare cloth and trip hammer blacksmith forges to make tools for trades and implements for farming were common. Eventually, the mills were set up on practically every possible site, even when the streams were only seasonal.

Other industries appeared in the 1800-

1830s. In Glens Falls, digging the feeder canal opened limestone beds near the surface. Waste from the saw mills was used in kilns to produce lime used in mortar that was then sold all along the Hudson/Mohawk corridor. Lime also had several other uses, such as in outhouses to sweeten the air and as whitewash to provide a plaster-like finish to wood.

Tanneries were set up in Greene, Fulton and Montgomery counties to utilize the oak, beech, birch and hemlock growth there. The quarries at Little Falls produced stone for the canals, as well as retaining and foundation walls and curbing. Quarries with rock used in the various aspects of building construction were also found in Amsterdam, Tribes Hill and Canajoharie, all in Montgomery County.

In the 1830s, Troy had already become known for its many ironworks. Eventually, they would specialize in specific items, ranging from nails and rivets to plate iron for stoves. They also produced the iron plates used to construct the Monitor in the Civil War.

Irish and German immigrants

Not all of the Irish were certified paupers; most were laborers from the rural working class. The men did not necessarily have a specific skill or trade to offer, other than general farm knowledge. Some of them were literate and left letters, but literacy seemed to be true more often of women. Boys as young as eight, nine or ten were bound out to a craftsman to learn a trade by practical experience after acquiring only rudimentary literacy. Girls, on the other hand, were usually kept at home longer to learn housework and to spin, sometimes to weave, sew and knit.

Freed of a master's time clock, they could pursue more book learning.

Many of these Irish were Catholic, having learned their letters from the local priest in a parish school. Universal elementary education was not mandatory in England until 1833 when governmental support was mandated. When parents could afford schooling, children were educated at home or in private schools, some affiliated with a specific denomination. This was one of the basic reasons many religious communities began in Europe. The Christian Brothers, the Daughters of Charity and other orders began with a desire to get the children off the streets and teach them skills so that they could support themselves and not steal.

Education and immigrants

In the New World, literacy was emphasized as early as the 17th century. Children were taught to read by using the Bible. Because of the dominance of Protestants, it naturally was a Protestant Bible. After the American Revolution, states encouraged neighborhood public schools which were built, maintained and supervised by the parents whose children attended. By the early 19th century, New York had public education statutes, but little control over the enforcement of what was taught or who attended. Because much of the United States was rural, farm planting and harvesting schedules interrupted the school year, and many children attended sporadically. It was not until much later in the 20th century that decentralization was abandoned, and mandatory school attendance with an obligatory school year could be enforced.

In urban areas, private or church-related schools often substituted for public schools for the middle class. Because poor children frequently worked, Sunday school often became their only vehicle for literacy. In order to get to Sunday school in the winter, warm clothing was needed. Thus, in Protestant churches, the Sunday school program was tied to the deacons' Poor Fund. Since Catholic and Protestant life mirrored each other so often, it is conceivable that Catholics also supplied winter clothing to poor children in order to entice them to Sunday school.

A majority of the German immigrants in the 1830s were Catholic, although some were Lutherans or Jews. At this time, the various German states were part of a loosely organized federation with the Hapsburg Empire still dominant. Each of the principalities maintained an army based on conscription, which was bitterly resented. The conscripts primarily were from the lower classes and hence could not buy their way out of serving in the army; but they could emigrate to avoid the draft.

Emigration was also spurred by other factors. First, the western part of the country (in what became roughly West Germany after World War II) was experiencing overpopulation. Second, while the aristocracy was willing to sell peasants some land, farmers could afford it only if they subdivided it so much that it could not give a productive return and yielded no profit. Third, among city dwellers, there were many skilled craftsmen who could not compete with the newly developing industrial world. Fourth, people remembered William Penn's posters, circulated along the Rhine over a century before, which touted the advantages of the New World. For some or all of those reasons, these Germans (not the more eastern Prussians) emigrated to the New World.

While not wealthy, they paid for their passage, and many times had a destination in mind before they set sail. They also generally came with a skill or trade. Many were butchers, blacksmiths and carpenters. While usually at least basically literate, it was in a language few people spoke in the United States. Unlike many of the Irish, they had to learn English in order to interact. Because of their desire to have their children maintain the German language and culture, as well as the parents' desire to have some control over their education, the Germans lobbied early on for their own churches and schools.

Churches multiply

With the influx of these immigrants, many of them Catholics, just before and during the 1830s, more churches were established in upstate New York. All would be on transportation routes. All would eventually end up in the dioceses of Syracuse or Ogdensburg, which were broken off of the Albany Diocese in the late 19th century.

The Syracuse area was a logical extension of the westward expansion along the Mohawk. The North Country was settled beginning in the 17th century by "canadiens," their Catholic church operating out of Québec. Many of the French were related to the Iroquois and Algonquins, some of whom were settled at St. Regis, a large area crossing the border between New York and Canada. Their concentration in this area gave them a 30 percent share of the immigrant population.

The "canadiens" often supported themselves by transitory and seasonal occupations. They were voyageurs, farmers, and, later, loggers and iron forge workers. They also traveled back and forth over the border continuously. Beginning in the 18th century, they resisted supporting their churches because churches were supported by the government in France. Thus, few churches were built and maintained beyond a few years. In spite of those problems, the actual continuing presence of priests there was probably much more consistent than what occurred farther south.

The origin and uninterrupted duration of a church is one criterion for its inclusion on a list of early churches. Another is an official status marker, whether it be a priest assigned full-time to a congregation (even if there were no building), a deed, a mortgage, a consecration, an incorporation of a church by the state legislature, or the publication of one of those legal documents in a newspaper. Just because a group petitioned the bishop for a priest or one came a few times a year to an area as a mission does not establish a permanent church. Such missions often existed in many places for as long as 20 years before a church was finally built. An example of an interrupted mission occurred at the town, still locally known as Corbeau, although officially Coopersville, near the northwestern part of Lake Champlain. In the 18th century, it was a French settlement on the Chazy River, having a priest out of Quebec. There was no resident priest from 1792-1806, then from 1812 until almost the mid-19th century. (Because of these varying ways of dating churches' beginnings, some celebrate their centennials and sesquicentennials based on hearsay evidence, particularly oral tradition. Oral tradition, while it plays a vital role in personalizing a history, is often notoriously inaccurate regarding specific dates and facts. For that reason, the dates of the churches discussed here are all documented even if tradition may indicate otherwise.)

North Country

The waterways around much of northern New York, the southwest-northeast arch of Lake Ontario and the St. Lawrence River, and the north-south Richelieu River-Lake Champlain corridor combined to create a semicircle of settlements with Catholic churches by the 1830s. On the eastern section of this area lay Plattsburg, where Father Patrick McGilligan, who had been the first resident priest of St. Peter's in Troy, arrived to organize St. John the Baptist church in 1827. A church was built in 1828 to serve the Irish who had come from the Montreal area to work in the lumber mills.

Farther northwest, nearer the St. Lawrence, St. Regis had an extra factor to contend with: the border with Canada. The Catholic church there was one of the earliest in the North Country, but it was located in

Canada. To the Iroquois there, who spoke French as well as their own language(s), and who lived on both sides of the border, it was incomprehensible to have this political line make a difference. To the English, however, it was equally incomprehensible to put an American flag on a Canadian church. A partial solution was found in 1834 when St. Patrick's was located in nearby Hogansburg for the burgeoning Irish population, a necessary addition, because they usually did not speak French.

Southwest on the St. Lawrence, Ogdensburg had been established as a French-Canadian, native American mission, Fort La Présentation, in the 18th century by Abbé Francois Picquet. Because the St. Lawrence is relatively narrow there, Ogdensburg became a port with close ties to Canada, the Catholics coming from there. A "Survey of the Catholick Chapel Lot made June 22, 1832, the Trustees of said Chapel for the sum of $.50 by Robert Tate and Son" documents the origins of the first church building.

South and inland on the Black River portage route from the Mohawk valley, the construction of St. James was completed much earlier in Carthage near Watertown in 1818. A Bonapartist, James Le Ray de Chaumont, bought miles of territory in Jefferson County and settled three colonies of Catholic immigrants: the French on the Saint Lawrence at Rosiere, the Germans at Croghan and the Irish at Carthage. What the parishioners could not raise themselves for the church at Carthage, James and his son, Vincent, supplied. James Le Ray went back to France after Napoleon's death, having signed over his properties to Vincent.

South and west of Carthage, Syracuse Catholics built a church in 1827. In addition to mills, Syracuse — then Salina — had been known ever since the 17th century because the natives living near there traded in salt, a very profitable necessity of life. After the construction of the Erie Canal, the salt works supplied most of the United States' needs until about 1870.

Northwest of Syracuse, Fort Oswego was the western terminus of the water route linking the Mohawk/Hudson corridor with Lake Ontario in the fur trade of the 18th century. In 1828, the Oswego Canal connected Lake Ontario with the Erie Canal, stimulating Oswego's growth. In addition to building the canal, immigrants worked in the grist mills and in the salt trade from Syracuse, as well as on farms. A combination of primarily Irish, many French Canadians and a few Germans formed the Catholic community which built St. Paul's in 1830.

The next group of churches were within what ultimately became and remained the Roman Catholic Diocese of Albany. In the early 1830s, many fledgling missions were developing, served primarily by St. Mary's in Albany west along the Mohawk and south down the Hudson, and by St. Peter's in Troy north up the Hudson and east to Vermont. Little Falls, Herkimer, Ilion, Frankfort and parts west were generally served by priests from Utica, but their orientation was west, rather than east.

At the same time . . .

1831: Egypt conquers Syria

1834: Abraham Lincoln, 25, enters politics as state assemblyman in Illinois

1836: The Alamo falls

1839: First electric clock built

Schenectady, founded in 1661, became important early as the terminus of the portage between Albany and the Mohawk to avoid the Cohoes Falls. Although the advent of the Erie Canal bit into this transshipment trade, people traveling west from the Hudson River preferred the faster stage route from Albany to Schenectady. When trains started running in 1831 between the two cities, trade started to improve, and warehouses were built. Irish settled there; and for years, Mass was celebrated in a broom factory by circuit priests from St. Mary's in Albany — Father Charles Smith and later Father John Kelly in particular during the 1830s. Among the church's members were Bernard Barry, Patrick Carey, Michael Gleason, James Giblon, Michael Hanlon, James Lunny, Patrick McDermott, Patrick McCarthy, Michael Mulcare and John McEncroe. In 1838, a deed for the land was obtained and a church constructed. The first trustees were Patrick Keys, Darriel O'Brien, Roddy Martin, John Brogan and Michael Carr.

Father John Kelly also served St. Mary's in Sandy Hill (later Hudson Falls) and its environs during the same time period. According to an early source, beginning in 1835, Father Shanahan would travel the circuit from St. Peter's in Troy to Lansingburgh, Waterford, Schuylerville and Sandy Hill. In 1840, Father Francis Coyle walked the following route carrying a blackthorn stick and his valise: Lansingburgh to Stillwater, Schuylerville, Fort Miller, Fort Edward, Sandy Hill, Glen's Falls and back via Argyle, Salem, Cambridge and then to Union Village (now Greenwich) where he said he found a lot of "corduroy Catholics" (Irish), then to Schaghticoke and back to Lansingburgh. The priest's reference to "corduroy Catholics" is telling; a young man writing home to Ireland cautioned his relatives to come with as few clothes as possible because the only people wearing corduroy were Irish, and it placed a red flag on the wearer wishing to assimilate.

Father Coyle was known as a good orator with ironclad arguments. On his route, he often gave lectures in schoolhouses to large crowds who came to hear the "Irish devil," as priests were called. He often began with a call for the Testament, which he then explained, and finished by refuting arguments tendered by some of the listeners. On a visit to "the Baptist church [at Schuylerville]...he had a large crowd to contend with as among them was a man named Delaney an Irishman but a false preacher and another named Murphy two hypocrites who preached against and cut down Catholics without scruple. Father Coyle proved Delaney was a fraud, and on his fourth visit in the Presbyterian church showed them the Catholic

church from the beginning to the present time. After that they thought very little of Delaney and Murphy, nor did they think when they met an Irishman they met a devil."

Mills and the developing logging trade were the primary industries in Sandy Hill. The Glens Falls feeder canal went through the town to connect with the Champlain Canal. In 1832, it was improved to be used for transportation. The people served were primarily Irish and some French. A church, built in 1834, was named Christ Church. Although it could hold 400 people, it did not become a separate parish in its own right until 1873 under the name St. Mary's.

Despite all of Father Shannahan's duties at St. Peter's in Troy, he found time in 1839 to start St. Patrick's Church in West Troy (Watervliet). The arsenal had been functioning for 27 years and the canals for 16. The Irish had formed a ghetto near the canal, and the new church was located there. Even before the church opened on Christmas Day in 1840, there had been a baptism and a marriage. Father James Quinn, Father Shannahan's assistant, became the pastor.

St. John the Baptist, Albany

The next church to attain official status in Albany was St. John the Baptist, not without a story. Father Charles Smith, a much beloved pastor of St. Mary's, was unexpectedly reassigned by Bishop Dubois to the Buffalo area. His assistant, Father Gregory Pardou, was appointed pastor. In an effort to cover deficits in the 1820s, the North Church

(Dutch Reformed) periodically sold its considerable real estate holdings, a significant share of which was in The Pastures, an area covering several acres in the South End of Albany along the Hudson River. The land was so named because livestock grazed there. Catholics were among the buyers who appeared at the auctions. Father Pardou, realizing that these Catholics in the South End outnumbered those closer to St. Mary's, initiated discussion with them and started a mission chapel there.

The trustees and many of the parishioners of St. Mary's were not pleased at the pending division in their church and petitioned Bishop Dubois for Father Smith's return. In 1837, Father Pardou was assigned to the new St. John's church but had to resign within a year due to ill health. Father John Kelly, the assistant at St. Mary's of circuit-rider fame, was sent to St. John's in 1837. In 1839, he purchased St. Paul's Episcopal Church at Ferry and Dallius Streets from the Episcopalians for $15,500. This church served Greenbush (now Rensselaer) and a large concentric area into the country for over 10 years as the main Catholic church in south Albany.

In the early 20th century, the present St. John's church was built at the corner of Westerlo and Green Streets, the old church becoming the grade school. (It can still be seen, one of the very oldest church buildings in the Capital District.) When the grammar

Above: Early baptismal records from St. John the Baptist, Albany (Kate Blain photo).

school was first started, probably shortly after the church, it was staffed by Irish lay teachers.

Temperance Societies

New organizations were forming, some entirely Catholic. In 1832, there were 14 exclusively male temperance societies in Albany alone, one of which was the Hibernian Temperance Association with 123 members. Father Charles Smith of St. Mary's (a convert from Anglicanism) was the president and P.M. Morange, a parishioner of St. Mary's, the secretary. Within a few years, there were temperance societies throughout the area, established particularly by priests, ministers and politicians, including one in 1840 at the arsenal in West Troy. The Fourth Provincial Council of Baltimore in 1840 recommended the establishment of temperance societies in all churches.

On March 17, 1841, Father Joseph A. Schneller, pastor of St. Mary's in Albany, started the Total Abstinence observance of St. Patrick's Day with a Mass at 8:00 a.m. The parade of 2,000 — to date "the biggest procession in Albany history" — started at

10:00 a.m., representing the membership of the Albany Catholic Total Abstinence Association (2,540) and the Hibernian Temperance Association (390). Father Schneller and two other priests headed the march. Of the many banners, one represented Father Schneller administering the pledge. Even children who had taken the pledge were allowed to march in the parade.

Also in 1841, the Hibernian Benevolent Society of East Troy, the West Troy Catholic Total Abstinence Association (organized by Father Quinn of St. Patrick's) and members of the army band from the arsenal met for a rally at St. Patrick's Church in West Troy (1839) and paraded from West Troy to Troy for a celebration.

Temperance was not restricted to the Troy/Albany area. The Father Matthew [sic] Total Abstinence Society was established at St. Mary's in Little Falls. While on his American tour, 1849-51, Father Theobald Mathew, an eloquent Irish Capuchin friar, coaxed millions to sign the temperance pledge, which was for a specific time period. People renewed their pledge when someone reminded them. Father Mathew appeared at St. Mary's in Albany in 1849 and again in 1851.

Temperance became a popular movement because of the even greater popularity of alcohol. The easy transport of grain on the Erie Canal precipitated the development of grain-based American spirits by the barrelsful. Hard liquor became a cheap commodity, as well as a means of pay. It also often accompanied accidental job-related deaths.

When the new Albany and West Stockbridge Railroad wanted to announce construction jobs, they asked Father Schneller to write a letter to the New York Catholic paper, the "Freeman's Journal," which was widely read by Irish immigrants, announcing that the contractors would hire only the men "who have taken the Temperance pledge."

Mill accidents were often alcohol-related. Everyone drank, even children. The main means of preserving fruit juices was to ferment or distill them. In the country, farmers depended on the apple crop to supply enough cider — which was always alcoholic — to provide a decent cash flow. Rum, which was associated particularly with earlier centuries, was still heavily drunk, as were imported wines. Beer had been brewed since the 17th century, beginning with the Dutch and Germans. The large, local New York State wine producers would come later in the 19th century.

As industrialization developed and became more widespread toward the mid-19th century, alcohol posed a daily problem, particularly among mill workers who had to perform repetitive tasks on large machinery for long hours. (There was no government control over safety practices of the mill owners until Al Smith was governor in the 1920s. Earlier, he had turned Tammany Hall in New York City into a champion of factory safety and so had allies for his battle at the state level.)

Other Catholic organizations were ethnically based. The self-help groups appealing to "race," as they called ethnicity then — such as the Hibernian Provident Society in Albany — provided social outlets, as well as economic aid in helping immigrants find jobs. St. Patrick's Society started in Albany in 1807. In 1813, they held regular meetings on the first Wednesday of the month. Thomas Harman was president; Hugh Flyn, vice-president; Cornelius Dunn, treasurer; and John Ready, secretary. Their annual meeting was held, of course, on the 17th of March. (Even earlier, Sir William Johnson had started St. Patrick's [Masonic] Lodge in Johnstown in 1766.)

The concept of ethnicity being called "race" provides an insight into the mentality of that era. Americans believed the Irish were a separate race and that people who spoke different languages were biologically distinct from one another and should not be mixed. That attitude — combined with the return in the early 1800s of many Revolutionary War loyalists from Canada and England who found their properties confiscated and resold — fueled a resentment and rivalry among hard-scrabble Americans who resented the arrival of immigrants perceived to be competing for the jobs they had. Although no outstanding incident occurred in upstate New York, there were anti-Catholic incidents in Charlestown, Massachusetts, in 1837 when a convent was burned, and in Philadelphia in 1844 when many churches and much of the Irish neighborhood were destroyed and at least a dozen immigrants killed by Protestant, native-born Americans.

Women entered the workplace in the 1830s; the collar and cuff factories in Troy assigned "women's work" to be done as piecework at home. That work eventually became mechanized in 1852 with the introduction of sewing machines, and the workplace was shifted from the home to a factory — still primarily employing women. For the first time, women worked outside of the home in a factory situation similar to most men's. Women naturally started acquiring many of the same attitudes that men had, including a desire to have some control over their lives in a society in which machines and the factory owner drove them. The men started organizing unions. The women looked to suffrage. Elizabeth Cady Stanton (born in Johnstown) and Lucretia Mott started campaigning in the early 1840s for equal pay and equal rights. They both were also abolitionists, an interesting corollary to women's rights.

The idea of freedom

The French Revolution unleashed the radical concept of representative government by the masses, an idea unheard of in any country. Everywhere else, only propertied men had suffrage. The leadership in even enlightened countries, such as the United States, believed in a classed society in which a skill for acquiring money outweighed intellectual talent. Although the constitutional amendment granting universal male suffrage regardless of race was not ratified until after the Civil War in 1870, its seeds were being sown in the movement to industrialize in which the common man was given responsibility yet little power.

At the same time, in the ecclesiastical

world, the Oxford Movement was creating havoc. Although it affected primarily Anglicans — and hence Episcopalians in the United States — it also influenced Lutherans and Presbyterians here. In 1829, the Catholic Emancipation Act became law in Ireland. Earlier in Ireland, Daniel O'Connell formed the Catholic Association, a national organization that first called in the aid of the Catholic clergy and then appealed to the Catholic public to give a penny a month to the association. Even the poorest could afford those dues, so the organization became immensely popular and rich, and created a positive morale that vitalized Catholics.

The money was used to convince Catholic tenant farmers, who could vote but not sit in Parliament, to vote according to their religion and not automatically for their landlord's nominee, who usually was against Catholic emancipation. What resulted was a united effort in which parish priests organized and escorted groups of voters to the polls. That solidarity established practical political know-how in those who were to emigrate around the world less than 20 years later and who would carry these methods to their new countries.

The strength shown by Catholics also laid the groundwork for various changes in England. Between 1828 and 1832, laws requiring that government office-holders receive the Eucharist exclusively in the Church of England were repealed. Concomitantly, most of the restrictions imposed on Roman Catholics were removed. As a result, their schools surfaced in an effort to provide elementary edu-

At the same time . . .

1841: New Zealand becomes British colony

1843: Charles Dickens writes "A Christmas Carol"

1845: First submarine cable crosses English Channel

1846: Pope Pius IX installed

cation on a voluntary basis for Catholic children. A year later, the government gave small building grants to these societies, as well as to Protestant ones, since it had become apparent that voluntary finances could not possibly provide universal education.

As a result of these relatively liberal governmental policies toward Roman Catholics, a re-examination of Roman Catholicism arose, particularly at Oxford University. Many discussions occurred during the 1830s and '40s centering around John Henry (later, Cardinal) Newman's contention that Catholicity, or communion with the universal Church of the first five centuries, was the true Church, "against such portions of it as protest and secede," a reference to the Anglican rule of fidelity to antiquity and the Fathers rather than the dogmatic authority of the Church per se. In 1845, Newman became a Roman Catholic, a move that would be imitated by several others. In the United States, several Episcopalian seminarians in New York City became Roman Catholic priests, some ending up in the Albany area after the Diocese was formed.

St. Mary's, Troy

With this as a backdrop, a remarkable man, Jesuit Father Peter Havermans (right), appeared in Troy in 1842 as pastor of St. Peter's parish. Within a year, he started St. Mary's Church in Irish South Troy, leaving St. Peter's to his assistant. By 1845, a rectory was built at St. Mary's that Father Havermans was to call home for the rest of a life full of accomplishments beyond his specific church.

In addition to St. Mary's, the 1840s witnessed the origin of several more churches. Originally, all of them were missions served by circuit riders. Lansingburgh and Waterford shared a mission. St. Augustine's in Lansingburgh was incorporated in 1842 as St. John's (its cemetery is still called St. John's). Keating Rawson, the convert who had been a trustee at St. Mary's in Albany and instrumental in starting St. Peter's in Troy, became a trustee for St. John's, finally getting a church in his own neighborhood. Other trustees were John Higgins, James B. Smyth, Thomas Halligan, George T. Gillespie, Barnett Evers, John Driscoll and Daniel Murray, once more primarily a group of Irishmen. Keating Rawson sold two lots to the trustees for $500 with the proviso that "the property was to be used solely for a church for the use of the Catholics of Lansingburgh and Waterford. Five of the trustees were to be from Lansingburgh and four from Waterford."

Schaghticoke Point (now just Schaghticoke) became the home of St. John the Baptist Church, incorporated in 1839 with the following trustees: Patrick Butler, John Brislan, James Ryan, Daniel Doherty, William Graham, Simon Bogan, James Conety, Anthony Wall and Edward Ward. Some of these predominantly Irish men worked in mills on the Hoosick River. It is believed that services were held in a brick schoolhouse on the Tibbits property. In 1841, George Tibbits, a Protestant, gave the land for the church and adjacent cemetery. By 1842, a small church was completed, which some church members bemoaned for years "looked like a barn" until it was appropriately decorated.

German Churches

Even before the Irish famine, the congregations of most of the churches in upstate New York were Irish. As German immigration increased in the 1830s, however, the demand for German-speaking churches and schools intensified. It is no coincidence that three German "national" churches were formed in Syracuse, Utica and Albany in 1842. ("National" churches were those formed by a specific nationality because they did not speak English and wanted to maintain their culture. They were not geographically based as "territorial" parishes came to be after the Diocese was formed.)

That year, Father Joseph Salzbacker, as the official representative of the Leopoldine Society in Vienna, traveled throughout the United States to assess the conditions of German Catholics. Through this Austrian missionary society, many German-speaking deacons and priests were recruited for the American missions, such as the future Bishop (later Saint) John Neumann, living in Philadelphia, who first served in Buffalo as a Redemptorist. The Leopoldine Society, along

Above: Holy Cross Church, Albany (A. J. O'Keefe photo).
Next page: Architect's original drawing of St. Joseph's Church, Albany (Parish anniversary book)

with the French Society for the Propagation of the Faith, also provided much-needed funds to build U.S. churches. The purpose of Father Salzbacker's trip was to see if the minority German Catholics were benefiting from that funding.

As a result, in Albany, Holy Cross parish was founded. Father Sebastian Bartholomew Gruber, as the first permanent priest, assisted not only the Germans in Albany, but also those who had settled in Nassau (St. Mary's), East Poestenkill (St. Mary of the Woods) and the Sand Lake/Averill Park area (St. Henry's). A long letter he wrote in 1849 to Bishop McCloskey, the first bishop of Albany, opened with: "Your Holiness shall pardon, that I have now yet less difficulty to write than to speak english particularly in the following matter of importance." He went on to discuss various problems that had developed concerning the purchase of land and construction of a church at Hamilton and Philip Streets. He refers to the school that was started in 1847 and staffed by lay teachers: "The worship as well as the school in the said manner can be continued in the old building without interruption of the services having happened hitherto."

After Father Theodor Noethen arrived in 1851, he became the circuit-riding priest for those German national churches in the eastern part of the area and later Vicar General for them. He also offered services in French (and spoke Italian as well as English).

On March 19, 1852, a newspaper noted: "St. Joseph's Day [was] celebrated by the St.

Joseph's Friends Society, a German association instituted for benevolent purposes, who marched in procession, with a band of music, to the church of the Holy Cross, and took part in the religious services of the day."

Benevolent societies were common among all ethnicities; but the developing — and prominent — celebration of St. Joseph's Day two days after St. Patrick's feast attracted attention. That year, "St. Patrick's day celebrated with unusual ceremonies" was all that was written in the same reference.

The Irish, however, were also active in 1842, organizing St. Joseph's church in Irish-saturated North Albany where they worked mainly on the canal and in the lumber district that eventually would extend for miles along the Hudson. The church's cornerstone was placed at the corner of North Pearl and Lumber (later Livingston) Streets and blessed by Bishop Hughes with the help of area priests: Father Joseph Schneller of St. Mary's, Father James McDonough of St. John's, Father James Quinn of St. Patrick's in West Troy, Father Francis Coyle of Sandy Hill and Father Michael Gilbride of Hudson. Also on hand was Father Edward O'Neil of St. John's College, Fordham. The first pastor was John J. Conroy, who would become the second bishop of the Albany Diocese.

Until recent times, in addition to St. Mary's, St. Joseph's has always been a key church in Albany. The current church on Ten Broeck and 2nd Street — designed by architect Patrick J. Keely as a copy of 13th-14th century middle-pointed, Gothic, Benedictine

architecture — was built in 1855-1860. Over the years, it has universally evoked admiration for its beauty, executed in materials very different from the Cathedral of the Immaculate Conception, another church designed by Keely.

Keely considered St. Joseph's his masterpiece. Along with St. Mary's, it has been considered a pivotal church in Albany, because it fostered many Church leaders until its core population moved to the suburbs in the 1950s and '60s.

Father Michael Gilbride, one of the attending priests at the blessing of St. Joseph's cornerstone, had recently arrived in Hudson where he spent the fourth Sunday of the month in sacramental duties. The first Sunday was spent in Hunter; the second and third, at Gilboa and Scienceville in Greene

County (now under the Gilboa reservoir) and at Middletown in Delaware County. By 1848, much of the remainder of Greene and Columbia counties was added to his circuit, and Hudson had a church: St. Mary's.

Growing toward a Diocese

The 1844 Catholic directory of the Albany area of the New York Diocese listed 12 full-time priests and one German-speaking priest from New York City "who sometimes officiates at Albany." A Father Imbert had a French congregation. Five priests had definite circuits. In general terms, one was south of Albany, two north-northeast, one north-northwest of Schenectady and the last along the Mohawk.

The priest who visited the most towns — 12 "occasionally" — was Father Francis Coyle of oratorical fame in Schuylerville; his circuit ranged from Lansingburgh, where he was based, to Ticonderoga and Minerva in the Adirondacks in what would eventually become the Ogdensburg Diocese. Each of six priests was based at one church, although from their records most of them probably traveled additionally to nearby towns.

While the directory lists only eight churches, three more were in existence among the circuits but were not yet dedicated. Albany had three; Troy, two; and Lansingburgh, Schenectady and West Troy, one each. If the rest of the Ogdensburg and Syracuse areas that became part of the Albany Diocese are also included, there were at least 19 chapels and churches, and 13 priests, two of whom were shared with the Albany area. Possibly three of them had their own churches and did not travel much, but the remaining had extensive areas to cover.

While the directory corroborates available information, any directory is only as accurate as the contributors are. If a contributor did not get his information to the New York Diocese or to the publisher on time, it could not be included. Furthermore, although this directory was published in 1844, the information was compiled in 1843. By the mid-19th century, directory and map publishers needed 12 months' lead-time in order to collect information, as well as payment for the advertisements and other contributions that underwrote publishing the volume. In 1854, advertisement pages covered roughly one-third of the volume. By 1858, the proportion was closer to half.

Famine in Ireland

Across the Atlantic, however, something horrifying was happening that would lead to those statistics booming in years to come. A fungus attacked the potato crop in Ireland in 1845. Years later, an old farmer described what happened in almost ethereal terms: "A mist rose up out of the sea, and you could hear a voice talking near a mile off across the stillness of the earth. It was the same for three days or more, and then when the fog lifted, you could begin to see the tops of the potato stalks lying over as if the life was gone out of them. And that was the beginning of the great trouble and famine that destroyed Ireland."

The blight returned annually from 1846 to 1850, but the worst year was "Black '47." A historian characterized the winter as the "harshest and longest in living memory" which set in to create additional misery at the end of 1846. From this time into the 1920s, Irish immigration to the United States involved the largest number of any ethnic group ever to arrive here. During and immediately after the famine, 2.5 million Irish emigrated. More hundreds of thousands came later. Some of those who arrived from the southern and western counties of Ireland did not speak English, adding to their woes.

Secret memories

The sheer horror of so many thousands of individuals left destitute by the famine and with no recourse for basic human needs was difficult to express. Much has been written and documentaries produced about the hideous side effects of the famine: the cargo ships that housed human freight...the cold-hearted attitudes of a few of the English government officials who welcomed the famine with Malthusian predictability — at that time widely held — as a means of ridding Ireland of its excess population...the make-work "relief walls" built around estates and the "famine roads" constructed to go nowhere, ordered by landowners with hearts who organized the work to give heads of families enough money to buy food while being reimbursed by the government for only half of the labor.

It is only now, years too late for firsthand accounts, that many of Irish descent are able to talk and write about the family histories they only half know because the subject was taboo in their homes. The memories were too monstrously painful to recall, and the guilt of being a survivor weighed heavy. Parents and grandparents cloaked family histories in such a dark mystery that a guilt was passed to the children — that of ignorantly believing that their ancestors had done something too horrible to mention (such as cannibalism). In reality, most of the "horrors" were probably more on the order of bodies not being buried with the proper religious services or denying food to neighbors.

Reporting news about Ireland in 1847, a New York City Protestant newspaper used a disapproving tone to express indignation at the injustice of the governmental authorities: "At Roundstone, in Connemara, four, five and six bodies have lain over ground for days, none being found to give them burial. The body of one old man was devoured by dogs. Four persons have been committed to prison for stealing a filly, which they were found eating. At Killucan (county Westmeath) petty sessions, on last Saturday, eight persons were brought up in custody of the police, charged with the crime of having stolen a few turnips! A female child was arrested for having in her possession a small head of cabbage, which it was suspected she had stolen."

There is one continuing Irish legacy of the famine, however, that surfaced in the third quarter of the 19th century and continues to this day: the disproportionately high, faithful and generous donations of money and time that the Irish give to places experiencing famine around the world, second only to Americans, many of whom are also of Irish descent. Irish physicians and social workers are also in the fore internationally in those destitute countries.

When the Irish arrived in the New World, it often was at Quebec. Canadian cargo ships routinely carried timber, salted fish or pickled pork to Europe and needed a return cargo in steerage. Diseases, particularly dysentery, typhus and cholera, spread easily in the overcrowded, unsanitary conditions. Ships carrying a high percentage of the sick made for Quebec, because Canadian passenger and landing laws were more lenient than American ones. As a result, a higher profit could be made on each crossing. In 1847, the year the Albany Diocese was founded, 35 percent of the Irish emigrating to North America died en route or at the quarantine sites. Grosse Isle, the "Isle of Death," was the Canadian quarantine in 1847 where thousands of victims died in the "fever sheds," leaving many children orphaned.

In the hands of con men

Many of those who survived made their way south to the United States. Once they arrived, sometimes bringing the diseases with them, they often were preyed upon by a web of "runners," brokers, bondsmen and boardinghouse keepers who extorted fees above the going rate. A "runner" was a con man who, grabbing their baggage, lured immigrants to a location, usually a boardinghouse, where they were fleeced.

By law, bondsmen posted a bond with the mayor to cover the cost of the immigrant's care if he became a ward of the state. The bond fee was paid for as part of the passage. Bondsmen were loath to repay the bond to the immigrant, so they manufactured "fees" or doctored the record or opened shelters for them in which they were packed in to cut the costs. One such was "the notorious James Roach," an Albany broker who employed a gang of thugs to intimidate the immigrant "cattle" (Roach's term). In 1847, he made $2,000 in three months, compared with $1,600 a year that the chief physician at Quarantine in New York City made in 1852.

In this milieu, the Hibernian Provident Society, the Hibernian Benevolent Society and other immigrant aid societies acted out of a sincere desire to help the new arrivals. In fact, the presidents of them were by law ex officio commissioners of the Board of Emigrant Commissioners. It was not until 1855, however, that they were able to procure one landing depot over which they had sole control. There, they could receive and forward immigrants without the interfering runners. This depot was the old fort and music hall at the Battery in New York, called Castle Garden.

Because of the sheer force of their numbers, the 1840s are associated with Irish immigration. In fact, although the numbers were fewer, there also was increased German immigration at this time. They, too, experienced "coffin" ships, runners, brokers, boardinghouse keepers and plug-uglies, but to a lesser degree. Ships registered at Hamburg and Bremen were better than those leaving Ireland and England because the German ports had improved their accommodations in order to woo the emigrant trade from the Atlantic harbors. Once in Albany, St. Joseph's Friends Society aided the German immigrants.

Orphans

Priests intervened when children were orphaned. In Canada, one took a darling little boy to Mass and told his congregation about 200 more who needed parents. People responded, but the numbers of orphans were overwhelming. Many of the French Catholic families allowed those adopted to keep their Irish surnames, an unusually charitable gesture.

When the Sisters of Charity left St. Mary's in Albany in 1844 in a dispute over the poor living and working conditions at their combination convent-orphanage-school, dismayed Albany Catholics held a meeting: "We view the departure of the Sisters of Charity as a great calamity and a loss which will be felt by every Catholic, more particularly on account of the education of the rising generation and the loss the Catholic orphans will sustain in being deprived of their motherly care and protection. Resolved — that if arrangements can be made for the return of the Sisters to Albany that we pledge ourselves as Catholics to use all exertions to sustain and support them in a proper manner."

When the Sisters of Charity returned in 1846, they were welcomed at newly erected St. Joseph's, where Father Conroy con-

structed a building for their use. That same year, St. Joseph's Industrial School was opened with Sister Mary DeSales again in charge. As they had done before, the sisters started a select school to pay for the orphanage and the free school. Parents of free school pupils who could afford to pay five cents for pens and a fee toward the cost of winter fuel did so whenever possible.

The industrial school was for the orphans, at that time a common means of combining education with work. In addition to literacy, young girls were taught practical skills, and the results were marketed to help support the orphanage. In some orphanages, they were taught sewing and fancy needlework, which was sold to individuals as well as retailers. Later in the century, other orphanages or "industrial schools" ran laundries for regular clients.

In 1848, the orphanage was called St. Vincent's Orphan Asylum and was located on North Pearl Street. In 1849, there were 50 children there. It was commonly referred to as the Female Orphan Asylum. That same year, the Sisters of Charity made $3,144.64 at St. Vincent's Orphan Fair.

It is no coincidence that the Albany Diocese was erected at this time: in the midst of the worst year of the Irish famine, when the need for spiritual, as well as physical, attention was so desperately required.

Above, the official crest of the Roman Catholic Diocese of Albany includes a beaver, representative of Albany's origins as a center of the fur trade. At one time, Albany was named Beverwyck, a Dutch word which means "area of the beaver." It is holding a bishop's crosier and the seal is topped by a bishop's mitre. The crescent moon represents the Blessed Mother. The Diocese is dedicated to her under her title of the Immaculate Conception.

PART II
A Time of Faith

1847 . . .

Cyrus McCormick builds a three-storey brick reaper factory in Chicago while John Deere constructs a factory in Moline to produce self-polishing plows.

George Caleb Bingham paints "Raftsman Playing Cards."

The Chicago Tribune and Philadelphia Evening Bulletin begin publishing. In Rochester, Frederick Douglass begins publishing "North Star," an abolitionist newspaper.

The first adhesive U.S. postage stamps go on sale.

Paris jeweler Louis Francois Cartier opens a small shop.

Iowa State University, Salt Lake City and Minneapolis are founded.

In Salem, Mass., steam powers a cotton mill for the first time in America.

A search party reaches the survivors of the stranded Donner Party in the Sierra Nevada Mountains.

Doughnuts with holes are introduced in Maine by a baker's apprentice.

Sir John Franklin and his crew of 129 die searching for the Northwest Passage.

Karl Marx and Friedrich Engels publish "The Communist Manifesto."

England's Parliament limits children between 13 and 18 to only 10 hours of work per day.

Henry Wadsworth Longfellow writes "Evangeline," which begins: "This is the forest primeval." Emily Bronte pens "Wuthering Heights" and her sister Charlotte creates "Jane Eyre." Herman Melville authors "Omoo."

Oliver Wendell Holmes is named dean of Harvard Medical School. Scottish doctor James Simpson introduces ether as an anaesthetic. The American Medical Association is founded.

Franz Lizst composes "Liebestraum."

Gen. Zachary Taylor defeats Santa Anna at the Battle of Buena Vista.

Liberia becomes an independent republic, populated by slaves freed from America.

Chinese and Irish immigrants begin to arrive in New York in large numbers.

Ebenezer Butterick begins his pattern company to speed the making of dresses.

Chapter Three
OUR DIOCESE IS FOUNDED

'We hereby found and establish a new
Episcopal See in the City of Albany.'

In May of 1846, the bishops of the U.S. met at their Sixth Provincial Council to ponder the rapid growth of Catholicism in America and recommended to the Vatican that four new dioceses be created. Nearly a year later, on April 23, 1847, Pope Pius IX (at right) established those dioceses. That

Cleveland and Galveston were among them indicated how the new nation was expanding to the northwest and southeast. That Buffalo and Albany were split from New York City proved how much the state was burgeoning, especially through immigration.

In his formal document, the Pope wrote that the American bishops "were convinced that the growth of the Catholic Church will be greatly promoted by the establishment of two new Episcopal Sees and Dioceses in the extensive territory of New York State, distinct from the See of New York, one of which should be centered in the City called Albany."

Pope Pius defined the borders of the Diocese of Albany as "identical with the northern and eastern boundaries of the State of New York; its southern boundary shall be the forty-second parallel of the north latitude; it shall extend westward to the eastern boundaries of the Counties of Cayuga, Tomp-

kins and Tioga.

"We furthermore confer upon the Bishop destined to rule this new See of Albany each and every power and privilege with which Bishops generally are endowed either by the law of the Church or by legitimate custom."

The first bishop

The "Bishop destined to rule" the Albany Diocese was once a 17-year-old who lay in a coma for days, badly injured after a terrible accident. Inexperienced in working with animals, he had tried to prod oxen left unattended by a farm hand out of the middle of the road. The beasts had spooked, overturning a wagon full of logs that had crushed him. The day after the accident, the position in the counting house that his mother had sought for him became available. After he regained consciousness, however, it was discovered that he was blind.

Weeks later, after recovering from his injuries — which left no marks on his body — and spectacularly regaining his sight, he returned to Mt. St. Mary's in Emmitsburg, Maryland, having decided against accounting in favor of becoming a priest.

As a young man, he deliberately learned to pace himself because he did not have the energy or endurance for extended physical effort. As a young adult, he became the first New York native son to become a diocesan priest. Later, he would be the first bishop of Albany and the first cardinal in the United States.

The young man, John, was born in 1810 to Patrick McCloskey and Elizabeth Harron, both of County Derry, Ireland. They had immigrated to Brooklyn shortly after their marriage in 1808. Patrick was a successful businessman, and John was sent to school early where he proved to be particularly adept at languages and math. In 1825, he graduated from Mt. St. Mary's in philosophy but could not decide on a profession. Through family connections, an effort was made to find him a position in a counting house, the 19th-century name for an accounting business. Then came the accident on the road and his September 1827 return to Mt. St. Mary's to study for the priesthood.

After training at Mt. St. Mary's and teaching Latin there, he was ordained in 1834. Appointed vice president of philosophy at a new seminary being built at Nyack, New York, he also taught there. After it was destroyed in a suspicious fire, he went to Rome to study further. Upon his return in 1837, he was assigned to St. Patrick's Cathedral in New York City and then as pastor of St. Joseph's in Greenwich Village, at that time a self-contained community used as a summer resort and almost an hour away from the city by horse car. He became the president of St. John's College at Fordham when it opened in 1841, where he also taught Rhetoric and Belles Lettres. Finding it too exhausting to be president as well as professor, Father McCloskey resigned and returned to St. Joseph's.

Previous page: Pope Pius IX (RNS photo)
At right: Bishop John Hughes (RNS photo)

Coming to Albany

In 1844, Father McCloskey was installed as coadjutor bishop of New York with the right of succession, the first native New Yorker so-designated. Three years later, on Sunday, September 19, 1847, the 37-year-old was installed, by Bishop Hughes, as the first bishop of the brand new Diocese of Albany. The new bishop was not given any time to acclimate himself to his new area; that afternoon, he laid the cornerstone of St. Joseph's church in Troy. The next day, he was in Watertown performing the same function. A day later, he went back to New York City in time to take part in the memorial celebration of Daniel O'Connell of Irish enfranchisement fame at Castle Garden. Before the end of the year, he had laid the cornerstone at St. Bernard's in Cohoes.

As presaged by his first acts as bishop, his episcopate would be characterized by the first official diocesan (i.e. geographically designated) churches. Previously, because of the huge size of the see, churches had been organized at the grassroots level, often by the laity. Now with a locally based bishop in residence, the Church in upstate New York was more closely organized from the top

down. While Buffalo became a see the same year, the Roman Catholic Diocese of Albany still enveloped a sprawling area that ran from Syracuse in the west to Massachusetts in the east, to the Canadian border on the north and southwest to Pennsylvania. The Albany Diocese was larger than the states of Massachusetts, Connecticut and Vermont combined.

Bishop McCloskey designated St. Mary's in Albany as the pro-cathedral. But less than a year later, on July 2, 1848, the cornerstone was laid for the Cathedral of the Immaculate Conception by New York's Archbishop Hughes. In 1846, the Sixth Provincial Council of Baltimore had made the Immaculate Conception the patronal feast of the United States. Pope Pius IX defined the dogma of the Blessed Mother's freedom from sin from the moment of her conception in 1854, six years after the Albany cathedral was one of the first to be so named.

The cathedral's corner-

stone was laid on the spine of isolated Robinson's Hill, known as "gallows hill" by Albanians. Madison Avenue — then Lydius Street — was at the edge of civilization, and the entire section was known as "the stone quarry." (It was still so isolated in 1855 that a mink attacked a policeman there.) The cathedral site was approachable only by footpaths.

Approximately 10,000 people gathered under a threatening sky at the site near Lydius

Cardinal McCloskey
(The Evangelist archives)

and Eagle Streets, some reputedly on rooftops, to witness Bishops Hughes and McCloskey in their pontifical robes attended by the Albany priests: John J. Conroy of St. Joseph's (who would become the second bishop of Albany); Thomas Kyle, pastor, and his assistant, Edward W. Putnam, of St. Mary's; Patrick McCloskey of St. John's; Sebastian Bartholomew Gruber of Holy Cross; Philip O'Reilly of St. Peter's in Troy; John Corry of St. Patrick's in West Troy; Bernard Van Reith of St. Bernard's in Cohoes; Anthony Farley of St. John's in Lansingburgh. Rev. Daniel W. Bacon of Brooklyn was the master of ceremonies. The festivities had scarcely ended when a cloudburst scattered the crowd.

In addition to those priests, there were 20 others in 1848, of whom seven were in what ultimately became the geographically reduced Albany Diocese. Peter Havermans was at St. Mary's in Troy, Thomas Martin at St. Patrick's in West Troy, Michael Gilbride at St. Mary's in Hudson, John McMenomy at St. Mary's in Little Falls, Daniel Cull at St. John's in Schenectady, Thomas Daly at St. Peter's in Saratoga and Michael Olivetti at St. Mary's in Sandy Hill.

Like given names, church names have "runs" in which certain ones are more popular at specific times. Of these parishes, five were named St. Mary's, including the Cathedral of the Immaculate Conception; three, St. John's (the Baptist); two, St. Peter's; and four with unique patrons: St. Joseph, St. Patrick, St. Bernard (the first pastor's name) and Holy Cross.

Through the years . . .

1847: The Mormons found Salt Lake City, Utah

1848: Wisconsin becomes a state

1849: Zachary Taylor inaugurated

While the Germans had Holy Cross, the French were accommodated at St. Mary's in Troy on Sundays, where Father Havermans instructed them in French. There were still many missions. Father Farley in Lansingburg took care of Catholics northeast at "Buskirksbridge, Hoosicksfalls, Shaticoke" in Rensselaer County and north at Mechanicville, Waterford, Schuylerville in Saratoga County on occasion. While Father Olivetti at Sandy Hill attended Cambridge occasionally, Forts Ann and Miller, Granville and Whitehall were "vacant." Father Gilbride in Hudson still traveled to Middletown in Delaware County, as well as Hunter and Scienceville in Greene County and Gilboa in Schoharie County. Father McMenomy in Little Falls attended to Schuyler in Herkimer County. Father Cull went to Amsterdam out of Schenectady.

Cathedral Built

For a time, nevertheless, the focus was on one church: the Cathedral. Shortly after Bishop McCloskey's installation in 1847, St. Joseph's parishioners responded to an early appeal for money to fund the construction of the Cathedral with a gift of $4,500 in a special collection. They were in the process of building their own church, so the money probably came from their own building fund. In 1849, the congregation of St. John's gave $300.

Ultimately, the cathedral would cost more than $250,000. Bishop McCloskey anticipated the high cost of the ambitious size of the Cathedral in a letter to pastors: "Will you please notify your people that we are about to commence the work of excavation at the Cathedral, that we hope to have it done by gratuitous labor, and that there will not be wanting those among your congregation who will cheerfully devote two or three days to the work. Those who can bring horse and cart will confer a great favor by doing so."

What was dug by pick and shovel only included trenches for the approximately 95 x 200-foot foundation and columnar supports. The floor was laid over a crawl space that eventually caused maintenance problems. Architect Patrick C. Keely of Brooklyn was engaged to design the Cathedral, which Bishop McCloskey envisioned as a replica of the gigantic 13th-century Gothic Cathedral of Cologne. It had finally been completed in the 19th century after a hiatus of more than two centuries. The Albany Cathedral of the Immaculate Conception was the first designated Roman Catholic cathedral in the United States in the Gothic Revival style.

The ceremony and mystery associated with the medieval Roman Catholic liturgy and personified in Gothic churches were stag-

Above: The view through a Cathedral window as workmen might have seen it during construction.
Next page: The Lady Window (Dave Oxford photos)

ing a comeback in the late 1840s, partly as a result of the recent Irish and German immigration. Previously, the building style of English architect Christopher Wren had dominated church structures, with his squarish floor plan, classical Greek or Roman ornamentation, superb acoustics, and clear window glass. That church style complemented the Protestant emphasis on being able to see the minister and hear the Word read. (It also personified the democracy of the fledgling republic, particularly in its emphasis on Greek motifs.) But after 1850, Gothic Revival architecture became au courant, particularly for churches. Ultimately,

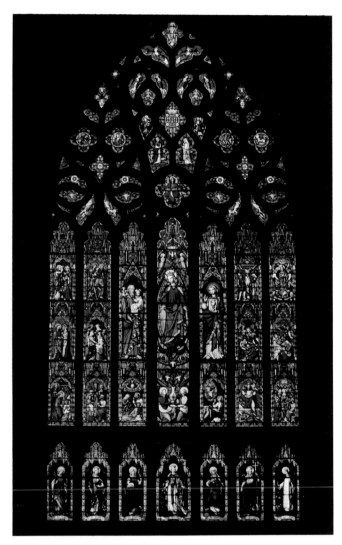

during the lengthy Victorian Era, it would become the norm for Protestant as well as Catholic churches for the next 50 to 60 years.

The cost of building a Gothic cathedral physically much more massive than any of the relatively modest churches in the area outstripped the means of the local people, both Catholic and Protestant, all of whom donated generously. So, in addition to appealing to the Catholics of New York City and Canada, Bishop McCloskey sought help from the Leopoldine Society of Vienna and the Society for the Propagation of the Faith in

Lyons, France. Writing to the latter in 1849, the Bishop worried: "Our Cathedral will be under roof before winter. We have been obliged to hurry on the work more than our limited resources would allow, in order to protect it from being exposed and opened during the severe frosts of another winter. For this reason, I will be obliged to incur even now a debt of eight or ten thousand dollars."

The structural components were of stone-faced brick. In November 1848, Patrick Keely wrote: "I wish you to get all the brick from the Rev. Mr. Haverman you can this year down to Abany [sic] as he has got about two hundred thousand of first rate bricks now burned and only promised me one[.] The bricks in the spring will be very dear, so if we had a good supply on the ground it would save money I will be in Abny [sic] on Saterday [sic] next—" (His spelling and punctuation are typical for the 19th century.) Father Havermans had acquired that many bricks to build St. Joseph's Church in Troy. For that reason, he had only "promised...one__" [hundred thousand, presumably].

This competition for the scarce capital — as well as other "competitions" that sprang up in other areas needing churches — resulted in the slow completion of the Cathedral. When it was dedicated in 1852, it looked very different from its current appearance. The two spires did not exist; but the Lady Window, made in England, and the Rose Window were in place, although the former was in its original location in the sanctuary. The Lady Window (refurbished in 1996) was designed in the 13th-century mode at New-Castle-on-Tyne in England to fit the Gothic style and was donated by the congregations of St Mary's, St. Joseph's and St. John's. The Cathedral interior was unfinished and 30 feet shorter than the present footprint. It was not to be completed until 1892 under the direction of an ailing Bishop McNeirny, trying diligently to finish it before his death.

On November 21, 1852, the feast of the Presentation, "Dedication of the cathedral by Archbishop Hughes [of New York], assisted by another archbishop, five bishops, and above fifty priests" was reported. "An audience of nearly four thousand people witnessed the ceremonies." According to another source, in addition to the prelates, there were 130 priests and acolytes. Whether there were "above fifty" or 130, the sheer numbers were impressive. In Albany, the Catholic Church had arrived.

Towering figures

At the dedication, Rev. Edgar P. Wadhams assisted Vicar General John J. Conroy, who was the master of ceremonies. Father Wadhams would become the first rector of the Cathedral and, in 1872, the first bishop of Ogdensburg. At this time, he was an assistant at St. Mary's, having been ordained there by Bishop McCloskey in 1850. Father Wadhams, 33, was not as young as most assistant pastors. After graduating from Middlebury College, he had entered the General Episcopal Seminary in New York City, had been ordained an Episcopal Deacon and, in 1843, put in charge of Essex County, his boy-

hood home. After much soul-searching and friendship with a fellow seminarian, Clarence Walworth — also destined to convert and become the pastor of St. Mary's — Wadhams was received into the Roman Catholic Church at Mt. St. Mary's Seminary, where he studied for the priesthood.

Clarence Walworth, born in Plattsburgh, was brought up in Saratoga Springs. His father moved the family there where he was a circuit judge, later becoming the last chancellor of New York State. Clarence was educated at Union College in Schenectady and in law at Canandaigua before he started at the General Theological Seminary (Episcopal) in New York City.

Both Walworth and Wadhams were part of the Oxford Movement, a religious upheaval in the Episcopal Church in the United States, as well as in England (where it was called the Anglican Church). The movement produced several prominent converts to Catholicism in the 1840s. The movement matured under John Henry Cardinal Newman, a theologian at Oxford University, who believed that the Anglican Church should revert to its roots in Roman Catholicism as a religion separate from the temporal government and divest itself of lay control, for example, over church appointments. The growth in England of certain Protestant religious sects that followed a decentralized, egalitarian tradition, such as Methodism, also influenced his desire to separate.

As part of the package, he and the other Tractarians, as they came to be known, sug-

gested that some of the attendant practices, such as wearing colored vestments, chanting and other rituals, be reinstated. Partly as a result of this movement, Gothic architecture was revived as an expression of the inexplicable sense of the mystery, the holy and the mystical of Catholicism. It was transferred to the United States by the substantial immigration from the 1840s on and fostered by priests centered in the United States who travelled from or around Europe.

It was a happy coincidence that the Oxford Movement impacted on mid-19th century America when the Church was deluged with the ethnic group that, in 20-30 years, would provide the Church with the most vocations per capita for years to come. The under-educated Irish first had to acclimate themselves to a new country's ways before they would become a part of the middle class that filled the need for priests (and nuns). The Tractarian converts took up the slack during this time, intellectually as well as physically, empowering the fledgling Church with a self-confidence imbued by the prestige associated with their names.

After all, they were former members of — or intimately knew the leaders of — the leading intellectual movement of the time, Transcendentalism, and its offshoots, such as the commune Brook Farm. Hence, they talked to

and corresponded with Ralph Waldo Emerson, Orestes Brownson, Henry David Thoreau and others. All of the converts were articulate, and their sermons and writings were published and disseminated nationally. Not all became priests, however; James McMaster left the seminary to become the combative editor of the New York Freeman's Journal, the leading New York City Catholic newspaper and one well-read in the Albany area.

Clarence Walworth (left photo) joined the Congregation of the Most Holy Redeemer, the Redemptorists, along with Isaac Hecker (below). Although the Redemptorists were primarily known as a Belgian/German/Bohemian (Czech) group, they were a missionary order of priests in New York City in the 1840s. When Walworth, Hecker (whose German parents had immigrated to New York City) and others from the Episcopal seminary sought out priests for their conversion, they were attracted to the Redemptorists precisely because they were missionaries. They ended up studying at the Redemptorist novitiate at St. Trond and seminary at Wittem in Belgium in the 1840s.

Although Walworth was received into the Church under the Redemptorists, Isaac Hecker (and his brother George) had already been previously welcomed by Bishop McCloskey. Both men

wanted to work specifically for the conversion of non-Catholics; because of that, Hecker founded the Paulists, the Congregation of St. Paul the Apostle, approved in 1858. They felt that because of their unique origins in the Protestant community, they had an angle on how to appeal to them, while the emphasis of the Redemptorists was on the parish mission or the revival of Catholics. In order to achieve his purpose, Hecker settled on publishing inexpensive literature on a national scale under the Paulists, in addition to giving public lectures. His efforts, along with those of McMaster, Brownson and Bishop John England (all but England converts and all liberal), helped bring the Catholic press to age in the 1850s.

Father Hecker's association with the Albany Diocese was twofold: His friendships with Bishop McCloskey and Father Walworth, and consequent time spent in Albany and at Saratoga Springs resulted in the Paulists being given the use of attorney (later Judge) William O'Connor's property for camping in the 1860s. In 1871, they bought the Harbor Islands for $100 on the eastern side of Lake George, and Hecker's presence became constant, though seasonal.

First Typewriter

Father Walworth took a different route, leaving the Redemptorists and going with the Paulists, but eventually becoming a parish priest at St. Mary's after the Civil War. His ambivalence partially resulted from his physical limitations. According to extant reports, he was a spectacularly powerful orator, probably along the traditional

Through the years . . .

1850: Hung Hiu-tsuen proclaims himself emperor of China

1851: James Fenimore Cooper dies; "Moby Dick" published

1852: Wells Fargo and Co. founded

hellfire-and-damnation tradition of the Redemptorists. Even a contemporary, the major Protestant evangelist, Charles G. Finney, admired Walworth, who "has been for years laboring zealously to promote revivals of religion...holding protracted meetings; and, as he told me himself...trying to accomplish in the Roman Catholic Church what I was endeavoring to accomplish in the Protestant church."

Yet all of his life, Walworth had tremendous eye problems. He was a prolific letter writer, and in most of them he referred to his eyes: Either they were better or worse. This limitation, as well as the malaria he had contracted, undoubtedly influenced his decision to settle down as a diocesan priest. Perhaps, as he matured, the itinerant life of a lecturer became less appealing. Whatever the reason, he was 46 when he started at St. Mary's in 1866, after spending some time at St. Peter's in Troy.

Possibly because of his eye problems, he purchased one of the first typewriters in the Diocese. The earliest typed letter extant in the Diocesan Archives is dated 1875, but the typeface looks as if it were designed in the mid-20th century: It has small capital letters completely sans serif (the little decorative lines on the edges of letters). The typewriter was probably bought for his niece, Ellen, who came to live with him and served as his personal secretary for the remainder of his life. With her help, he was able to publish books chronicling Wadhams' life, the Oxford Movement and his own life, among others.

On Gallows Hill

In spite of its remote location on Gallows Hill, Father Edgar Wadhams created such a desirable atmosphere in the Cathedral of the Immaculate Conception that even non-Catholics went to Mass there. Lewis Coon, a college student, wrote his parents in 1856 to say: "On Sunday I usualy attend meeting from one to two or three times each Sabbath. At the various Churches in this City last Sunday I went to the Roman Catholic Cathedral, which is built of Stone and is the largest best finished and most Costly Church in the city — I understand it cost near $150,000 and its interior the greatest and most beautifull piece of Architecture of any Church that I have seen in this or any other City — there was over 1,200 members in attendance at this church and I understand that is their usual congregation. All of the churches that I have visited as yet have

the best Choir and Instrumental music that I have ever heard."

Father Wadhams, musical himself, hired an Irish-born organist, Robert J. Carmody, who created a 47-voice choir and won accolades for creating the best church music in Albany. In 1859, Charles Mackay, a British visitor, wrote in his travelogue: "The Roman Catholic cathedral is internally one of the largest and most magnificent ecclesiastical edifices in America...[where] high mass is sometimes performed with a splendour and completeness, orchestral and vocal, not to be excelled even in Paris or Vienna, and to which London, as far as I know, can make no pretensions."

Know-Nothings

In the mid-1850s, the protectionist Know-Nothings were gaining strength in politics across the U.S. However, except for an incident on March 17, 1835, when an effigy of St. Patrick was hung from a tree near West

Anti-Catholic riot in Philadelphia (RNS photo)

Troy, nativist outbursts did not occur in the area. By 1854, however, after several years of serious Irish and German immigration, isolationist, anti-immigrant and, hence, anti-Catholic attitudes had solidified.

That was the first year that any of the 1847 Irish arrivals — who had been savvy enough to have registered — could have acquired citizenship and voted, and the native-born were afraid of losing control. In the November election, the American Party garnered enough votes to win state elections for the first and last time. Rather than a party, it was more a quasi-secret society. When asked to clarify the party's aims, members responded, "I know nothing." In addition to the obvious limitations in attracting a universal following when it would not tell its platform, its sole modus operandi, based on the hate that is engendered of fear, fizzled; and its efforts to take over the fledgling Republican Party failed. Abraham Lincoln remarked on the unconstitutional nature of the bigotry: "When the Know-Nothings get control, the [Declaration] will read: 'all men are created equal except Negroes, and foreigners, and Catholics.'"

At the height of the Know Nothing movement, Father Augustus J. Thebaud, a Jesuit at St. Joseph's in Troy, commented that he did not feel threatened because "I was surrounded by an army of Irishmen, mostly from Tipperary, and all the Know-nothings of Troy combined would not have dared to attack me in my fortress."

Except for the Putnam Bill passed by the State Legislature in 1855 forbidding Catholic bishops from holding property in their own names — the normal procedure in the Catholic Church for passing a church from pastor to pastor — Bishop McCloskey weathered the Know-Nothing scare relatively unscathed. He did so by working behind the scenes with state officials to effect changes. In 1863, the Putnam Bill was quietly repealed. At the same time, the trustee system was changed to accommodate the Catholic method of governance — but not until Bishop McCloskey had weathered many a storm over the politics of power in various churches. A friend from Bishop McCloskey's school days at Emmitsburg grasped his personality: "He will not fight, but he will conquer."

Bishop McCloskey's Reputation

In 1864, when he left the Albany Diocese to become Archbishop of the see of New York, his regional prestige was so great that 36 of the most prominent Protestant leaders in Albany invited Bishop McCloskey to a testimonial dinner to "bear witness to the results of your episcopal labors, the reflected light of which we see in the elevated condition of your people. It is for us to recognize the successful mission of one, who has united in his person the character of a learned prelate and a Christian gentleman, and whose influence in society had been exerted to soothe and tranquillize, to elevate and instruct."

Bishop McCloskey declined the invitation, saying: "The time remaining to me is so brief, and my occupations so urgent, that with much reluctance I must beg to decline."

Bishop McCloskey's sense of humor was dry and ironic. An example dates from when the trustee law was changed to include a board comprised of the bishop, vicar-general, pastor and two lay trustees (the latter two chosen by the first three, a method more hospitable to the Catholic hierarchy). An inordinate amount of Bishop McCloskey's time was spent mediating pastor/trustee problems. In 1858, prior to this change in the trustee law, Bishop McCloskey patiently heard the complaints of a faction from Utica against Father MacFarland. When they had finished, the Bishop replied: "Gentlemen, your petition shall be granted very shortly. I have just received from Rome the bull appointing your pastor Bishop of Hartford." (Rev. Francis P. MacFarland became the third bishop of Hartford on March 14, 1858.)

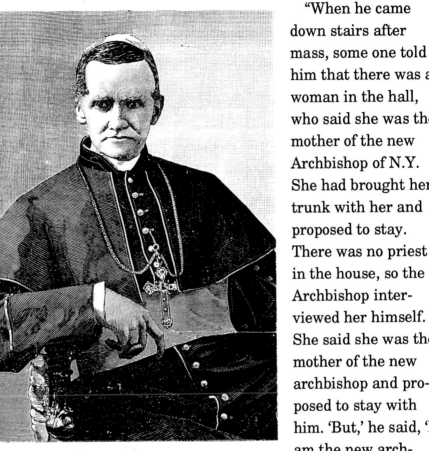

Another incident also served to illustrate his dry manner of dealing with what could have been a difficult situation. After his appointment as Archbishop of New York, Bishop McCloskey arrived in New York City on the night boat on August 7, 1864.

He celebrated Mass at 9:30 a.m. Shortly afterward, he was surprised by a newly arrived "relative."

"When he came down stairs after mass, some one told him that there was a woman in the hall, who said she was the mother of the new Archbishop of N.Y. She had brought her trunk with her and proposed to stay. There was no priest in the house, so the Archbishop interviewed her himself. She said she was the mother of the new archbishop and proposed to stay with him. 'But,' he said, 'I am the new archbishop and you are not my mother.' 'I know,' she said, 'but you are not the new archbishop, you are the Bishop of Albany; is not that enough for you?' The archbishop had to send for a policeman.

"Meanwhile she locked herself in the reception room, and refused to open the door. When the policeman came he was obliged to enter the room through the balcony window of the reception room. She was taken to the station-house, where the archbishop had to go to make a charge against her. When he entered, the official in charge told him what the woman had stated, adding that she told a very straight story for a crazy person. She was then called up from the cell below where she was kept, and repeated her story: that she was the mother of the new archbishop, etc. The archbishop then made his statement how she had introduced herself into the house and had refused to leave: after which he turned to go — whereupon she cried after him: 'Are you going to leave me with these rascals. They attempted to ruin me, etc., etc.' The archbishop turning to the now indignant official, said, 'She tells a very straight story,' and left."

Bishop McCloskey weathered more than trustee problems and fake mothers. His tenure was the first attempt to create some continuity and order in a 28,204-square-mile area in which large numbers of newly arrived Catholics were clamoring for priests. His legacy left increased numbers of institutions; in what became the Albany Diocese, both churches and priests increased three times to approximately 40 of each.

Women Religious

Acting on his own initiative, as well as that of some of his stronger priests, Bishop McCloskey brought several religious communities into the Diocese, primarily to educate children and to help the poor, especially orphans, and the sick. In the 19th century, a significant number of religious communities were founded — several in the U.S. and particularly women's groups — that were devoted to remedying social problems. Fewer groups began that limited themselves to a contemplative life. Previously, travel had

been accessible primarily to men religious, but now these religious women also journeyed to foreign missions, including the United States, to fulfill their vocations, an unprecedented option. Furthermore, even up to the present times, women constituted a higher percentage of all religious.

Laying aside the spiritual aspect, a timeless given for entering religious life, what pragmatic reasons made a vocation such an attractive option when weighed against marrying or remaining single in an extended family situation in this particular era? First of all, religious, regardless of their personal gifts, were easily recognizable because of their clothing. By the 19th century, particularly as new religious communities were founded, distinctive garb characteristic of each group was adopted to differentiate the members from the laity. The purpose was to create a sense of coherence to a community with common goals; but the habit also became a means of controlling their behavior in public, as well as public behavior towards them. Because their professions were often in education or medicine, they were accorded at least a distant respect befitting the middle class when seen on the street. Furthermore, in the case of the sisters, habits protected them as they moved into male-dominated areas previously not open to respectable women, such as army hospitals during the Civil War.

Since their professions were among the people rather than being confined to a monastery or convent, many of these "walking" women religious — as Catherine McAuley, foundress of the Sisters of Mercy, called them — achieved positions of esteem beyond what they might have had if they had been married and subject to a husband, or single and working in a mill under a male supervisor. This difference gave them an enviable independence, although they were still subject to the rule of their order or congregation and the bishop or parish priest. For example, it was assumed by society that unaccompanied nuns out on the street were performing some necessary function of charity; the same people might question why an unaccompanied married woman was out. In a sense, they had safety in numbers because their reputation depended on that of the group. If the group was viewed as being able to successfully educate large numbers of children, for example, the resultant esteem would reflect on the individual sister as being a representative of the group.

Married women could not own property or vote, but they paid taxes when widowed, as seen on the assessment and tax lists. That listing — the only time they were mentioned on official town- or city-related documents — was always as "Wid. Johnson," not even with her first name. If a husband died when the children were still young, they often were taken from her by the courts and placed under the guardianship of another man. While it usually was a neighbor or relative, it did not have to be, nor was it necessarily in her neighborhood. If there were several children, there might be several guardians, men who guaranteed that if the child were old enough, they would take the boy on as an apprentice

Through the years . . .

1853: Pedro V becomes king of Portugal

1854: Dogma of Immaculate Conception declared

1855: Alexander II becomes czar of Russia

or the girl as a servant as if they had been "bound out." Orphanages received these "half-orphans" when a guardian was not assigned.

In one documented case, the file of guardianship papers for the mother of several minor children contained pathetic notes written to the judge, begging that the children be kept with her. Instead, they were farmed out among three men. Within a couple of years, she had married one of the men and brought her family together again, opening to speculation her motives for marrying him.

Another secular reason a woman might have wanted to become a sister could have been the chance to help people beyond her own family. In addition to cottage industry jobs done at home, such as laundry, sewing and tailoring, mill jobs and positions in music or art, women had been teachers of elementary-age children for centuries. But in addition to teaching, a sister could work in an orphanage or a hospital, both situations in which suffering could be alleviated, an emotional reason for becoming a woman religious that should not be glossed over.

Two 19th-century orphans cared for by the Daughters of Charity (Daughters of Charity archives)

Society of St. Vincent de Paul

In 1848, Bishop McCloskey brought to St. Mary's the Society of St. Vincent de Paul, a lay group of men devoted primarily to the temporal service of the poor. It had been founded only 15 years previously in Paris by Antoine Ozanam and his fellow students at the Sorbonne. In the 1850s, "conferences" were formed at St. John's, the Cathedral and St. Joseph's, all in Albany, and later in new parishes as they formed. Each conference was associated with a parish and organized around weekly visits to the homes of the destitute. Locally, it was known as St. Vincent's Charitable Aid Society. In addition to providing help for individual families, it raised funds for St. Vincent's Orphan Asylum, thus supplementing and complementing religious communities.

Father Peter Havermans

Amidst the growth of more religious available to help the developing Diocese, Father Peter Havermans launched the construction of St. Joseph's Church in Troy. Bishops McCloskey and Hughes — who had consented to building it — officiated at the laying of the cornerstone on May 21, 1847. The next year, the property was conveyed to the Society of Jesus for $6,000.

Father Havermans had been trained as a Jesuit at Georgetown after he emigrated from Belgium where he had been ordained in 1830 at Ghent. After learning English at Georgetown and working in Philadelphia, he asked for a dispensation of his Jesuit vows, so that he could return to being a secular parish priest. Father Havermans then traveled to Troy where he made a tremendous impact as the first prominent priest universally respected by all in that city. He still retained his Jesuit connections, which explains their arrival in Troy in 1848, where they remained until 1893, when the order decided to remove priests from all churches not affiliated with upper-level schools, such as colleges, or mission work.

Also in 1847, Father Havermans brought the Frères des Ecoles Chrétiennes, the Brothers of St. John Baptist de La Salle (better known as the Congregation of Christian Brothers) to St. Mary's, where he was pastor, to teach the boys at the parish school. The first director, Brother John of Mary, translated from French to English the daily community prayers — still employed in the 20th century — as well as the Brothers' series of arithmetic texts utilized in parochial schools in the 19th century.

Their next school in the Albany Diocese was St. Joseph's Academy in Troy, founded in 1851. It eventually became La Salle Institute. It was a boarding school designed to supply boys with "all the advantages of Christian education and at the same time solid instruction preparatory to commerce and the arts." Board and tuition cost $100 for the long school year, which ran from September 1 to July 20.

In 1848, Father Havermans asked the Sisters of Charity — also known as the Daughters of Charity because of their affiliation with the French Daughters of Charity of Saint Vincent de Paul — to open a school for girls at St. Mary's and St. Mary's House of Charity. The latter became the Troy Hospital in 1851 after an 1849 outbreak of cholera focused attention on the need for a place to quarantine people.

Help for boys

When cholera broke out again in 1852, Father Havermans collected 40 orphaned boys and placed them under the care of Brother Jeremie de Jesus in a part of the academy building that he called St. Mary's Orphan Asylum.

After this latter epidemic, Bishop McCloskey asked the Christian Brothers to start a male orphanage in Albany to complement St. Vincent's Orphan Asylum (informally known as the Female Orphan Asylum), which had been opened in 1849 by the Sisters of Charity. In 1854, St. Vincent's Male Orphan Asylum started accepting boys. In addition to children orphaned by cholera, 25 were added who had been previously housed in the Protestant asylum. A large structure was built on a farm a little over one-and-a-half miles west of the Cathedral on the present site of La Salle School, the modern descendant of the orphanage. In 1859, the director, Brother Urban, opened a pay school with 80 students in part of the building, the forerunner of Christian Brothers Academy.

In 1859, the Christian Brothers started a school for boys at St. Joseph's in Albany and used the old church building after the beautiful, new Gothic church was completed in

1860. When the old church was sold in 1863 to the Albany Steam Bakery Company to pay off the debt on the new church, the boys' school was discontinued until a new building was completed for them in 1873. Rev. John J. Conroy, the pastor of St. Joseph's, felt obligated to sell the old church to pay for the debt when an offer was tendered. Earlier, the rectory had been sold. When he was made bishop in 1865, Conroy still remained pastor of St. Joseph's. Father Thomas M.A. Burke, who would be the fourth bishop of Albany, was the second in command. It was under his scrutiny that the second boys' school was built.

In 1861, the Christian Brothers started teaching the boys at the Cathedral School, while the Sisters of St. Joseph taught the girls. In 1863, the Brothers started teaching at St. John's, also in Albany, with a mind-boggling enrollment of 600 boys and only five Brothers. Earlier at St. John's in 1852, Bishop McCloskey had brought the Daughters of Charity to start an elementary school and a Select School, the latter an upper-level paying school for girls, which served to financially support the parish elementary school. The Brothers now relieved them of the education of the younger boys.

Society of the Sacred Heart

In 1852, three nuns of the Society of the Sacred Heart at Manhattanville began their apostolate in Albany with help from the Sisters of Charity, who brought meals to them daily as they struggled in the summer heat to ready the Westerlo mansion — recently a Stephen Van Rensselaer home — for school

in September. Bishop McCloskey had asked the foundress, Mother Madeleine Sophie Barat, for a foundation in Albany similar to Manhattanville.

A few students — mostly Protestant — arrived for school that year. A year later, there were 36 of them. Within a few years, they had outgrown a second house, so in 1859 the Gothic Tudor-style Rathbone Mansion at Kenwood was purchased. It had been built in 1841 and included 53 acres. In 1861, the school was incorporated as the Female Academy of the Sacred Heart. The bond with the Sisters of Charity continued, with the students making sets of clothing for the children at the orphanage and those children enjoying picnics at Kenwood.

That same year, the Religious of the Sacred Heart started a day academy and a parish school, both separate from the boarding school. It was unusual for this society to open a parish school, but St. Ann's Academy continued after St. Ann's opened in 1867 and lasted until 1920. Father Walter Torpey, pastor of St. Paul the Apostle in Troy, who was from St. Ann's parish, used to say kiddingly that he "went to Kenwood, the school for poor children," but he thoroughly appreciated the education that he received there and went back for graduations for years.

Sisters of St. Joseph of Carondelet

The 1860s were to witness the arrival of yet more religious groups, partly as a result of the Civil War, but also because 15 years after the large immigration from Ireland, the increasing Catholic population needed their services.

The next group to come into the Albany Diocese included six sisters of the Congregation of Saint Joseph, who arrived in July 1860 at the invitation of Father Thomas Keveny at St. Bernard's in Cohoes. This was their second mission in the Diocese. Two years earlier, six sisters had gone to St. Mary's in Oswego from their original U.S. home in the Diocese of St. Louis, where they had arrived in 1836. In October 1860, they opened a parish school for 500 children in Cohoes. Because it was a mill town, many of the children worked during the day, so the sisters also conducted evening classes at the convent. A year later, a select school was started for 40 young ladies.

Three years later, what came to be fondly remembered as the "mammoth sleigh-ride" occurred. During a severe snow storm in the winter of 1863, Father Keveny organized 50 carryalls on runners containing children, teachers and himself for a long sleigh ride to Albany to the Cathedral School where they were entertained by equally happy students eager for a day of hooky with the approval of Bishop McCloskey and Father Wadhams. The Sisters of St. Joseph had also been teaching the younger boys and girls at the Cathedral School since 1861, so the occasion was an unexpected reunion for them as well. The Christian Brothers were teaching the older boys there, with the total enrollment at 200.

Also in 1861, two German-speaking Sisters of St. Joseph arrived to teach at Holy Cross in Albany, while other English-speak-

Through the years . . .

1856: George Bernard Shaw and Oscar Wilde born

1857: Irish Republican Brotherhood (Fenians) founded

1858: Blessed Mother appears in Lourdes, France

ing sisters went to Troy to teach at St. Joseph's. Father Joseph Loyzance, the Jesuit pastor, had enticed the community there because his superiors had intended to open a college. As a result, he had built a large school building capable of accommodating more than 400 pupils. It was soon filled to capacity.

A year later, Father Cull at St. Peter's in Saratoga Springs requested the services of the Sisters to staff a day school that soon had 200 students. Then it was back to Troy in 1864 at Father James Keveny's request; there, seven Sisters took charge of St. Peter's School. Four lay teachers had been teaching the 400 children in one of the largest parishes in the Diocese. Soon, a select school for girls was also organized.

Meanwhile, Troy, specifically St. Joseph's parish, was selected by the Sisters of St. Joseph for their novitiate and regional headquarters for the Eastern Province. The first postulant, Ellen Sheehan of Balltown, was received on the Feast of the Immaculate Conception, December 8, 1864.

Troy and West Troy came of age as a premier industrial city in the 1860s. It was

Above: The interior of St. Joseph's Seminary, Troy (The Evangelist archives)

known internationally for stoves, horse-shoes, bells and fine scientific instruments, among other items, many of which still surface today in the most remote places. The opportunity for expansion was provided by the Civil War. The Union needed manufactured iron parts in various forms to win the war. The mill owners, many of whom were also inventors, supplied those parts — from the plates on the ironclad Monitor to the millions of horse shoes and mule shoes needed to move men and supplies. The War Department planned to take over H.[enry] Burden and Sons to insure that enough shoes could be produced, but officials changed their minds when they saw how the company

could keep up with demand. The shoes were so critical an item that the Confederate government gave orders to secure first the cars carrying the shoes after commandeering a train.

The wealthy mill and factory owners in Troy were primarily New England Protestants, who supplied the city with culture in the form of Rensselaer Polytechnic Institute (founded by the last Patroon, Stephen Van Rensselaer, in 1824), Emma Willard's Troy Female Seminary, modern brownstones, beautiful churches, and Troy University, a Methodist-affiliated institution, started just before the Civil War in 1858 and graduating its first class during the war in 1862.

Partially due to the war, the principals were unable to pay their subscriptions on the mortgage, and the one building completed at almost $200,000 was sold to the ever-alert Father Havermans for $60,000, along with its lake and nearly 40 acres. Father Havermans, acting as agent for Archbishop Hughes, and Bishop McCloskey recognized its potential value as a seminary to supply parish priests for the entire state. Named St. Joseph's Provincial Seminary, it was considered in an ideal location on the rail line halfway between New York City and Montreal.

The seminary was headed by the Very Rev. Canon Louis Joseph Vandenhende from the Grand Seminaire of Ghent and staffed by three professors trained at the newly founded American College at Louvain, Belgium. The latter group included Father Henry Gabriels, who became the second Bishop of Ogdensburg. This seminary would train priests for 32 years until Dunwoodie opened downstate in 1896. It would be remembered as a seminary that united men of different ethnic backgrounds (many the first generation born in the United States) into a cohesive, American-educated clergy.

Part of the reason New York wanted the seminary closer to home was to ensure that enough of the young priests stayed downstate. When the seminary was in Troy, many men requested assignments in the more rural Albany Diocese or similar dioceses, only returning home to the more urban downstate area when forced. Over the course of 32 years, out of the 750 students ordained, only 328 went to the New York Diocese — about 10 a year and less than half of what was needed. Albany shared the remainder with 34 other dioceses and four religious commu-

nities. Eventually, in the early 20th century, the Sisters of Saint Joseph acquired the seminary as their provincial house and used it until the last quarter of the 20th century when it was sold to Rensselaer Polytechnic Institute as an extension of their nearby campus.

Sisters of Mercy

While St. Joseph's Seminary was being developed and the Sisters of St. Joseph were establishing their strongholds in various parts of the Diocese, in southern Rensselaer county Father John Corry of St. John's in Greenbush (now Rensselaer) was waiting for his niece to finish her postulancy in the Sisters of Mercy. The order, founded in Dublin in 1827, had arrived in New York City in 1846. In the middle of the Civil War, a group of four sisters arrived in Greenbush, having used up most of the 80 cents they had among them on the ferry from Albany. The sisters were supposed to have brought more money; the one in charge of finances believed that the mother superior had been given the purse. The 80 cents found in another's pocket was money she had inadvertently forgotten to give to a poor woman back in New York City. They had to borrow the carriage fare for the ride to the newly built convent.

Father Corry, who had recently died, had previously contracted with an agent to purchase property for the convent, a common practice that continued until the 1950s as insurance against anti-Catholics refusing to sell to the Church. The agent would then transfer the property from his name to that of the pastor. The money, of course, usually came from the Diocese for the initial deed. In this case, part of the land transaction was paid for with 100 pounds of grade A sugar.

After tremendous scurrying to ready the convent, a paying school was opened within a week. The children who could already read and write paid 12 cents a week; those who could only read, a dime; and those in the beginning class, 6 cents. A select school was started at the same time. In spite of the fees, 200 children were soon enrolled. (At least one family, the children of a widowed mother, was admitted free.)

A poster advertising for postulants at the Institute of the Sisters of Mercy, their novitiate in Greenbush, written in the 1880s, states succinctly the requisite qualities the girls must possess to enter the convent. (While details may vary from community to community, the requirements also reflect the standards of contemporaneous religious groups.) The tenor firmly establishes them as preferably middle-class, 16-25 years old with "the qualities indispensably required" being health and "a lady-like appearance, without any serious apparent deformity, the abilities either to acquire the necessary instruction, or to exercise some of the ordinary offices in the Community" and "a docile and amiable disposition, detachment from worldly goods and interests, zeal for the glory of God, for those committed to her care, and for her own perfection." She could expect to work visiting and relieving the sick, teaching poor girls and protecting "distressed women of good character." The community would not consider applicants who were ille-

gitimate or from a family of "bad or doubtful reputation," or those who supported their parents, had "any grave or apparent deformity," were deaf or had "bad sight" or if there were insanity in the family. From the list, it is obvious what social values prevailed at that time.

A prospective applicant brought with her a letter of recommendation from her pastor, her baptismal certificate and the consent of her parents if she were a minor. If too many girls wanted admittance at a particular time beyond the available funds, she or her parents would pay a dower of $200 a year during her probation for her maintenance and "all other necessaries." These stringent qualifications precluded some from entering; not everyone could become a sister or a nun, and there were similar requirements for brothers and priests.

Augustinians and the Franciscans

In 1858, Bishop McCloskey brought in the Fathers of the Order of Saint Augustine as parish priests to staff St. John's, which soon became St. Augustine's, in North Troy (Lansingburgh), and St. Mary's in Waterford. In 1862, they also supplied Immaculate Conception in Hoosick Falls and by 1864, St. Patrick's in Cambridge. All Augustinian parishes in the Diocese were northeast of Albany and served large, primarily rural towns in which many water-powered mills manufactured a variety of items and where potatoes were grown for starch used in the collar and shirt industry in Troy. The Irish Augustinians had been in the United States since 1796 in Philadelphia and came north to minister to the predominantly Irish millworkers.

The Germans outside of Albany were served occasionally by Father Theodore Noethon, who succeeded Father Gruber at Holy Cross. In 1862, those in Schenectady petitioned Bishop McCloskey for a German-speaking priest and a parish. A Franciscan Father of the Order of Friars Minor Conventual, Father Oderich Vogl, soon came from Syracuse. The first group of Franciscan Conventuals had arrived in America in 1852 at the request of a bishop in Texas, specifically to help the Polish as well as Germans. Bishop McCloskey had then invited the Franciscans to Utica, as well as Syracuse, then in the Albany Diocese. That same year, the former Cameroonian Church building was purchased in Schenectady at a sheriff's sale for $2,000 and refitted for $300. St. Joseph's was born.

Civil War

While much of this Catholic expansion was occurring in the Albany Diocese, the Civil War raged. At its beginning in 1861, both North and South depended on volunteers; but within a year, each side realized the need for conscription in which the names of draftees were drawn from a pool of eligible men. Federal law allowed draftees to buy their way out for $300, which angered laborers, who generally made only $500 a year.

Those laborers, many of them Irish and Catholic, also worried that their jobs could be taken by emancipated Negro workers. Furthermore, prominent Catholic plantation owners in Maryland and Virginia owned slaves. Recognizing all of those factors, the

national Catholic Church did not take a political stand on the emancipation issue and was roundly criticized by abolitionists, mostly Northern Protestant ministers, for not preaching against slavery. They, in turn, were quoted in the Republican papers that blamed Irish Catholics for bringing on the Civil War because they were Democrats and, therefore, by default supported the Democratic South and slavery.

During the draft riots of 1863 in New York City, sparked by conscription and the potential job threat if abolition were to occur, a mob in Troy descended on the Liberty Street Presbyterian Church, a Negro church, only to be met by Father Havermans, who calmed the mob and sent them home.

In addition to the draft, recruiting was done abroad, particularly in Ireland and in Canada among the French, assuring men American citizenship as a reward for their service. While those efforts were thwarted, especially in Ireland, they did produce an increase in immigration, thus further swelling the Catholic population.

The primary object of the North in fighting the Civil War was originally to prevent the

ANNUAL REPORT OF THE TRUSTEES OF
ST. PETER'S CHURCH
FOR 1880.

EDWARD BOLTON, *Treasurer, in account with St. Peter's Church.*

Dr.

1880.		
To cash from discounted notes	$12,397	92
" pew rent	5,414	32
" Plate and door collections	2,228	95
" Special collections	1,610	13
" Steam-heating collections	1,277	00
" Bequest of Rev. Jas. Keveny,	1,000	00
" Cemetery	665	85
" Sale of old iron	6	50
Total receipts	$24,600	67
Overdrawn from bank	20	70
	$24,621	37

Cr.

1880.			
Jan.	6, Overdrawn from bank (see last report)	$73	03
"	9, Broderick & Ellis, mason work, in full	221	00
"	12, G. V. S. Quackenbush & Co., carpets, matting, etc.	278	25
" "	Jas. F. Lee, stone and labor	68	00
"	13, Bolton & Hartney, coal for church, vestry, schools and house	309	63
"	14, E. F. Leahy, oil, tapers, etc.	16	77
"	15, H. S. Church, chamberlain, taxes, city, state and county, 1879	112	70
Feb.	2, Manufacturer's bank, note and interest	4,072	33
"	6, King & Blakeman, carpets	306	00
" "	Dodds & Ferguson, gas fixtures	98	00
"	9, McWilliams & Ensign, goods for house	4	44
"	10, Geo. J. Brennan, painting, etc., in full	300	00
" "	C. N. Stannard, sprinkling street,	10	00
" "	Jas. Dennin, candles	10	50
"	16, Wm. J. Woods, incense	4	25
Mar.	4, Rt. Rev. F. J. McNeirny, Irish relief fund	1,025	00
"	27, T. J. Hurley, printing reports, &c.	28	00
April	19, James Laudrigan, flour for altar breads	14	86
"	22, Troy Whig Publishing Co., printing resolutions of respect — Father Keveny	6	75
May	4, Manufacturers' Bank, discounted note	4,000	00
"	10, Jas. Hanlon, labor, blow'g organ,	2	00
"	18, Jas. G. Stead, flowers for altar	20	00
" "	John C. Hoellinger, refrigerator	18	00
"	20, Rt. Rev. F. J. McNeirny, seminary	210	00
July	1, Daniel Hennessy, labor at church,	2	50
"	6, M. F. Collins, Sunday Observer, printing resolutions of respect	2	70
"	7, Manufacturers' Bank, discounted note	1,000	00
" "	M. B. Kelly, labor and gas fixtures	12	00
"	8, Geo. H. Lasure, repairing lightning rod	5	00
" "	John Nugent, sec'y sunday school,	10	30
" "	A. L. Hotchkin, furniture and bookcase for house	455	60
"	10, Jas. Liney, goods for church and school	10	98
"	13, Donnelly Bros., altar wine	66	08
"	16, Jas Hilton, cotton girdles	2	50
"	19, John F. Wolf, tuning organ	20	00
"	20, Rev. Wm. B. Hannett, salary in full	914	00
Aug.	2, M. Timpane, goods for house	16	50
"	4, Hudson, Bolton & Co., insurance	147	50

Aug.	4, McLeod & Reardon, goods and labor	$234	52
" "	Thos. I. Walsh, goods for house and church	17	10
"	5, W. C. Winne & Co., goods for house	141	81
" "	John Phelan, carpenter work, in full to date	441	00
"	6, Thos. Ha ch, repairing pumps at convent	4	00
" "	John Burns, wood	40	00
"	9, E. Bolton, treas., check stamps	2	00
"	10, Green & Waterman, draping, church	250	00
"	19, Thos. D. Eagan, palm	13	75
"	21, Very Rev. P. Ludden, altar wine account	60	00
"	24, Evening Standard Publishing Co., printing resolutions of respect,	5	40
Sept.	1, Wm. Keefe, labor in cemetery	23	75
" "	Winifred Hennessy, cleaning the school-house	11	25
"	12, John H. O'Brien, insurance	5	50
"	13, John J. Brassell, bell-hanging	2	50
" "	Wm. Campbell, repairing slates on church and schools	40	00
Oct.	1, Wm. Kelly, blowing organ	90	00
"	7, Henry Erben & Son, organ acct	180	00
"	8, Citizens' Gas Light Co	210	79
"	11, Louis Davs, music	10	82
"	15, Warren & Taylor, pump at convent	9	25
" "	H. S. Church, chamberlain, city taxes, 1880	98	70
" "	Green & Waterman, furniture for choir	18	50
"	19, Jas. Young, crockery for house	22	83
"	27, Sisters St. Joseph, parish schools,	1,000	00
"	30, Thos. Fitzgerald, draining cemetery	189	00
Mar.	3, Very Rev. P. Ludden, salary acct.	500	00
"	7, Manufacturers' Bank, note and interest	4,122	00
"	22, Rt. Rev. F. J. McNeirny, for Holy Father	230	00
Dec.	2, Herbert R. Flanigan, salary	28	60
"	3, Judge & Cavanaugh, mason work on organ loft	66	00
" "	Enoch Copley, painting, &c	60	00
" "	Rt. Rev. F. J. McNeirny, cathedraticum	210	00
"	10, J. B. Parmenter, Troy Press, printing resolutions of respect	6	25
" "	Thos. Gaffney, labor at church and school-house	6	00
"	11, T. S. Sutherland & Son, steam-heating acct	700	00
"	20, Bonesteel & Boyle, lumber for cemetery	16	25
"	23, Christopher Crape, evergreens and wreaths	14	88
"	27, Louis Davis, organist, salary in full to Jan. 1st, 1881	600	00
" "	Rev. Jeremiah Heffernan, salary in full to Jan. 1st, 1881	600	00
" "	John H. Curley, sexton, salary in full to Jan. 1st, 1881	400	00
"	28, Dennis Murnane, wood	57	50
" "	John M. Francis & Tucker, printing resolutions of respect	6	25
	Total expenditures	$24,621	27

LIABILITIES.

Due Manufacturers' National Bank ... $3,500 00

EDWARD BOLTON, Treas'r.
JAMES LINEY, Sec'y.

T. J. HURLEY, PRINTER, HARMONY HALL, TROY.

A STATEMENT

Of the the Cost and Expenditures of the two Houses bought of Frank Forshew, Esq., for the use and benefit of St. Mary's Church. Hudson, N. Y., in the years of 1868 and 1869.

Amount of the Houses bought of the above,
being $3,000 for each house, - $6,000.

RECEIPTS:

Receipts towards the first house by subscriptions, -	$3,269
Receipts towards second house, -	2,768
Nett Proceeds of the first Fair in 1869, -	933
Do. do. for the second Fair, -	796 51
By Concert, -	819 60
By Excursion, -	246 13
Received and collected at the church doors on Sundays, -	1,876
	$9,708 24

EXPENDITURES:

Paid Frank Forshew for the Pastoral residence, including interest and lawyer's fees, -	$3,080 60
Frank Forshew, for Sister's House, including lot attached to the same, -	2,246 34
Messrs. Avery & Hildreth, for repairing and remodelling school house, -	1,607 27
John Burdwin, for painting church, &c., -	423 81
Thomas Brennan, for cellar and church, -	97 81
Messrs. Traver and Son, for Lumber, -	55 54
Messrs. Macy and Son, for the same, -	50 00
Houghtaling, for do. -	5 88
Benedict, for Nails, &c., -	21 00
Lawrence Maker for side walk, -	12 00
Messrs. Thompson, Winslow and Carter, -	80 00
Labor, -	8 50
Messrs. Coffin and Brothers, for stone, etc. -	97 52
Messrs. Avery and Hildreth, second bill, -	55 90
Patrick Henchy, for work done in school house, church, &c., -	225 00
John C. Ball, for painting school house, etc., -	194 00
Messrs. McKinstry & Co., for paint and oil for the same, -	102 87
James Fitzgerald, for mason work, -	68 18
Messrs. Macy and Son, for second bill, -	28 90

Benedict, for second bill, -	39 54
Messrs. Thomas and Son, for repairing furnace, -	27 55
John C. Ball, for second bill, -	19 60
James Fitzgerald, for do, -	29 32
Traver and Son, for second bill, -	58 36
Patrick Henchy, for do., -	28 05
Expenses attending three different Orders of Sisters, in visiting and inspecting our school houses, -	164 20
Due to and advanced by me since last Report in the past year,	138 00
Expenses attending pastoral residence in May, 1868, including taxes, -	51 09
Two year's interest on school note, -	140 00
Messrs. Mulreign & Co. for work done in both houses, -	524 15
Moore on account of Water Co., -	66 80
Labor attending the same, -	2 00
Water for Sister's house, (-) -	18 75
Sundries, -	11 25
Wardrobe and clothes reel for Sister's, -	14 00
Wm. D. Morange for transferring property to St. Mary's Church,	10 00
Willard Peck, for the same, -	16 00
Rev. J. J. Moriarty for expenses to and from Canada to engage Sisters, -	50 00
Insurance on houses, -	48 75
Revenue stamps on transfer deeds, -	9 00
Insurance on School house, -	21 00
Cash refunded furnace men, -	15 00
Herrick for carpenter work, -	29 88
Canny for the same, -	17 00
Labor, -	15 50
Trees and labor in yard, -	13 80
Fitzgerald, mason, -	5 00
House cleaning, -	10 90
Expenditures in furnishing the Sister's house and that of the Pastor, -	1,304 00
Total expenditures, $11,353.22	$11,353 22
Total receipts, 9,708.24	
Balance due to Pastor, -	$1,644 98

JAMES S. O'SULLIVAN, PASTOR.

We, the undersigned, have carefully examined the above accounts, and hereby certify that they are perfectly correct.

JOHN C. BALL,
MAURICE WOULFE,
JOHN BROWN, } AUDITORS.
FENTON SHAW,
THOMAS TYNAN,

Universalist Church bought by the Rev. James S. O'Sullivan, for the use and benefit of St. Mary's School, Hudson, N. Y.:

Paid the Trustees of the above Church for the same, -	$1,500.
Mortgaged to the same, and transferred to Mary O'Sullivan, for	1,500.
	$3,000.
Cash raised on my note to pay the first installment, -	$1,000.
Nett Proceeds of a Horse Raffle, -	374.
Cash advanced by the Church, -	126.
	$1,500.

N. B.—The "Black Hawk" Horse, worth Five Hundred Dollars, given by me as a present or gift to the Congregation to enable them to purchase the above property, is now an act ill-requited and badly rewarded by a few unfortunate and ungrateful rebels.

The above School House is now and still indebted by note for -	$1,000.
By Mortgage, for -	1,500.
Indebted for the total amount of -	$2,500.

JAMES S. O'SULLIVAN, PASTOR OF ST. MARY'S CHURCH.

Dated at Hudson, N. Y., this 9th day of November, 1871.

We, the undersigned, have carefully examined the above accounts, and hereby certify that they are perfectly correct.

JOHN C. BALL,
MAURICE WOULFE,
FENTON SHAW, } AUDITORS.
JOHN BROWN,
THOMAS TYNAN,

secession of the Confederate states, not to abolish slavery. It was on this issue that the Irish laborers justified their participation in the war. The idea of a nation divided north and south reminded them of the repugnant situation in Ireland, which was emotional to them then (as it is now). The conscripted Irish joined the war to save the nation, not to free the slaves. To demonstrate Catholic patriotism, Father Havermans flew the American flag over St. Mary's in Troy, beginning on April 13, 1861, the day after the firing on Fort Sumter.

Slavery had long been condemned in Catholic history. In 1435, for example, in "Sicut Dudum," Pope Eugene IV condemned the enslavement of the African natives of the newly colonized Canary Islands. In 1537, Pope Paul III's "Sublimus Deus" condemned the forced servitude of the Indians of the New World: "Indians and all other people who may later be discovered by Christians are by no means to be deprived of their liberty or the possession of their property...nor should they be in any way enslaved." Thus, both Negroes and Indians were specifically mentioned in separate decrees. This teaching was reiterated by Gregory XIV in 1591 and Urban VIII in 1639. As late as 1890, Leo XIII also wrote against slavery.

Ironically, the Irish — who feared losing their jobs — were to gain much from the Civil War: recognition of their patriotism, leadership and fighting abilities; social acceptance; and the development of their political organizations. It also was the first war in which Irish Catholic chaplains accompanied Irish Catholic regiments, an extension of the already-existing chaplaincies at the poorhouse and penitentiaries. Father Noethon was the chaplain for the Albany Penitentiary, while Father Thebaud helped at the poorhouse in Rensselaer County.

In addition to men receiving recognition in the Civil War, Catholic women, such as the Sisters of Charity, worked as nurses for soldiers returning from the battlefront to Troy Hospital. This was done at the request of General J.F. Rathbone, related to the Rathbone family of Kenwood, which had been bought by the Religious of the Sacred Heart.

There was another side to the legacy of the Civil War. Many of the Irish who served in the Civil War, both North and South, were Fenians, and Albany became the gathering point for the ill-fated 1866 invasion of Canada after the war. By that time, Bishop John McCloskey had become Archbishop of the New York Diocese. While he attempted to stop their secret meetings, they still went en masse to Albany via steamboat on June 1 and brawled with anti-Fenian Irish in Albany. Only about 150 men under the leadership of Irish Civil War officers attempted to go north on June 7. Their officers were arrested and jailed within a couple of days by the U.S. Army, and the issue ended.

The end of the Civil War in 1865 proved to be a turning point in the Catholic Church, as well as in the Albany Diocese. Father John J. Conroy was appointed bishop July 7, 1865 and consecrated on October 15, 1865 as the second bishop of Albany.

Chapter Four
YEARS OF GROWTH

*'I just walked alone from
the sacristy to the throne.'*

The Civil War sounded the death knell for the Know-Nothings. Because of their intense focus on Catholics and Catholicism, the historical function of that movement would be, ironically, to interest people in the religion, to which many of them then converted. The performance, and hence promotion of Catholic men in the war, often to officer status, changed the anti-Catholic focus from suspicion to praise. And the praise translated to accommodation and acceptance of Catholics.

For example, the trustee law had been changed in 1863 to accommodate Catholicism. Catholic chaplains were accepted in traditionally Protestant domains, such as the poorhouses and penitentiaries. Some hospitals, such as the Troy Hospital, although private and religious, were "from the commencement...under city patronage...the city paying the Sisters $1.50 per person per week for their care and medical attendance, the sum they would pay if they were sent to the County House....Persons of all creeds and color are admitted, the only qualifications of a candidate is to be sick." Albany County paid the Christian Brothers $1.25 a week for each orphan at St. Vincent's, raising it to $1.50 in 1869.

It was into this liberal atmosphere that Bishop Conroy stepped. From his birthplace in Clonaslee, Leix, Ireland, he went as a boy to Montreal to be educated at the Sulpician

College. He then attended St. Mary's College in Emmitsburg before finishing at St. John's Seminary at Fordham and being ordained in 1842. Three years later, he was assigned to St. Joseph's parish in Albany. He remained pastor there even while he was bishop, an unusual circumstance; he did not resign from active ministry there until 1874. A measure of his stature in the Diocese is that after the Cathedral was dedicated in 1852, Father Conroy was made chairman of the committee to assess each parish to help remove "the heavy indebtedness" of $25,000. By 1860, he had overseen the construction of the new Gothic St. Joseph's and several attendant buildings, including schools and a rectory. He was also Bishop McCloskey's vicar general.

A more touchingly personal sign of his esteem occurred on the day before he became Bishop McCloskey's successor when the congregation at St. Joseph's presented him with a well-written, five-page address, praising him as a wonderful pastor. The testimonial was signed by 13 trustees. They also gave him the bishop's mitre, crozier and ring that signified his office. He left St. Joseph's in the well-organized hands of Father Thomas M.A. Burke, who would become the fourth bishop of Albany in 1894. But something sadly wrong happened as Bishop Conroy eased into his new duties. The first clue can be seen in his handwriting, which lapses at times into unintelligibility. A second sign can be found in letters, written years later to his successor, Bishop McNeirny, in which priests, trustees, laity and lawyers try to

Opposite: Bishop Conroy, second bishop of Albany
(The Evangelist archives)

make sense of what did and did not happen during Bishop Conroy's tenure. Sorting through those letters, one finds that apparently not all legal papers, such as deeds, were executed by all of the pastors, some of whom also still had several missions that were rapidly growing into full-fledged parishes and stations where priests said Mass on occasion. The well-organized priest who had been put in charge of so many important matters was becoming a bishop who had trouble writing, much less keeping his finger on the pulse of a far-flung, expanding diocese.

Bishop Conroy — although he tried to centralize the administration of the Diocese — did not seem to be on top of what was happening; as a result, he did not leave a good paper trail for future bishops and pastors to follow. To make matters worse, he had a couple of rascals among the dissenters, men only too eager to give their skewed version years later after Bishop Conroy resigned.

There were other, more subtle signs that something was amiss. For example, when Bishop McNeirny was made coadjutor bishop in December 1871 (meaning he would automatically succeed Bishop Conroy, a step often taken when a bishop is ill or thought to be otherwise in a tenuous state), it was not mentioned in the Catholic directory until 1873. Thus, the information from that 1873 directory is the first time McNeirny is mentioned in a secondary position to Bishop Conroy, a position he holds until the 1875

directory. There, McNeirny is listed first as administrator of the Diocese, while Bishop Conroy is named as the second bishop after McCloskey's listing, as if Conroy were dead. Bishop McNeirny continues to be listed that way until 1878, when he is identified as the present bishop. There, Bishop Conroy is listed as the second bishop, this time with his resignation date: October 16, 1877.

While those developments seem convoluted, they reflect the position taken by the hierarchy of that time on how to deal with an alcoholic bishop who periodically tried very hard to stay sober. After a trip to Oswego in 1872, he wrote from Montreal that he was going to Quebec and on the way home would stop in Saratoga Springs, the site of many health spas. In the 19th century, people often "took the waters" as a cure for alcohol-

The closing session of the First Vatican Council (CNS photo)

ism as well as rheumatism. In 1872, when the Diocese of Ogdensburg was established, it was suggested that Bishop McNeirny be transferred to the empty Diocese of Newark "on the grounds that Bishop Conroy had fully recovered his health and no longer needed an assistant."

First Vatican Council

In spite of his personal problems, Bishop Conroy did attend the First Vatican Council, in 1869-70. In fact, he was "appointed special bearer of despatches without compensation" by the U.S. Department of State. As a courier for Washington, he received "a special passport," probably a diplomatic one. Bishop Conroy wrote from various cities that he visited while on the trip, giving directions on several financial matters pertaining to St. Joseph's and the Diocese. In Rome, doctrinal questions occupied his mind. In a letter home, for example, he mentioned the great issue of that Council: "We are still occupied with the question of infallibility which may not be proclaimed for two or three weeks."

Archbishop McCloskey also attended the Council. When the final vote was cast, he and most of the other bishops voted for infallibility, even though he had voted "non placet" (literally, "it does not please") in an earlier vote. Cardinal Gibbons of Baltimore remarked years later (in 1910) that Archbishop McCloskey's position was not in opposition to "infallibility in itself" but that he "declared himself against the expediency of declaring it an article of faith at that time." Apparently, a number of bishops feared that some European governments would use the

Through the years . . .

1862: Bismarck becomes prime minister of Germany

1863: Henry Ford and William Randolph Hearst born

1864: Tolstoy begins writing "War and Peace"

teaching as a pretext for persecution — as the German government did, in fact, afterward.

Humiliation

A little over a year after Conroy's return from Rome, Bishop McNeirny was appointed coadjutor. At the same time, in 1872, the Diocese of Ogdensburg was separated from the Albany Diocese to make the latter more manageable. Father Edgar P. Wadhams, rector of the Cathedral of the Immaculate Conception in Albany, was made Ogdensburg's first bishop.

Assisted by a coadjutor, his Diocese split and the rector of his own cathedral now the bishop of the newly severed diocese, Bishop Conroy obviously felt humiliated. A letter written from Manhattanville to Kenwood in 1873 stated that those at Manhattanville "understand perfectly the state of affairs with regard to the government of the diocese, but...we are all the more for that circumstance in a very delicate position with regard to Bp. Conroy. [Nothing] should be done to wound his feelings, and she [the mother superior] thinks he would be hurt if he were passed over on this occasion." Apparently, a celebration was being planned, which precipitated discussion over whether or not Bishop Conroy should be invited.

Foi, Langue et Moeurs

While this preoccupation with the governance of the Diocese was a priority among those at the upper levels of the Church hierarchy, Church life continued to progress by leaps and bounds. The late 1860s through the 1870s, for instance, witnessed an increase of French and German parishes. The Franciscan Order of Friars Minor Conventual, already established in Schenectady, arrived in Albany to attend to the German community near the Bowery, and Our Lady of Angels parish was born. The French had become a strong factor in the mill towns, particularly in Cohoes where a number of huge mills, particularly textile mills, were built in the 1850s and expanded in the 1860s and 1870s.

The French were French Canadians, who had always treated the Champlain valley — and the North Country for that matter — as their personal bailiwick. After the aborted rebellion in 1837 when the French attempted to reassert their ascendancy in Canada, many of them, discouraged, moved to the border areas around Lake Champlain and Burlington, Vermont. What they called "the exodus" from Quebec, however, did not occur until after the Civil War when the mills that had been geared up for wartime levels changed to domestic production. Because inflation was rampant — prices so high and demand artificially elevated — the temptation to migrate was strong. Mill owners from New York and New England actively recruited in Quebec, competing for the largest families with the best work ethic.

Unlike other ethnic groups, the French had developed a unique approach to work. If the entire family had to work, it was likely that they all labored in the same mill. Husbands would choose a workplace where their wives could also get a job, often in a textile mill where strength was not a requirement (as opposed to a steel mill or a mine), and the children followed suit, contributing as much as one-third of the family income. In that way, papa could oversee what was happening to his family, and women were not automatically relegated to the cook stove and laundry room. In fact, their work on certain machines was considered just as valuable as the men's.

In 1868, Bishop Conroy established two new parishes for them: Assumption in Albany and St. Joseph's in Cohoes. Our Lady of Angels in Whitehall was established by the Irish just to counteract the strong French influence at Notre Dame des Victoires, established in 1844. Also, the parishioners of St. Jean Baptiste in Troy built a new church at this time. For the French, the parish was more than a church jurisdiction; it was their basic social and political unit. Since the English conquest in 1760, the French Canadians had fought for "survivance" (survival) of three essentials in their lives: "foi, langue et moeurs", that is, faith, language and customs. Because of active lay participation in Canada, there was a strong tradition of local control and independence.

Due to his education in Canada, Bishop Conroy felt a camaraderie with the French and often went to Montreal and Quebec for vacations. In 1865, he brought the Sisters of the Holy Names of Jesus and Mary to St. John's parish school in Schenectady. These Sisters, established at Quebec in 1844 for the education of children and young girls, were French-speaking. In the 1880s, they would open a convent and a private academy, which still exists today on New Scotland Road in Albany.

Education and Health

Bishop Conroy was particularly interested in education. Under him, the Sisters of St. Joseph, the Sisters of Mercy and the Christian Brothers all expanded their schools in

---

Above left: Bishop Conroy's coat of arms with his motto, "Health and Hope."

Right: Bishop McNeirny's coat of arms with his motto, "What God Wishes."

number and enrollment. In 1869, before he went to Vatican I, Bishop Conroy asked his priests to lobby for the passage of a state law to secure a "fund for the permanent aid and support of our Catholic schools." This was the beginning of 30 years of school controversy, which continued under Bishop McNeirny. For the first time, the importance of universal education was being actively touted in America as well as in England and the remainder of Europe.

A major event during Bishop Conroy's tenure was the 1869 opening of St. Peter's Hospital on Broadway in Albany, right near the heart of sweat labor and the scene of many accidents in the lumber district, two railroads, the Albany Basin and the Erie Canal. In the patient accounts, the most common problem was trauma caused by job-related accidents. Before that time, there had not been a Catholic hospital in Albany. After the

"The City of Albany, N.Y." by L. F. Tantillo shows the Capital circa 1868. At the far left is the Cathedral with its unfinished spire. Arrayed along the waterfront are several other churches.

death of Peter Cagger, a prominent Catholic lawyer, politician and philanthropist, his widow and daughter donated $15,000 as seed money for a memorial. The hospital took its name from him and has become one of the premier hospitals in the Diocese.

After the Troy Hospital was started to care for the poor who were ill — often because of epidemics — Catholic hospitals for paying patients were added primarily for two reasons. First, crucifixes, shrines and Extreme Unction (now called the Anointing of the Sick) were not allowed in regular hospitals, although chaplains eventually were. Second,

because of Catholic beliefs, certain procedures, such as abortions, were not performed in their hospitals.

Another French group that Bishop Conroy brought to the Diocese after his return from Vatican I was the Congregation of the Little Sisters of the Poor, who established homes for the aged in Albany and Troy. This order, founded in France at St. Servan in 1839 by Jeanne Jugan to care for the indigent elderly, had arrived in Brooklyn only in 1868. Their work continues today at Our Lady of Hope Residence in Latham.

In 1877, by the time Bishop McNeirny became the full bishop of what is the present Roman Catholic Diocese of Albany, there were 63 parishes with at least one full-time pastor, 33 missions (that is, church buildings served by circuit-riding priests) and 64 stations where a priest came on occasion to someone's house, warehouse, schoolhouse or other public location to offer Mass. In the interim, the numbers of priests had not kept up with the growing Catholic population, so missions and stations were a means of accommodating Catholics in rural areas where many of the jobs were. The missions and stations often were placed in or in close proximity to workplaces: the quarry, mine, forge (Iron Works), tanneries (Gloversville), mills (Steam Mills, Union Mills), boat basins (Spraker's Basin), springs (Richfield Springs, Sharon Springs), etc.

The creation of missions and stations at workplaces continued to the mid-20th century, especially in the rural parts of the Diocese. It was not until after World War II that the automobile became the primary means of transportation, and people were willing to travel more than two or three miles to work, shopping or church that demography played a role in centralizing churches.

The total of 96 church buildings in 1877 represented an increase of approximately 59 churches in only seven years since Bishop McCloskey's departure, a tremendous increase and a tribute to Bishop Conroy's ability to guide the Diocese in spite of his problems. Among the growing portions of the Diocese was the southwestern tier, including Oneonta, due partly to the completion around 1865 of the Albany and Susquehanna Railroad. The train was probably how a priest got there from Cobleskill to celebrate Masses in homes and halls. By 1883,

Through the years . . .

1865: Abraham Lincoln assassinated; Civil War ends

1866: Degas begins painting ballet scenes

1867: Karl Marx writes first part of "Das Kapital"

Oneonta Catholics had reached such numbers that Bishop McNeirny okayed their own parish, St. Mary's, headed by Father James Maney from St. Mary's in Albany. Within a week of his arrival in town, he had baptized three babies; within six months, construction on the church had begun. When the formal dedication was held in 1885, two special trains were run from Albany and Binghamton to bring guests, including McNeirny, who used the occasion to confirm dozens of young Catholics.

Bishop Francis McNeirny

Although Bishop McNeirny had been working as coadjutor and, later, administrator since 1871, it is only from 1877 on that he can claim exclusive responsibility for whatever occurred in the Albany Diocese. Born of Patrick and Margaret (Sheridan) McNeirny in New York, Francis was educated, as was Bishop Conroy, by the Sulpicians at Montreal College. Afterward, he attended the Grand Seminary in Montreal. After his ordination in 1854, he immediately was made secretary to Archbishop Hughes and, upon his death, to Archbishop McCloskey. During the Civil War, Father McNeirny accompanied Archbishop Hughes and Bishop McIlvaine, along with Thurlow Weed of Albany newspaper fame, when they were commissioned by Washington to visit Paris in order to counteract the influence of Southern delegates searching for financial support there. Thus, he served in New York City only until he was appointed coadjutor bishop to Bishop Conroy (with the right of succession to the Albany Diocese) in 1871.

Since his tenure was entwined so closely with Bishop Conroy's, it is difficult to separate precisely what he initiated from what Conroy did in the years between 1871 and 1877. While much of the daily running of the Diocese may have been shared in some fashion, without a daily log it is easiest to give Bishop Conroy credit for all that transpired before 1877 and to recognize Bishop McNeirny's accomplishments after that. In fact, Bishop Conroy was still performing episcopal duties to aid his successor even into the 1890s. Between them, the division of responsibility remains a bit vague.

What is known is that Bishop McNeirny was a no-nonsense man who brought stature, literally, to his role: He was over 250 pounds, even as a young man. His work to centralize and regularize his large Diocese would bring him recognition as an administrator. In modern parlance, he might be characterized as an upper-level bureaucrat who fit within the College of Bishops. However, he did not demand to be the center of atten-

tion. Upon the resignation of Bishop Conroy when Bishop McNeirny went from being the administrator to the third bishop of the Diocese, there was no ceremony. "I just walked alone from the sacristy to the throne," said the blue-eyed, fair-skinned bishop who was only 5'7".

Welcome home

When he was recognized, however, he loved it. Upon his return from Rome in 1886, the Knickerbocker reported that a crowd of thousands, including about 1,000 men sodalists representing the Albany City parishes and headed by the Albany City band, awaited his train in order to accompany him to the Cathedral. Hon. Thomas J. Lanahan delivered an address greeting the Bishop. "The response of the bishop was modest and appropriate. [But] he could not conceal his great affection for his people and the effect produced on him by the magnificent evidence of their love and affection. All Albanians, irrespective of creed or race, join with the young men in extending a joyous 'Welcome Home' to Bishop McNeirny."

Part of the joy may have been in celebration of an award he received while in Rome: the Grand Cross of the Knightly Order of the Holy Sepulchre, a decoration given to a select few. It was a highly prized award.

Before leaving for Rome, Bishop McNeirny had written Mayor John Boyd Thacher to ask if he could find a job for Mr. Thomas Kearney, an elderly, "infirm" man. The mayor replied that there were "no appropriate jobs under my immediate control" but

Opposite: Bishop McNeirny (The Evangelist archives)

that he would "hope to find a position...under the Capitol Commission, when they start work, as one of the Gatekeepers." That minor example, coupled with the use of the city band to greet the Bishop, is yet one more illustration of the almost small-town chumminess in this part of New York that has blurred the division between church and state.

Inspired by St. Francis

Bishop McNeirny placed a statue of Francis de Sales, his patron saint, under a Gothic canopy in the northern transept of the Cathedral (where it remains). While that particular saint was undoubtedly chosen partly because they shared a given name, among the writings of St. Francis was an apologia for the pontiff's primacy of jurisdiction and infallibility, written in the 1590s. Since Vatican I had just reiterated those very same topics, St. Francis' comments were uncannily apropos almost 300 years later at a time when the Church was centralizing its authority.

Bishop McNeirny's veneration of his patron saint illustrated a characteristic of Victorian-era Catholicism: devotionalism in which the sacred was sought via sacramentals and rituals that acquired an importance in and of themselves. The Irish and Germans had brought some of their favorite religious customs along with them when they crossed

Next page: On March 15, 1875, Archbishop McCloskey became the first American to be named a Cardinal. He is shown receiving his red biretta from Archbishop James Bayley of Baltimore in St. Patrick's Cathedral, New York City. (RNS photo)

Through the years . . .

1868: Tchaikovsky composes his first symphony

1869: Cincinnati Red Stockings become first salaried baseball team

1870: First Vatican Council promulgates dogma of papal infallibility

the Atlantic to America. The Irish had the Rosary, for instance, while the Germans stressed the Forty Hours Devotion. In the 1880s, when immigration from Eastern Europe started, the Polish also brought a preference for Forty Hours. European farmers, particularly the French and Middle Europeans, clung to the Angelus tradition.

Early in 1875, Bishop McNeirny published a list of plenary indulgences that could be gained "once at any time during the present year." A plenary indulgence was the remission in full of the temporal punishment incurred by a sinner for wrongs he or she committed. Basically, an indulgence shortened the time a person spent in Purgatory atoning for sins. The conditions laid down in Bishop McNeirny's letter included: "First. A true repentance and heartfelt sorrow for sin, joined with a good confession and worthy communion." Children who had not yet made their First Communion were not left out: "The pastor or confessor may substitute some other work of religion, or piety, or charity."

The second condition involved visiting four churches once a day for 15 days, "either con-

secutive or otherwise." Four churches each were listed for Albany, Troy, Oswego, Syracuse and Utica. In Albany, they were the Cathedral, St. Ann's, St. Mary's and St. Joseph's, all English-speaking. In Troy, St. Joseph's, St. Mary's, St. John the Baptist and St. Peter's were designated. (It is unclear whether St. John the Baptist referred to the church that had become St. Augustine's ten years previously or if it was St. Jean Baptiste, the French church. If it was, it would have been the only French church in the group.) There were two German churches listed, one each in Syracuse and Utica.

The third condition for Bishop McNeirny's plenary indulgences was that prayers be devoutly said during the church visitations for a list of prescribed intentions, although one could choose which prayers to say.

Pope, Bishop, Priest

This devotional Catholicism fit within the emphasis on centralized authority. The bishops represented the pope and his decisions as verbalized in encyclicals, and passed them on to the priests. Because of his elevation above ordinary humankind and since the priest verbalized what the pope had written, the automatic transfer of authority down the hierarchical chain gave him undisputed stature. In a sense, each was a monarch in his own jurisdiction; but in cases of dispute, "Roma locuta est; causa finita est: Rome has spoken; the case is closed" became the operative phrase guiding internal Church affairs.

Because of their elevation over lay people,

priests — perhaps unfairly — had the responsibility to conform to the expectations of the people in terms of personality, ability, behavior and godliness. They were to be examples a child could emulate. A non-conforming priest was placed under the thumb of a strong pastor. Numerous letters in Bishop McNeirny's file were written by and about priests in which a petitioner requests reinstatement because he has not been drinking for a long time, or a pastor — such as Father Havermans in Troy, who often was saddled with such problems — vouches for another cleric for the same reason. In another case, a letter tells about a priest who wanted to be transferred to another parish because he could not get along with the pastor, and it was making the associate ill.

There were also letters from parishioners about priests, expressing a variety of problems, ranging from perceived slights to carousing to legal or financial matters. The reason for this rather large body of correspondence may be simply that the Church was experiencing growing pains in which the demand for priests was too high for the supply. As a result, unqualified people were sometimes accepted into the seminary in the hopes that they would show some redeeming qualities and be useful in secondary roles.

Limits of history

But also — and this cannot be overstressed — all historians can write only from those documents still extant from any given period. Because they must deal with the records at hand, the historical perspective is, by necessity, skewed to how a newspaper re-ported an incident, what documents happened to be kept, what books were written, which articles were saved and what someone remembered, often many years later. Furthermore, no one will ever know what articles, books, letters and other parts of the culture were discarded in order to hide less admirable qualities or events, or to twist the results.

What is truly regrettable, though, were the so-called unremarkable events that were so readily accepted as a part of daily routine that they were left unmentioned and unrecorded. For example, in writing about heating systems historically, it is not written that many people living in mid-20th century regularly turn back their thermostat at night to 65 degrees or lower to save on relatively costly central heating systems, as well as a belief that lower temperatures while sleeping are healthy. At different times in history, common events are not recorded, such as the average time people get up to get to work on time and/or how much time it takes them to get to work.

No one imagined how, 150 or 200 years later, anyone would ever want to know, for example, that the reason people did not settle what became the New Scotland Avenue area for years was because there was no trolley line. Working class laborers had no horse and wagon to take them to work the mile or mile-and-a half away in downtown Albany, and they avoided walking unless they had to. Women did not want to trudge a mile or so to a store or church in long skirts on dirty lanes with no sidewalks. They did laundry only every two weeks or so because it was such a major chore and took all day; they did not want to wear muddy or dusty skirts for days until the next laundry day. (Ironically, partially because wheelmen — bicycle riders — lobbied nationally, roads were improved, so their spills were less frequently due to potholes.) Thus, the letters in Bishop McNeirny's file reflect only a small proportion of the total volume written; and in most of the cases, they were ones written to him, not ones he wrote.

Rituals

A third element of Victorian devotional Catholicism was its emphasis on sin and impurity in which salvation and holiness were open to everyone but had to be earned by struggling victoriously over sin, often by performing rituals. That was accomplished, for example, by devotional guides, such as the Sacred Heart devotion; through the intercession of Mary and the saints; by saying certain prayers, especially the Rosary; and particularly by going to Mass and receiving the sacraments of Baptism, Confession, Communion and Marriage. At that time, the Eucharist was not received weekly; monthly reception was considered the norm. "Good Catholics" referred to those who took monthly communion and sometimes monthly confession, although the latter was less common.

Sex and Alcohol

As might be expected of Victorian times, the sins that were perceived to be the worst were related to sexuality and alcohol. Although temperance had never disappeared

Through the years . . .

1871: Jehovah's Witnesses founded

1872: James Whistler paints "The Artist's Mother"

1873: Remington, a gunsmith, begins producing typewriters

as a movement, it experienced a revival when the American bishops decided, at the Third Plenary Council of Baltimore in 1884, to warn Catholics who sold liquor to ponder the occasion of sin that surrounded their business and to consider a more becoming way of making a living. Bishop McNeirny sent a letter to be read at all Masses in which he directed that certain regulations be followed "concerning pic-nics, excursions, fellowships etc. encouraged by so-called Catholic societies, and very notably by that one bearing the chivalrous, sacred name of Knights of the Holy Cross." Societies organized for beneficial purposes for their own members could not have public functions to raise money unless the proceeds went to some public charity. No fund-raisers for Church purposes or public charity that involved "round dancing, night dancing, dancing in halls or ball-rooms" were to occur. Absolutely, no wine, beer or any kind of intoxicating liquors were to be sold at church events. "Any meetings...where morals or good behavior are endangered, such as moonlight excursions, [or] pic-nics continued till after night-fall were forbidden." Finally, the bishop's permission was required for all fund-raisers. While this directive was all-inclusive, because Bishop McNeirny focused on the Knights of the Holy Cross, he was probably targeting the German affinity for picnics at which beer was consumed. The organization was a social club probably organized initially as a fraternal society to aid immigrants.

In the 1880s, summaries of Father John J. McIncrow's sermons, given at St. Mary's Church in Amsterdam, were published in the Amsterdam Daily Democrat and The Evening Recorder. His sermons often prohibited various activities, much like Bishop McNeirny's directive; but many also appeared quite modern. For ex-

ample, Father McIncrow (above) spoke in scathing terms of parents who allowed their children "too many privileges," such as the practice of midnight sleigh rides and parties, and he railed against teenagers (listed as boys and girls 16-20) hanging out at night, a practice he called "street walking." He himself went out at night to shoo them home, particularly the girls. He insisted that the excise board not grant liquor licenses to men who sold to minors and drunkards, and objected to "the terrible habit of smoking ciga-

rettes [which] is prevailing to an alarming extent among the young." Obscene pictures should not be found in the possession of little boys; and promiscuous gatherings, such as circuses and "vile" performances of travelling performers, should not be attended.

In sum, Father McIncrow talked about guilt by association; he earnestly entreated his parishioners not to "disgrace themselves, their priest, their nationality or their holy religion." He also spoke directly from the pulpit about prostitution and was concerned about "impure expressions and ribald jests" that "our virtuous Catholic girls have to listen to" in the mills. In 1883, in a letter to Bishop McNeirny, Father McIncrow wrote about a bill being brought before the State Legislature at his request, prohibiting the State Board of Health from performing abortions in the name of public health.

Customs Christianized

Many of our favored American traditions, such as those associated with Christmas, Santa Claus or card-giving, evolved during the Victorian era, as did a revival of many of the customs associated with marriage, some of which harked back to Roman times. Marriage involved consent and property transferral (a woman's services, as well as her personal wealth), both legal, financial aspects of temporal life; and classical Roman tradition sanctioned them. Therefore, they became one of the foundations of the basic body of marriage customs in the Church. Constantine, the first Christian Roman emperor, gave the Church authority to act as the judiciary in civil cases, which included marriage and divorce, as well as the attending problems of property loss and, at times, remarriage. As the Roman Empire declined, the authority of the Church grew in order to compensate for the collapse of the civil judiciary system. As the Church became increasingly involved with these matrimonial decisions, its own canonical body of literature, as well as sacramental theology, underwent further development and refinement. Then throughout the centuries as different ethnic groups were christianized, their views on marriage and their attendant customs were, variously, incorporated, modified or rejected. Over the course of time in some cases, the situation developed where marriages could be civilly recognized but canonically invalid. (In France to this day, for example, only civil marriages are recognized by the state, so couples are often married twice. There were also instances when a couple was married in a Protestant church.)

Of course, different cultures brought their own customs to the United States. Then when they arrived here, set up housekeeping in rural areas, had children, and those children wanted to marry, it was not unusual for them to be married civilly or to just live together until the circuit-riding priest came to witness their marriage. There were many cases of couples being married in the Church at the same time their child was baptized. That should not be considered a stigma. It was only with the advent of canals and trains, literacy and the publishing business, all of which popularized trends, that wedding ceremonies performed by a circuit-rid-

Through the years . . .

1874: Robert Frost, Winston Churchill and G. Marconi born

1875: Bizet's opera "Carmen" debuts in Paris; he dies

1876: Korea becomes an independent nation

ing priest became more common.

This devotional Church contrasted with earlier Catholic practices that placed more emphasis on a personal, more spiritual Catholicism in which a more congregational tone prevailed. The earlier Church was a religious institution designed to satisfy spiritual needs. The change to a more ritualistic religion based on what was now a community institution in which various societies were formed — such as the Rosary Society, the Sodality of Mary or the Confraternity of the Holy Childhood — occurred world-wide. In 1895, for example, "the girls who are employed in the collar shops" of Troy organized a Purgatorian Society to raise money for Masses to be offered for the souls in Purgatory. Each of 40 women donated five cents a week to the group, resulting in 85 Masses being offered.

The last element of Victorian devotional Catholicism was a belief in the miraculous. New sciences and technologies were dominating the workplace, illuminating mysteries which heretofore were inexplicable in the practical world. But the inner, spiritual, emotional world was still an enigma. Religious processions evoked this atmosphere, as did the popularization of reported miraculous cures, especially at such shrines as Ste. Anne de Beaupré in Canada.

Schools

Many of these elements of devotional Catholicism could not have taken place without universal literacy promoted from the pulpit. And universal literacy came to mean parish schools in all Catholic neighborhoods. That tradition had its origins in the public schools where a Protestant Bible was used to teach reading and blatantly anti-Catholic tracts were used as readers for older children. In Troy, for example, Father Thebaud sent two Irish girls, daughters of Michael O'Grady, to the Rensselaer County poorhouse to teach catechism to the Catholic children in order to prepare them for their First Communion. He became incensed when he discovered that the Methodists had received $50 from the Board of Supervisors to buy "moral and instructive books," which were in fact "abusive tracts against the Catholic religion." The Methodist New Testament and prayer-books were also distributed to all the children, and Father Thebaud reacted.

Catholics reasonably requested that if their children were to learn to read by using the Bible, that they should be given their own Bible. But that request was almost universally denied, opening the way for the Poughkeepsie Plan, by which the local government paid Catholic sisters and brothers to teach Catholic children in parish schools. That plan was sporadically accepted in some places in the Albany Diocese, such as in Troy

in the early 1880s at St. Joseph's where the school building itself was leased to the city school system; its pupils and teachers, the Sisters of St. Joseph, were considered an integral part of the public schools. In spite of those isolated instances, the Poughkeepsie Plan never gained enough credence for a state law to be passed.

Generally, however, Catholic schools were not accepted into the public school system, partly due to the intellectual controversy among the Catholic bishops concerning whether or not Catholic children should be educated in public schools or in parish schools. Since the Albany area had always been known for its more relaxed and accepting attitudes toward its different neighbors, it was not surprising that the issue never became a heated one. While there may have been instances in which other counties paid for services rendered in Catholic institutions, to date only Rensselaer County and Albany County statistics on Troy Hospital and the poorhouses and orphan asylums have come to light. While both involved shelter and sustenance, except for the hospital, education of children also took place.

In time, because of Catholic complaints, because readers were developed (such as McGuffy's), and ultimately because of how courts interpreted the separation of church and state, anti-Catholic teachings were expunged from schoolbooks, and the Bible was dropped as a reader from the public school curriculum. In the minds of many Catholic parents, those developments absolved them from seeking an obligatory Catholic school education for their children, particularly in rural areas where there were not enough children to warrant a parish school.

In contrast, at this time, of eight parish elementary schools started under Bishop Conroy, three of them taught in German and one in French. Under Bishop McNeirny's auspices, 14 schools were added, of which four were French and taught by French-speaking nuns: Assumption in Albany, St. Jean Baptiste in Troy, and St. Joseph's and Sacred Heart in Cohoes. The Sisters of the Holy Names taught at Assumption; Sisters of St. Joseph briefly, then the Sisters of St. Anne at St. Jean Baptiste; the Sisters of St. Anne at St. Joseph's for the girls and laymen for the boys; and lay teachers at Sacred Heart. The Sisters of St. Anne, founded at Vaudreuil in Quebec in 1850, specialized in teaching both boys and girls in bilingual schools, especially in rural areas.

St. Joseph's in Amsterdam, the only new German school, was taught by laypeople. The rest of the nine schools were taught in English by laypeople and/or the Sisters of St. Joseph and Mercy nuns — and one new group, the "Black Cap Sisters of Charity" from Mt. St. Vincent-on-Hudson. They taught at Catskill, the southernmost school in the Diocese at that time. It would be their first and only school in the Albany Diocese. Sacred Heart in Castleton had only lay teachers for all of its life. The northernmost school was in Whitehall; the most westerly, in Little Falls.

In addition to founding more schools,

Bishop McNeirny spent part of the last year of his life, from May 1893 until he died in 1894, on the New York State Board of Regents. At the same time, Melvil Dewey of the Lake Placid Club fame, as Secretary of the Regents, exercised his unique ideas regarding education and, especially, promoted phonetic spelling. Although the Bishop was on the board, by that time he was quite ill. From about 1885 on, in practically every letter he received, the writer hoped that the Bishop was feeling better.

Cathedral finished

Long before he died, however, Bishop McNeirny completed work on the Cathedral. It began with music; Bishop McNeirny had a "superb baritone" and was known as perhaps the best of New York State's "singing bishops." When he was still administrator of the Diocese, upon the resignation of the Cathedral music director in 1876, he invited Leandre Alexandre Du Mouchel to become the organist. Du Mouchel, who was from Rigaud, Quebec, had studied in Leipzig under master organists after his education in Montreal. In 1880, Bishop McNeirny had the organ extensively improved to show off Du Mouchel's virtuosity.

Under the maestro's guidance, the choir consisted of 38 sopranos and altos, and 37 basses and tenors; it was supplemented at times by a chorus of 40 voices. In addition, the 40-voice orphan girls' choir and the 70-voice Academy girls' choir sang on special occasions. On great feasts, a permanent orchestra supplemented the organ. Later, a boys' choir was added. One press account

Cathedral of the Immaculate Conception

Drawing of the Cathedral by Martin Gieschen

installed in the tower.

Those developments were the beginnings of the final completion of the Cathedral. In 1882, renovations were started on the sanctuary and nave. By 1891, the final press had begun, and parishes were assessed to pay for the renovations and repairs. Several newspapers, including The Argus, the Albany Express, the Albany Times, the Press & Knickerbocker, the Albany Evening Journal, The Evening Union, The Catholic Weekly and the Catholic Mirror, discussed the project, how much it cost, and how the money would be raised.

Along with the construction of the Episcopal Cathedral of All Saints at this time, finishing the Cathedral of the Immaculate Conception was one of the costliest non-public, religious projects in the area. Meanwhile, work on the new State Capitol appeared never-ending. Standing for 20 years, the stonecutters' sheds for the Capitol appeared to have become a permanent addition. Almost an entire generation grew up unaware that the sheds sprawled over Capitol Park, which reappeared in 1899 when the struc-

praised the results: "Never was the choir under Prof. Du Mouchel heard to better advantage." In improving the grand organ, over the years water-powered wind bellows were

tures were removed.

In 1884, a German stonemason wrote Bishop McNeirny from New York City, asking for a recommendation for an altar he had designed, which had been requested by Father Farley in Newport. During the 1880s, there was ample work in stone in the area for two reasons: Economic prosperity was soaring and would remain so until the Panic of 1893; and the sparks from coal-burning trains had forced insurance companies to insist that town and city buildings be made of brick and stone.

Labor Movement

The day that Mr. Patrick McCann, the general contractor for the foundation and carpentry at the Cathedral, started dismantling the wall to extend the sanctuary west 30 feet, Bishop McNeirny "was seated in a pew, viewing the work, with a smile of deep satisfaction on his genial countenance." When the contract was awarded to Mr. John Smith to construct this sanctuary addition, the Bishop "inserted a clause requiring that the work be done by organized labor workmen; the hours of the men and their wages to be in accordance with the rules of the Federation of Labor or other organization having authority in such matters."

Earlier, in 1885, in one of his fiery sermons, Father McIncrow had also indirectly promoted the Knights of Labor: "In our mills our virtuous Catholic girls have to listen to impure expressions and ribald jests....Should a boss, or any other man in any of our mills use such language to our girls, that girl

Through the years . . .

1877: Thomas Alva Edison invents the phonograph

1878: Leo XIII becomes pope, succeeding Pius IX

1879: Anti-Jesuit law introduced in France

should immediately inform the Knights of Labor and get the man who so insulted her Christian modesty...discharged from the mill."

Those events foreshadowed a major change in Catholic policy concerning trade unions. Because unions feared reprisals from mill, forge and factory owners, they were formed originally as secret societies. But ever since the upswing in Masonic membership in the 18th century, the Catholic Church had opposed any secret society and condemned men who joined labor unions. In this area, however, the lack of the extreme violence resorted to by union members elsewhere (such as in the mines of Pennsylvania) to fight sub-human working conditions tempered attitudes in general toward union membership in the Albany Diocese.

By the 1890s, Albany — and undoubtedly Troy and other small cities — had assemblies of the Knights of Labor representing brewery workers, gas and steamfitters, painters, railroad workers, dock laborers, iron workers, and stove mounters. They had struck several times and successfully bargained for higher wages and fewer hours.

These men also complained over the injustice of competing with child and prison labor, and training boys under the "Berkshire system" by which journeymen were required to take time from their jobs — in which they were paid by the piecework system — to train young boys, thus losing precious time for their own income.

The international opposition by the Catholic Church toward unions by the end of the 19th century threatened to alienate the working class forever from the Church until bishops like McNeirny — and, earlier, Archbishop Elizear Taschereau of Quebec — and Cardinal James Gibbons of Baltimore helped convince Pope Leo XIII of the rights of working people. It was an easily justified decision and avoided the mass exodus of Catholic men from the Church. By this time, Polish and Slovak workers had been added to the French, German and Irish laborers, the last group the most articulate in English and often forming the leadership in the unions in the Albany area.

Women at work

Labor unions were not exclusive to men. With the advent of the collar and shirt industry in Troy, and even before the sewing machine enabled the industry to mass-produce garments, women were employed in large laundries to wash the items. The first women's labor union was one of laundry workers in Troy in 1864. By the 1890s, suffragettes, such as Susan B. Anthony (from Rochester) and Elizabeth Cady Stanton (from Johnstown) frequently lobbied at the State Capitol. They had come a long way

from their first convention in 1848 in Seneca Falls. Now they were recognized as being formidable enough to merit the opposition of a group of prominent Albanians, including Mrs. John V.L. Pruyn and Episcopal Bishop Doane.

Long after the secret ballot was made law and political parties were barred from lobbying near polling places in the early 20th century, voting was still a physical event. It often involved alcohol, fist fights and bribes. Even after the Nineteenth Amendment in 1920, alcohol and $5 bribes were given by politicians outside the polling places in some rural towns, as well as in Albany. People turned out to vote in part to collect their dues. In the 19th century, few self-respecting, middle-class aspiring women wanted to be associated with such "low-class" snarling.

The Cathedral acquired a new look that would last until the mid-20th century when Connecticut brown stone was deposited on the Madison Avenue side of the building and stonecutters' sheds were erected behind the sanctuary. Derricks were used to lift the stone for the new sacristy and the south tower. A century later, the match of the stone that was quarried at two distinct times and which, therefore, aged at different rates is still amazingly good. The south tower of the Cathedral (on what was Jefferson Street and is now a state parking lot) was completed to match the 210-foot height of the north tower, both overseen by the same man — Jewell — who had finished the Madison Street tower in the 1860s. It is probably because the towers were overseen by the same individual that they match so well in spite of the 20-year difference.

As the sacristy was enlarged, the much acclaimed Lady Window was moved to the north transept. Various stained glass windows toward the front of the Cathedral, in the sanctuary and in the transepts were added. The look of the interior decoration was distinctly of the heavily carved, ornate high Victorian design. In 1892, one of the last improvements made was an electrical connection between the organs that allowed Du Mouchel to operate 62 stops from one location when all three organs were in use. In addition to the great organ, the south transept organ had eleven stops; the smaller one in the north transept, only eight.

Church Finances

Bishop McNeirny beautifully timed the completion of the Cathedral. Within a year, the United States was feeling the Panic of 1893, fueled by the recall of European securities investments, which caused the New York Stock Market to collapse. Unemployment was rampant with the usual attendant woes. Before that happened, however, the improvements on the Cathedral were paid for by a variety of means. Church projects, in general, in the 19th century were paid for in predictable, but always problematic ways. No one wanted to deny anyone access to the sacraments; but if nobody financed construction of the churches or heating them so they lasted, there would be no place to receive the sacraments. In addition to the previously mentioned lotteries and outright grants of money, one grassroots method of financing

in all churches — Protestant as well — involved collecting pew rents. Families rented a specific pew and placed therein their accoutrements, such as prayer books. They felt as proprietary about their possessions being there as if they actually owned the pew. The pews nearer the front were more socially desirable, especially if there were a daughter to marry off, because parishioners could see who was there. Nameplates embellished the ends of the pews, identifying those who belonged there. Therefore, rivalries sprang up over the choice pews, and prices for them rose in proportion. Since wealthier families could outbid poorer ones, the atmosphere became decidedly more socio-economic than religious. Priests, ministers, parishioners and bishops in all denominations were equally appalled at this development, which, at times, even ended up in the courts. This method of financing slighted the poor parishioner, who had just as much chance of going to heaven but less of being in the front row in church. That pew rental lasted in some parishes well into the 20th century indicates its popularity among the upwardly mobile seeking status wherever they could. Sometime after World War I, though, and definitely by the '20s, rentals were replaced by weekly contributions in many parishes.

This evolved from "seat money," terminology a tad removed from pew rental, although the concept was the same. Those wanting to sit down in any pew during Mass plunked a fee — perhaps 15 or 25 cents — in the basket at the door. Those willing to stand did not pay. In one situation prior to World War

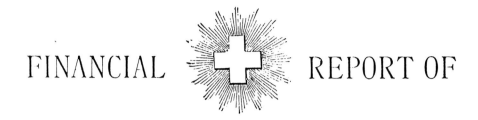

FINANCIAL + REPORT OF

THE CHURCH OF
THE IMMACULATE CONCEPTION,

HOOSICK FALLS, N. Y.,

FOR THE YEAR ENDING DECEMBER 31st, 1887.

1887. RECEIPTS.

Jan. 1, Balance on hand, last report..		$40 79
Dec. 31, Pew rent for year............		2,600 00
Plate collections............		600 00
Coal collection.............		90 00
Library collection		50 00
Cemetery lots........		159 50
House rent, less repairs.....		160 00
Collection for side altars.....		320 00
Proceeds from festival.......		950 00
School fund collection.......		385 00
Donation from Augustinian Fathers...		800 00
Indian and Colored people's collection..........$45 00		
Propagation of the Faith 25 00		
Seminary collection.... 70 00		
Papal collection... ... 80 00	220 00	
		$6,375 29

1887. EXPENDITURES.

Town, corporation and school taxes....................	$146 77
Organist and leader, etc......	250 00
Sexton's salary.............	408 00
Easton & Co., lumber, paint etc	105 85
F. Riley, coal........... ...	302 00
Two side altars.......... ...	600 00
Cemetery, ditching, pipe, etc..	140 00
Insurance..................	153 00
Cathedraticum..............	250 00

1887.

Maintenance of clergy.......	$1,600 00
Chimes for sunday school....	50 00
Cleaning church........	20 00
Gas	49 53
Altar wine.................	25 00
Clerical fund..............	5 00
Morgan, balance on chancel window....................	75 00
Collections, forwarded to Rev. Chancellor..	220 00
Interest on note of $4,000.00, since Oct., 1884.	650 00
	$5,050 15

RECAPITULATION.

Total receipts for the year 1887.......	$6,375 29
" disbursements for the year 1887,	5,050 15
Cash on hand, *reserved for School Fund*,	$1,325 14

LIABILITY.

A note of $4,000.00, bearing interest at 5 per cent, from Jan. 1, 1888, is the only debt on the church.

Rev. J. D. WALDRON, O. S. A.,

Pastor.

Many other bills have been paid that could in justice be charged to the treasury of the church.

I, this practice evolved not from a desire to increase the coffers but from a directive to reserve the 9 a.m. Mass exclusively for children. Since priests did not want to alienate adults by sending them away from that Mass, some charged a seat fee to entice those without children to attend another liturgy — and to keep the children from feeling crowded in the pews.

Another means of income for the Church was the direct gift, the primary method for collecting sizeable amounts. As so often happened in the Diocese, some of the gifts came from prominent non-Catholic individuals, such as $50 — as well as an autograph of Pius IX — given by Protestant Mayor John Boyd Thacher at the Cathedral Fair. Protestant President Grover Cleveland also sent $25 for that fair. Earlier, in 1850, Thurlow Weed had written Bishop McCloskey because he wanted to "consult with [him] about the best mode of proceeding" in relation to collections for the Cathedral.

Ever since St. Mary's had been founded, fairs were a popular way to pay for projects and routine expenses; thousands and thousands of dollars were acquired at these events, which sometimes lasted two weeks. For example, funds to build the third St. Mary's in 1867 were raised at a two-week fair that netted $10,000, a figure that compares well with the extended weekend church fairs of the 1950s. In 1887, the Cathedral table of the Grand Fair made $8,570.16, falling $1,646.75 short to pay for the erection of the Jefferson Street tower. After a special collection netted an additional $1,400, some-

Through the years . . .

1880: General Lew Wallace publishes "Ben Hur"

1881: Pablo Picasso born; Fiodor Dostoevsky dies

1882: U.S. bans Chinese immigration for ten years

one contributed the final $246.75 needed to meet the $10,217.07 cost.

Most of the grassroots fund-raising efforts in use today were also employed then. Performances, such as dramatic readings, were given. Concerts or excursions on the Hudson were held. Du Mouchel conducted a concert by the Cathedral choir at the Leland Opera House for the benefit of the Cathedral window to Saint Cecilia in 1892. And whenever a special event occurred, such as Bishop Burke's installation, a collection was taken up.

Two still current methods of grassroots giving — annual or biennial tithing and weekly donations in the basket (or box) at the entrance or when it was passed during the Offertory — were new to American Catholics in the 20th century. Weekly envelopes started in the 1920s in many parishes, secondarily as a means of church registration. They also became a weekly record of tax-deductible donations that could be used to reduce income tax after it was mandated in 1913 by the 16th Amendment. In spite of this incentive, a high percentage of people do not use envelopes because they do not want the parish priest to know how much they contribute; some parishes never even started to employ them.

Then there were site-specific financial arrangements. In 1892, for example, Father Denis B. Collins wrote from St. Joseph's Church in West Winfield that "the subscriptions of the people cannot come in until after the hop season" harvest. In 1881, at Our Lady Help of Christians parish in Albany, individual parishioners mortgaged their own homes in order to provide the cash needed for the new "German Gothic Cathedral." That same year, Father Jno. P. Gilmore from St. Mary's Church in Waterford wrote Father J. Collins: "Please send me dispensation from all calls for Jno. [John] H. Lynch and Hannah Griffin. If called they would have to remain from work in mill three weeks and thus suffer financially. They are well known here as respected parties." Presumably, Hannah and John wanted to get married but needed dispensations; yet they could not take the time from work to appear physically and therefore needed a favor from their pastor, who, as the underlying assumption implies, would be rewarded by their contributions in the future. As a corollary, their plight also points out the predicament of mill workers at the mercy of owners unconcerned about their personal problems.

In addition to church buildings and attendant property, the Diocese owned burial grounds. In Albany, that involved considerable property, extending between Ontario Street and North Main Avenue, and Western to Singer Street, parallel to and beyond Kent Street. Because property owners were assessed to pay for costly improvements — water and sewer lines, as well as for paving — in 1889, the Diocese decided to move the burials completely to St. Agnes Cemetery in Menands, which had been purchased under Bishop Conroy in 1867. Part of the property in Albany that had been bought in 1851 by Bishop McCloskey was then sold to avoid paying for the improvements.

Thus, diocesan dealings in real estate tended to be incidental, rather than part of a regular investment portfolio. While the Albany Diocese did not specialize in real estate as a means of financing churches in the 19th century, the Dutch Reformed Church did. Some individual parishes did own real estate, sometimes willed to them. Individual pastors, however, negotiated in real estate periodically in order to finance construction of a school or rectory. Their personal worth was more likely — although not commonly — to have been based on railroad stocks, for example, or securities, as can be seen in their wills. Pastors were more apt to negotiate a favorable interest rate on a construction loan from a friendly, perhaps Catholic, officer at the local bank. After all, any construction also improved the economy by creating jobs — and more bank depositors.

Finally, there was the la Propagation de la Foi — the Vatican's Propagation of the Faith office — which financed many projects until 1908 when the Church in the United States was removed from being a mission area with accountability to the Congregation for the Propagation of the Faith. Bishop McCloskey had relied heavily on that office, as well as the Leopoldine Society, to finance the original construction of the Cathedral from 1848-1852. By the end of his tenure in the Diocese, Bishop McCloskey was sending money to the former, carefully recording the current exchange rate. Collections sent in 1874 amounted to 1,090.40 francs; in 1875, they increased to 5,927 francs (based on exchange rates at that time, the latter amounted roughly to $1,185.)

Bishop McNeirny also sent money east, particularly to a variety of bishops in Limerick, Loughrea, Killarney, Longford, Monaghan, Skibbereen, Waterford and Mayo, Ireland. In 1880, the first Irish Catholic mayor of Albany, Michael N. Nolan, president of the Quinn and Nolan Brewery, appealed to Bishop McNeirny and Episcopal Bishop Doane, in a letter printed in the Argus, for money for the relief of Ireland. Both bishops promised to oversee collections. Bishop McNeirny's letter to the pastors began: "A wail of distress comes to us, borne over the waters of the broad Atlantic, and falls mournfully upon our ears. It is the voice of Ireland's poor, appealing to our brotherly love and sympathy."

In addition to collecting for the poor here and abroad, and building churches and schools, pastors filled out forms that Bishop McNeirny had developed in his efforts to centralize and regularize the administration of the see. He expected annual reports and all property documents to be in order: deeds, mortgages, debts, insurance, etc. along with a map showing the buildings. The Bishop

Through the years . . .

1883: Marx, Manet and Wagner die

1884: Mark Twain publishes "Huckleberry Finn"

1885: "The Mikado" by Gilbert and Sullivan debuts in London

also established a "diocesan bureau of accounts" with auditors appointed to check over the reports.

Additionally, he acquired a new political level in his administration. It was not a new duty, since it was assumed that all bishops of Albany de facto should be involved in politics at the state level. For the first time, however, that status was formalized when Bishop Corrigan of New York suggested $500 for "the employment at Albany of a competent person to watch the proceedings of the Legislature, and report on all measures affecting our joint interests in this State: the various Dioceses contributing pro rata for services so rendered." The words "lobbyist" and "spoils system" were both coined — and used — in Albany as early as the 1820s. (Lobbyists were so called because only legislators were allowed in the legislative chambers; the men wanting favors hung out in the lobby.)

Reacting to Social Problems

Two groups of women religious appeared in the Diocese who were primarily involved with social work in institutions, as well as educational work for those in the homes. In 1884, Father Havermans of Troy brought the Sisters of Our Lady of Charity of the Good

Above: St. Vincent's Male Orphan Asylum, founded for children orphaned by a cholera epidemic. It would evolve into LaSalle School for Boys in Albany. (LaSalle School archives)

Shepherd, a French group, to work with wayward girls who had gotten in trouble with the law. The girls were placed in the sisters' monastery on the "Troy Road," rather than being sent to jail. In 1887, they opened an additional home in Albany where their institution was chartered as Saint Anne School of Industry and Reformatory of the Good Shepherd. Since 1888, it has remained in the same location, now known as St. Anne Institute.

Schools of Industry were designed to produce profit-making goods or services to pay for the care of the group. In addition to basic literacy, the residents learned practical skills, such as commerce, homemaking and trade sewing. In addition to the girls, there were women who wished a life of prayer and penance, sometimes in reparation for past misdeeds. The institute supported itself by running a laundry and doing commercial sewing, crocheting, embroidery and fine needlework.

Also in 1884, the other new group, the Irish congregation of the Sisters of the Presentation of the Blessed Virgin Mary, were invited by Father William F. Sheehan, pastor of St. Patrick's in West Troy, to found an orphanage where brothers and sisters could live together. He chose this community because they had helped his widowed mother, who had had eight mouths to feed. The sisters had petitioned the bishop to pay for Father Sheehan's seminary education, and his sister was a cloistered Presentation nun in the small town of Fermoy, Ireland, where he was born.

Orphanages were ordinarily divided by sex. When children were orphaned in infancy, they might never know of siblings of the other sex who lived in another orphanage. Father Sheehan had read of a situation in which it was discovered that a young pre-nuptial couple were actually brother and sister, and he wanted to avoid similar situations. St. Colman's Industrial School and Orphan Asylum of Watervliet was incorporated in 1884 (and still operates today as St. Colman's Home, now specializing in helping emotionally disturbed children with autism and developmental disabilities).

A third group, the Dominican Sisters of the American Congregation of St. Catherine de Ricci, OP, appeared in the Diocese in 1880. The order was founded in Glens Falls by convert Lucy Eaton Smith, "with the permission and approval" of Bishop McNeirny "for the Work of Spiritual Retreats." They also would staff a home for women. When they first got started, they taught at a school at St. Alphonsus parish for both boys and girls, and were supported by the church; but records do not indicate if it was a parochial or private school. Later, they were in Saratoga Springs. In 1901, they ended up in Havana, Cuba, possibly through connections with Augustinian Father William Ambrose

Through the years . . .

1886: Statue of Liberty dedicated

1887: Sir Thomas More beatified

1888: Frederick III becomes emperor of Germany, dies

1889: Adolf Hitler born

1890: Van Gogh dies; Dwight Eisenhower born

Jones, who was born in Cambridge, in Washington County, but who was in Cuba at that time as a parish priest.

Transitions

As Bishop McNeirny's illness progressed and it became apparent that trips to spas, such as Carlsbad in Bohemia in 1889, did not help, he pushed to see his projects completed. Cardinal McCloskey had died in 1885, a victim of Parkinson's disease. He had worked beyond the time when his handwriting had begun to fail in, at least, 1881. In a letter he wrote to Bishop McNeirny that year, he expressed the hope that the latter's health had improved. It hadn't.

In 1885, Father Patrick Ludden, McNeirny's Vicar General and pastor of St. Peter's in Troy, wrote that Bishop Wadhams of Ogdensburg was ill in the hospital and had had several "delicate operations," looked "quite old and shaky," and had been taking "things easily for some time." Two years later, in January 1887, Father Ludden would be named the first bishop of the new Diocese of Syracuse, which had been severed

RT. REV. JOHN J. CONROY. D.D.,
DIED NOV. 20. 1895.

*Twentieth-century workmen inspect Bishop Conroy's crypt
in the Cathedral's undercroft. (Dave Oxford photo)*

from the Albany Diocese in 1886. Bishop Wadhams would last until the end of 1891. His successor in Ogdensburg was Belgian Father Henry Gabriels, who had been the professor of Dogmatic Theology at St. Joseph's Seminary in Troy in 1864 and rector in 1871.

Bishop McNeirny died of "typhoid-pneu-

monia" on January 2, 1894. Ironically, Bishop Conroy outlived his successor. In 1878, "Bishop Conroy from Albany" was one of four bishops at a fund-raising fair for St. Patrick's Cathedral in New York City. As late as 1892, Bishop Conroy was asked to put in writing for the fourth or fifth time the dividing line between St. Mary's and St. Joseph's churches in Albany, a bone of contention between the two parishes for years. Bishop Conroy died almost a year after his replacement — on November 21, 1895.

Chapter Five
INTO A NEW CENTURY

'My great-grandfather couldn't get a job at the mill
as Capobianco, so he changed it to Riley!'

In 1894, a newspaperman learned via telegraph that a new bishop had been named for the Albany Diocese. (Albany had had the telegraph since 1846, a year before the Diocese was founded; even Bishop McCloskey had sent messages on it.) The journalist rushed to St. Joseph's Church to congratulate the pastor, Rev. Thomas Martin Aloysius Burke, on his elevation. The congratulations came as a surprise to the fourth Bishop of Albany, who learned at that moment of his appointment.

He had been appointed vicar general of the Diocese upon Father Patrick Ludden's elevation to Syracuse in 1887. Father Burke had become pastor of St. Joseph's in Albany after Bishop Conroy resigned that position in 1874. While still assistant pastor, Burke oversaw the construction of the schoolhouse for boys, which was placed under the charge of the Christian Brothers. Burke was consecrated on July 1, 1894. Afterward, at a banquet at the Kenmore Hotel in downtown Albany, he was presented with a purse of $7,000 by the priests of the Diocese.

Born in Ireland, Thomas was the son of Dr. Peter Ulic Burke, who had graduated from the University of Edinburgh and brought his family to Utica. Thomas was one of the first boys to go to the newly established Christian Brothers Academy in Utica. He was also probably the first Albany bishop

Next page: Bishop Burke and his coat of arms with his motto, "God Is My Hope."
Overleaf: The photo presented by Bishop Burke to Pope Leo XIII (Jas. H. Lloyd, Troy).

not to be fluent in French. While his predecessors had studied in French-speaking Quebec, he had opted to go to St. Michael's College in English-speaking Toronto before he prepared for St. Mary's Seminary at St. Charles College in Maryland.

Bishop Burke had a twinkle in his eye and a zest for living that enhanced his appealing Irish charm. People remembered him fondly from his introduction to them as children: "My name is Tommy Mary Ann." From a young child's point of view recalled in later years, one man recollected him as "very old and very tiny." His delight in living would take him outside the Diocese on a regular basis. Almost immediately after his consecration, for example, he made an ad limina visit to Rome with a report on the Diocese. ("Ad limina" means literally "to the threshold" of Peter and refers to the regular visits bishops make to the Vatican to report on the progress of the Church in their dioceses.) The Rome trip kept him out of the Diocese from September 11 to early December 1895. His route across the Atlantic took him from Albany to New York City, aboard the steamer New York to Southhampton, England. From there, he went to Amsterdam, Berlin, Dresden, Vienna, Venice, Milan, Florence and finally Rome. During his 26-minute October 29 audience with Pope Leo XIII, Burke noticed that the Holy Father, whom he had not seen in six years, looked old and "not physically strong." The Bishop presented him "with a photo of the Cathedral here with the bishop and priests represented as being present in the sanctuary. He expressed his

pleasure with the picture."

Never one to pass up a chance to visit other places, the Bishop's return route took him to Naples, Geneva, Nice, Marseilles, Lyons, Paris ("which is as everyone knows," he said, "full of life and gaity, but among many there is the greatest spirit of religion manifest") and back to Southampton. Between Paris and Southampton, Bishop Burke was informed that Bishop Conroy had died (willing $32,000 to Cardinal McCloskey and Archbishop Williams of Boston, both of whom had predeceased him). Burke telegraphed Albany to order the funeral arrangements. Arriving in New York, the peripatetic prelate did not hurry home; instead, he made a side-trip to Washington.

"The voyages both ways were pleasant and fortunately we experienced no storms," Bishop Burke told friends when he finally got to Albany. "On my return voyage, we cele-

brated Thanksgiving aboard ship. Services were held and at dinner, of course, the great American bird, the turkey, was served, as were the accompanying pumpkin pies."

Burke continued to travel considerably, going to Plattsburg and Burlington, Philadelphia and New York, often leaving on the night boat. Among many other treks, he visited Yellowstone and California.

Within three years of his consecration, the jubilee of the Cathedral was celebrated —

Copyright by
Jas. H. Lloyd Troy. NY. USA.
1895

just two days after a stained glass window from England illustrating "The Last Judgment" was put in place, a gift of Bishop Burke. In 1898, after the Stations of the Cross were installed, another gift from him, the Cathedral was officially completed.

With Ogdensburg and Syracuse now dioceses in their own right, the Albany Diocese inherited by Bishop Burke was its current size of 14 counties (including only parts of Hamilton and Herkimer), the smallest geographically ever. Notwithstanding, it contained 135 churches, 51 chapels and 80 stations. Because the definitions of those categories changed through the years, it is difficult to make an accurate comparison with previous statistics; but if churches with resident and non-resident pastors and chapels are added together, and compared with the 1877 statistics of 63 parishes and 33 missions, the totals indicate an increase of 90 buildings in 18 years. In 1877, there were only 64 stations, so those had increased by 16.

Those churches were served by 145 secular priests and 62 Franciscans, Augustinians, Redemptorists and Jesuits. The Paulists were stationed at Lake George in the summer. The Franciscans had expanded to other German churches, especially Our Lady of Angels in Albany and St. Lawrence's in Troy. The Redemptorists had arrived in Saratoga Springs to start a House of the Second Novitiate, named St. Clement's College.

In addition to the Christian Brothers, who staffed orphan asylums and private schools,

Through the years . . .

1891: Earthquake in Japan kills 10,000

1892: Tchaikovsky's "The Nutcracker" debuts in St. Petersburg

1893: Henry Ford builds his first car

1894: Korea and Japan declare war on China

there were the French Brothers of St. Viateur, who taught at Sacred Heart Academy at Cohoes. The Brothers of Our Lady of Lourdes served at St. Joseph's Seminary in Troy.

Of the 13 different communities of women religious, six were exclusively dedicated to education: the Ladies of the Sacred Heart at Kenwood, the "Black Cap" Sisters of Charity in Catskill, the Sisters of St. Anne in Cohoes and Troy, and the Sisters of the Holy Names at Assumption Academy in Albany. The latter two taught in French, while the German-speaking Sisters of Christian Charity and the Sisters of the Third Order of St. Francis, the latter out of Syracuse, taught at the schools connected with German churches. The other orders to have only one function were the Little Sisters of the Poor with their homes for the aged poor in Albany and Troy, and the Dominicans, who gave private ladies retreats in Saratoga Springs.

There were five other orders. The Sisters of the Presentation had an orphan asylum and school in West Troy. In Troy and Albany, the Sisters of the Good Shepherd operated female reformatories and attendant schools. The Sisters of Charity ran the Troy Hospital, in addition to teaching at schools in Albany and at their orphan asylums in Albany and Troy. The Sisters of Mercy were the most diversified with combined efforts in three areas: education, social service and health care: education and an orphan asylum and its attendant school in East Albany, a school in West Troy, and St. Peter's Hospital in Albany. By far, the largest group, the Sisters of St. Joseph, were primarily educators in parochial schools throughout much of the Diocese, including Albany, Amsterdam, Catskill, Cohoes, Glens Falls, Hoosick Falls, Hudson, Lansingburgh, Little Falls, Schenectady, Troy, West Troy and Whitehall. But the order also ran an orphan asylum and related school in Troy. In addition to those duties, three communities had novitiates: the Ladies of the Sacred Heart, the Sisters of Mercy and the Sisters of St. Joseph.

The Catholic population of the Diocese was approximately 130,000. Of those, about 13,000 were enrolled in parish schools and 1,600 in colleges, academies and select schools. It was estimated that the "total [number] of young people under Catholic care" was 15,233, only about 12 percent of the total Catholic population. If it is assumed, conservatively, that 30,000 of the total population were school-age children, those 15,233 children represent only about

In its February 29, 1896 issue, The Vatican reported on a fire at St. Vincent's Male Orphan Asylum in Albany. Fifteen cattle perished in the blaze. The Vatican was a Catholic newspaper that preceded The Evangelist.

half of the children needing schooling. The remainder were in public schools or possibly taught at home, but some never received even basic literacy. Nationally, in the 1880s and 1890s, 37-38 percent of the communities supported Catholic schools. By 1920, it was down to 35 percent, where it remained until mid-century.

Bishop Burke was the first to establish a diocesan school board, composed primarily of the principals — who were usually the pastors. Father William R. Charles, later the founder of Vincentian Institute, was the first superinten-

UP IN SMOKE.

Fire at St. Vincent's Male Orphan Asylum.

CATTLE ROASTED TO DEATH

Tons of Hay Make a Brilliant Conflagration.

FLAME FIGHTING IN ZERO WEATHER

A Sad Blow to One of Albany's Greatest Charities—The Asylum Barn a Total Loss—Fire Was Probably of Incendiary Origin.

Tuesday evening at about 7 o'clock the large barn situated in the rear of St. Vincent's Male Orphan asylum on Western avenue was completely destroyed by fire.

When the alarm was sounded and the apparatus arrived on the scene it was found that some of the fire plugs in the immediate vicinity were frozen, which delayed the firemen in getting a stream on the flames. When finally this had been accomplished the barn was one mass of flame, brilliantly lighting up that section of the city. The reflection could be seen in the sky for miles around.

The fire was discovered by one of the Brothers of the asylum, who immediately gave the alarm.

In the barn were four horses, fifteen cows, a heifer and a bull. The mounted patrolmen who responded at the first alarm succeeded in saving the horses, but the panic stricken cattle crowded against the barn doors on the inside, preventing their opening. All of the cattle perished in the flames.

Stored in the loft were about ten tons of hay and a large quantity of grain. The hay and grain, together with a number of wagons, a carriage and all the farm implements, were totally destroyed.

The cattle were valued at $500. The insurance carried on the cattle, barn, hay, grain, wagons and farm implements was $1,800. The total loss will reach $2,020.

Some time previous to the fire one of the farm hands employed by the Brothers found two suspicious characters lurking in the neighborhood of the barn and drove them away. The employee then left the asylum grounds for the purpose of transacting some business in the city. He had not been away more than fifteen minutes when the alarm sounded.

From these circumstances there seems to be no doubt but that the fire was of incendiary origin. The night was too dark for the asylum employee to identify the strangers.

Chief Higgins and the firemen, who battled with the flames in zero weather and under most unpleasant conditions are loud in their praise of the Brothers of the Asylum, who furnished the half frozen men with hot coffee and lunch.

The barn was built about four years ago and was a most substantial structure. The loss of the barn and cattle is a severe blow to the Asylum.

dent. In the 1880s, Father McIncrow in Amsterdam lobbied for all schools to be chartered under the Board of Regents, particularly the academies. By the early 20th century, most of them were. Around 1906, on an informational pamphlet put out listing accredited schools of higher learning in Albany, 14 out of the 24 listed — almost 60 percent — were Catholic high schools and academies, along with Albany Medical College, Albany Law School, Albany Business College, Albany College of Pharmacy and the

Above: Father McDermott with the "Public Examinations" group from St. Mary's Church in Glens Falls. Students were quizzed in public to demonstrate their learning and prove the excellence of Catholic education.

Next page: A group of Irish immigrants at the end of the 19th century. (Balch Institute for Ethnic Studies)

State Normal College.

During Bishop Burke's tenure, 14 more parochial schools and three more secondary schools were opened. The academies were in Schenectady, Albany and Troy, while the elementary schools were in Albany, Troy, Hudson Falls and along the Mohawk in Cohoes, Schenectady, Amsterdam and Gloversville. One of those, St. Francis de Sales in Gloversville, was a German school, while three were French: St. Anne's and Mater Misericordiae (now St. Marie's) in Cohoes, and St. Paul's in Hudson Falls. Significantly, five of the schools were Polish: St. Mary's and St. Adalbert's in Schenectady, St. Casimir in Albany, and St. Stanislaus and St. Casimir in Amsterdam.

Upon graduation from Catholic schools,

one could look forward to membership in the Catholic Union. Started in 1887 under Bishop McNeirny, it blossomed under Bishop Burke as a social and educational club with its own building in Albany that hosted receptions, dinner dances and similar events for special occasions. There was also a billiard room for members. Classes in French, German and advanced English literature were taught there, and its free library had more than 5,000 volumes. The large Victorian building was one of many Catholic buildings demolished during construction of the South Mall in Albany in the 1960s. Among its 19th-century officers were many well-known names of the steam-heat Irish.

Immigrants

The immigrant population that began to arrive in the United States in the 1880s came as migrant workers planning to make their fortune and return to their homeland. Overpopulation on a finite amount of land disenfranchised many a landless peasant; and when the industrial economy of Europe went into a tailspin, the jobless were driven abroad. Unable to find jobs in other parts of

Europe, they resorted to emigrating across the Atlantic. More than half of this first Polish immigration and 40 percent of the Italians who came to America returned home. The Italians were dubbed "birds of passage." Of those arriving after 1900, in the second wave of immigration when it took more time to accumulate the fortune, many who wanted to return home were stranded in America because World War I broke out.

The Polish began arriving in larger numbers in the 1880s. The Kingdom of Poland had been dissolved in the 18th century and divided among Germany, Austria and Russia. Those who returned to Poland before World War I were hoping for a reunited Poland. The Polish who came to the United States were primarily young, over half of them single men of peasant stock, most unskilled and with little education. Looking for industrial jobs, they had exhausted the other countries of Europe before coming to the United States. Because their English was limited, they naturally gravitated to the places where mills and factories already employed Polish men.

The new Polish schools in the Albany Diocese defined their pockets of influence in Schenectady, Albany and Amsterdam. Because many Poles planned to return to Poland, they particularly wanted their children taught in their own language. Education in general was important to them, as was the preservation of their culture. In 1892, Matki Boskiej Czestockowskiej — Our Lady of Czestochowa or St. Mary's — was formed in Schenectady as the mother church. As early as 1886, scarce Polish priests were sought to act as circuit-riders for various dioceses. The Bishop of Newark, New Jersey, wrote Bishop McNeirny about one who was "of good standing," meaning that he could be accepted officially within a diocese.

The Italians started trickling into the United States in the 1880s, but it was not until after 1900 that their arrival became a tidal wave. In spite of their high return rate, they eventually became the third most populous Catholic group after the Irish and Germans. Typically, three-fourths of them were young men; one-third had a trade, such as masonry; one-third were agriculturalists; and one-third were unskilled. Those who were married came alone and established themselves before sending for their families. In one study, the average wait for a reunion was about four years. In

Father Joseph Dereszewski, first pastor of Our Lady of Czestochowa Church in Schenectady (Parish Anniversary Booklet)

some cases, the family had to wait until the husband got his citizenship papers. Some of them did not return to Italy until they were of retirement age and went back as "Americani," as they came to be known in their towns. In the first 25 years of the 20th century, of the 3.8 million Italians who arrived in the United States, 2.1 million returned. In some years, more left than arrived. They were the last major Catholic group to arrive before immigration was restricted drastically in 1920 by federal legislation setting quotas on the numbers of individuals coming from Eastern and Southern Europe. That legislation effectively ended the immigrant church. It would take another generation to phase out the national churches; St. Joseph's in Cohoes may be the last remaining church in the Diocese to still have parishioners who confess and sing some hymns in French. With a few exceptions to aid specific groups — such as apostolates for Blacks, Hispanics, Vietnamese or Koreans — the national churches long ago stopped using their own languages, and the sacraments were celebrated uniformly as Catholicism was americanized.

As always happens in any country experiencing phenomenal immigration, protectionist policies came to the fore; in the 1890s, a modern version of the Know-Nothings, the American Protective Association (APA), became actively anti-immigrant, which also meant anti-Catholic, even against second-

and third-generation Irish and Germans. The anti-immigrant attitude was virulent during World War I; even President Woodrow Wilson waged an anti-German campaign, effectively destroying any remaining semblance of what could be identified as German culture in America. In Albany, that meant the demise of about four regular German singing clubs, groups of men who used to rehearse in the back rooms of bars and give performances on a regular basis in a formal music tradition. It also meant the complete avoidance of speaking German. A man being brought up by maiden German aunts remembered going to the store for them as a very young boy so that they did not have to appear in public with their accents and be questioned about their patriotism. German ceased to be taught in high schools or used as a medium of bilingual instruction at German parish schools.

Wilson also waged an anti-Irish campaign, believing that the ancient Irish animosities against the English might cause Irish immigrants to sympathize with Germany. The anti-immigrant phenomenon resurfaced in the 1920s when a redefined Ku Klux Klan emerged to expand its platform to include anti-Catholicism and anti-Jewish elements with its anti-Negro program.

Ironically, the immigrant Irish, who had become fiercely loyal to the Church, also waged an anti-immigrant campaign against what they perceived as more relaxed attitudes toward the Faith. Before the potato famine, pre-Christian beliefs in pilgrimages to holy wells and particularly in fairies who

Through the years . . .

1895: Babe Ruth and Jack Dempsey born; Pasteur dies

1896: William Ramsay discovers helium

1897: First U.S. comic strip, "Katzenjammer Kids, debuts

had to be appeased and fairy trees that must not be touched prevailed in Ireland over Catholic doctrine, and churches were not well attended. After the famine, however, the common man became convinced that not only were these pagan beliefs completely ineffectual in confronting such a horrible disaster, but also that God had punished them for not following the Church's teachings. Also, it had been the clergy, rather than the government, that wrote the letters to America to beg for relief that brought dollars to build churches and schools. The Irish became convinced that only good would come of participating wholeheartedly in Catholicism. That fervent attitude came with them to the United States. As a result, by the end of the 19th century, many priests and nuns were produced from Irish families, creating a heavily Irish hierarchy.

When other immigrants arrived, until they were numerous enough to convince the bishop that they needed their own "national" — that is, ethnic — parish, they were forced to attend territorial parishes, which were often strongly Irish. While practices varied from church to church in the early 20th century, many anecdotal stories tell of certain ethnic groups being excluded from Mass at churches with assimilated congregations. At that time, when Catholics entered the church, the collection was often taken up in a basket at the door. In some churches, a velvet belt stretched across the door, and only those who plunked their money into the basket were allowed into the main church. "Such was the Christian greeting awaiting immigrants," said one person. "[I] guess the dominant group forgot they were in God's house." Italians in particular remember being directed to the basement to hear Mass "in the annex."

Similar stories are told about some of the high schools. Poor Irish children, unable to pay the fees, were accepted; but a Polish or Italian child in the same situation was told that the classes were full. Thus, it was understandable that different ethnic groups requested their own parishes where they would not be treated as second-class citizens. It is also significant that the only Negro school in the Diocese was at the outset segregated, as was their church, St. Philip Neri in Albany, a practice conforming to the times.

(In spite of the lack of "political correctness" of these facts when seen from current times and our contemporary embarrassment over their very existence, it must be acknowledged that these situations occurred, and we should recognize them for what they were: an attempt to maintain power so dearly won in middle-class politics and society, as well as religion. We must try to understand the historical era in which prejudice was — and still is, although perhaps more subtly — a commonplace method of attempting to maintain dominance over any group that was deemed to be threatening. As a corollary, a story must be told. An Italian-looking woman visited the author and said her maiden name was Riley: "Riley? But I thought you said your family was Italian." "They are. My great-grandfather couldn't get a job at the mill as Capobianco, so he changed it to Riley!" He got the job. That was the power of the Irish!)

National Churches

By the end of Bishop Burke's tenure in 1915, there were 11 Polish churches, all located in small factory or mill towns or cities: Albany, Amsterdam, Cohoes, Granville, Herkimer, Little Falls, Schenectady, Troy and Watervliet. Six had schools, but only two had sisters: the Felician Sisters at St. Stanislaus in Amsterdam and the Sisters of the Resurrection at St. Mary's in Schenectady. The schools with the highest enrollment were those two (with 687 and 562 students respectively) and St. Adalbertus — today Adalbert — with 748 children taught by lay teachers. At this time, St. Adalbert's had added to their high school a Kollegium level, which was an optional college preparatory course for students in grades 7-12.

The French had ten parishes, the next largest number of churches: four in Cohoes and one each in Albany, Hudson Falls, Schenectady, Schuylerville, Troy and Watervliet. An additional couple of churches that had been started earlier as national churches were no longer exclusively French.

There were seven schools, all taught by sisters. In addition to the French-speaking orders mentioned earlier, the Sisters of Mercy, St. Joseph and the Dominican Sisters also taught at those schools.

The Germans had only seven churches, but all had schools. In fact, in some cases, the Germans started a school before they had a church, an emphasis on education that they were known for. All were taught by German-speaking sisters as well as by the Sisters of St. Joseph. Four schools were located in Albany with one each in Amsterdam, Gloversville, Schenectady and Troy. In Al-

Above left: St. Anthony's Church in Albany served Italian Catholics.
Above right: St. Anthony's Church in Johnstown served Slovak Catholics. (Kate Blain photo)

bany, the parish school at Our Lady Help of Christians was so demanding that it became known as Krank Street College.

The Italians had six churches, but only two schools; and only St. Anthony's in Albany was taught by Italian sisters, the Baptistine Sisters (Sisters of St. John the Baptist) from Rome. St. Anthony's in Troy was staffed by lay teachers. The other churches were in Amsterdam, Cohoes, Schenectady and Watervliet.

Much has been written about Italian Catholicism, which — not unlike the pre-famine Irish religion — had a popular set of magical beliefs and superstitions that coexisted with official Catholicism, sometimes in unholy alliance or as inculturation in which parts of popular and official Catholicism were intertwined. In any case, the humanistic attitude of the Italians by which they expressed frank opinions of the clergy (often Irish) was the antithesis of Irish training, and was interpreted by them as being anti-clerical. Perhaps, in the minds of the Irish, the perceived anticlericalism justified relegating the Italians to the basement. Part of the reason for this may also have been that most of the Italians being sent "to the annex" were those without power — women and their children; typically, the men were at home, which was also part of their cultural heritage.

Italian Catholicism was often based on the mutual aid society, and they named their churches after the popular saints of these societies. Devotional Catholicism, such as novenas to St. Anthony and blessings of houses, was brought to its height by the Italians, who fervently placed much importance on these rituals, sometimes over the celebration of Mass. Italian men would turn out for a religious activity required as part of a society without hesitation, but they might not attend Mass weekly. Italians were a people for whom religion was all-pervasive, but that did not necessarily mean that practices deemed conventional by other ethnic groups were followed. It was undoubtedly due to such attitudes, a cultural lack of emphasis on formal education, the want of teaching sisters and, perhaps, a mistrust of the Irish hierarchy that schools were not universally started in Italian parishes.

The Slovaks had two churches, St. Anthony's in Johnstown and Saints Cyrillus

Through the years . . .

1898: Lewis Carroll, Bismarck and Gladstone die

1899: Philippines demand independence from U.S.

1900: Sigmund Freud publishes "The Interpretation of Dreams"

1901: Walt Disney born; Queen Victoria dies

and Methodius in Schenectady. This group emigrated from what was a part of Hungary and today is Slovakia for the same reasons other Eastern Europeans came —jobs. The majority were laborers in industrial positions.

The Lithuanians were the last Eastern European group to have a church during that era: St. Casimir's in Amsterdam. They also had a school with 108 students taught by lay teachers. This group, long closely associated with the Polish because of conquest, came mainly as unskilled male migrant laborers who intended to return home, much like the Polish; but only about 20 percent did before World War I.

Eastern Rites

Two Eastern Catholic rites became associated with the Albany Diocese in the early 20th century: the Byzantine and Maronite. Within the Byzantine tradition in this area, there are two groups, the Ukrainians and Ruthenians. While these groups have liturgies and customs similar to the Latin Rite, believe the Pope is the head of the Church

and are fully Catholic, mountains and bodies of water literally separated them from the western tradition. As a result, their churches developed differently. The most obvious difference is their preservation of ancient traditions in their celebration of Liturgy. They have also preserved the custom of marriage of priests; although this was discouraged in the United States after the early 1920s, the custom is gradually being restored in many of the Byzantine parishes within the boundaries of the Albany Diocese.

These groups still exist in the area but are affiliated with their own dioceses. Of these three, the largest group was the Ukrainian Byzantine Rite composed of some people

First communicants from St. Nicholas Ukrainian Church in Watervliet, 1913 (Joseph W. Felock photo)

from Galician Austria, but also of Ruthenians from western Ukraine in an area called Ruthenia, at that time a part of Austria and Hungary. Living south of the Carpathian mountains, they had developed a language and culture separate from the Galician Ruthenians. Both groups came for the same reasons the other Eastern Europeans did: work; but in their case, the Ukrainians and Ruthenians had a tradition of mining, so were attracted to the quarries in Granville and Hudson.

The Ruthenian church was — and still is — in Granville; the Ukrainian churches were — and remain — in Amsterdam, Cohoes, Hudson, Little Falls, Troy and Watervliet. (In 1962, one other church was added to the latter group at Hunter.)

The Maronite rite is completely different

from the Byzantine in that it follows the Syriac tradition developed in the Mid-East. By 1905, the Maronite Church of St. Ann in Troy served Catholics from the Middle East, primarily the Palestine area. It was the second Maronite Church in New York; the first was in Brooklyn. Although people probably worked at factories when they first came here, they soon established their own businesses, such as bakeries.

These various national or ethnically centered churches provided an opportunity for immigrants to adjust to the American way of life by easing the change from their background into an all English-speaking environment. One of the favorite church-related activities was for a group to rent passenger cars on the railroad to make a pilgrimage from their town to Auriesville. People would take the night boat from New York to Albany to join with others going on the train. In 1886, the first national pilgrimage was organized, and German Catholics crammed into 20 cars in a special train that left Schenectady for Auriesville. French-Canadian, Polish, Italian and Lithuanian pilgrimages, among others, also went to Auriesville. (Some of these groups continue to visit there every year.)

Incorporation

During the establishment of the Eastern Rite churches, as well as additional Roman Rite parishes, including ethnic Italian, Polish, Lithuanian and Slovak churches, Bishop Burke was particularly concerned with properly incorporating these churches. In 1886, as a stopgap measure, Archbishop Corrigan

of New York had written Bishop McNeirny on the importance of incorporating all of the churches, if not one by one, at least in a general deed to the Bishop, which was not to be filed until his last illness so that property could be conveyed via a deed rather than just in a will as had been done heretofore. At that time, however, Bishop McNeirny's illness was progressing, and he was more concerned with finishing the Cathedral.

The limitations of the vehicle Bishop Corrigan had suggested were obvious, so Bishop Burke set out to incorporate all Church property individually. The "Act for the incorporation of benevolent, charitable, scientific, and missionary societies," was passed in 1848, but it would be well into the 20th century before all of the diocesan properties accumulated since it began would be legally registered. In addition to churches, that included St. Peter's and other hospitals, the Catholic Union, religious communities, as well as all of the chapels, schools, rectories, convents, orphan asylums and so on found in the Diocese. The main motivation for this activity was to avoid taxation: Once incorporated as missionary and charitable societies, the institutions did not have to pay property taxes.

Practical methods on how to incorporate were addressed at the Diocese's Sixth Synod in 1895. A synod is a gathering of all of the priests in a diocese at which the bishop communicates specific rules and regulations as well as the forms needed to comply with them. It is significant to note what was considered important enough to be addressed at each of the diocesan synods because the topics reflected current problems. For example, matrimony almost always was addressed in some fashion.

During Bishop Burke's tenure, synods were used as a means of convening priests to hand out personnel assignments for committees, courts and councils, as well as changes in regulations as needed. Synods occurred every three years beginning in 1895 and totaled six. Before that, Bishop McNeirny also called them every three years. Under Burke, a synopsis and the forms were summarized in English, while the specific appointments and rules were in Latin, down to the priests' names. Bishop Gibbons did not call any synods, but he did have the use of the telephone, a means of communication more expedient and less cumbersome than convening a meeting. By the time Bishop William Scully assembled the Fourteenth Synod in 1958 — the last one to date — the information was written completely in English.

Expansion

Additional institutions had been set up in the Diocese under Bishop Burke. St. Mary's Hospital in Amsterdam was operating by the Sisters of St. Joseph by 1915. Also, a new type of hospital had been started: the maternity hospital. The Daughters of Charity had opened The Maternity Hospital and Infant Home on North Main Avenue in Albany (where the Pastoral Cen-

Staff members from St. Mary's Hospital, Troy (St. Mary's archives)

ter is today). The Sisters of St. Joseph had begun St. Joseph's Maternity Hospital in Troy. The Seton House, a home for working girls, and the Day Nursery, the first daycare center, were operated by the Daughters of Charity in Troy. In addition, St. Anthony's on the Hudson in Rensselaer was in operation by the Franciscan Fathers, the same Minor Conventuals out of Syracuse who had been established at the German churches for years.

In addition to the sisters already mentioned in discussion of the ethnic schools, other communities came to the Diocese. The French-speaking Sisters of the Congregation of the Assumption out of Nicolet, Quebec, were at St. Alphonsus in Glens Falls. The Dominican Nuns of the Second Order, a strictly cloistered group, were at the Monastery of the Immaculate Conception on State Street in Albany. The School Sisters of Notre Dame out of Baltimore had come to teach at St. Mary's in Albany.

A Catholic Governor

In 1913, Martin H. Glynn became the first Roman Catholic to serve as governor of the State of New York when he served out the term of William Sulzer, who was impeached and removed from office. Glynn, editor and publisher of the Times-Union, hailed from Valatie. While governor, Glynn prefigured Al Smith in his interest in labor. He established workman's compensation, farmers' cooperatives, a state employment agency and a limited work day. In 1914, Glynn and Bishop Burke reviewed the parade in celebration of Burke's golden jubilee as a priest.

Bishop Thomas Francis Cusack

The day following the sudden heart attack and death of Bishop Burke on January 20, 1915, both houses of the State Legislature and the county court adjourned out of respect for him. Monsignor John L. Reilly, pastor of St. John the Evangelist in Schenectady, was appointed administrator of the Diocese. But soon, Thomas F. Cusack, Auxiliary Bishop of New York, was appointed the fifth bishop of Albany.

Although born in New York City, he had connections to his new diocese: He had studied for the priesthood at St. Joseph's Seminary in Troy and was ordained by Bishop McNeirny in 1885. After ordination, he returned to New York City where he gained experience in pastoral work for 12 years. When he was made

---

At right: A memorial tribute to Bishop Burke published in The Knickerbocker Press on January 24, 1915.

Opposite: Bishop Cusack with his coat of arms and motto, "Other Sheep I Have."

Through the years . . .

1902: Enrico Caruso makes his first recording

1903: Pope Pius X succeeds Leo XIII

1904: World Series between N.Y. Giants and Boston Red Sox called off

1905: Theodore Roosevelt inaugurated

auxiliary bishop to Cardinal Farley in 1905, Bishop Burke attended the consecration.

At that time, there was an apostolic Mission House at Catholic University in Washington, D.C., where priests studied mission methods under Fathers Walter Elliott and A. P. Doyle, Paulists aflame with missionary zeal who spent summers at Lake George.

One of the popular methods was to have a mission band, much like the Salvation Army bands that still exist today. Bishop Cusack, who had studied at Catholic University and was a charter member of the New York Diocesan Missionary Band, was appointed its

head and became known for missionary work. After he became Bishop of Albany, he organized a Diocesan Missionary Band with headquarters at Haines Falls in the Catskills.

Father James Pritchard, the longest-tenured priest in the Diocese at the time of the writing of this book, remembered Bishop Cusack well; in fact, he was confirmed by Cusack. Father Pritchard vividly recalled the Bishop's habit of taking daily walks on South Pearl Street and speaking to everyone he met: "He ingratiated himself to all citizens of Albany." Once, he helped a boy reload a sled carrying firewood after the strap holding it had broken.

As a 12-year-old boy himself, out playing

with his friends, Jimmy Pritchard would tip his hat to the strolling Bishop, who would return the gesture. "He was a large, well-built man with silver hair and a face that shone with benevolence toward all." Bishop Cusack was renowned for a question box he installed in the Cathedral during Lent. Sometimes, he gave funny answers to the inquiries placed there. When asked if it was a sin to throw a snowball at a priest's hat, for example, the Bishop responded: "No, as long as it isn't the

Above: Chaplains in World War I included, left to right: Father John McCann from St. John the Baptist Church in Valatie, Father Paul Leduc, who served at St. Joseph's Church in Cohoes, and Father William Brennan of St. John the Baptist in Albany.

Right: A World War I veterans' ward in St. Peter's Hospital, Albany (Sisters of Mercy archives)

Bishop's hat!"

His tenure coincided with World War I, which witnessed the beginnings of two Catholic groups that would end up characterizing two prominent aspects of the Catholic Church in the 20th century: chaplains and the Catholic Women's Service League. The chaplains served an urgent need. In 1890, Bishop McNeirny had been informed by Archbishop John Ireland that the army and navy immediately needed priests to serve as chaplains because "a large number of the men in both services are Catholics." Twenty-six years later, Bishop Cusack lobbied to establish proportionally more Catholic chaplains since positions were filled only upon attrition of those already serving. Thus, a disproportionately high number of Catholic chaplains was needed, because there was a higher number of Catholic men in the service. In 1917, he opened a campaign to raise $80,000 toward maintaining Catholic chaplains wherever American soldiers went.

During the Great War, Rev. Francis Kelley from Cohoes enlisted as a military chaplain while pastor of St. Vincent de Paul's in Albany. General Pershing awarded him the Distinguished Service Cross personally: "During operations of his regiment against the Hindenburg Line, he was constantly at the front, caring for the wounded and supervising the burial of the dead, often under heavy shell and machine gun fire." In all, Father Kelley was awarded two decorations, seven citations and the British Military Cross for refusing to leave wounded

Through the years . . .

1906: Shaw's "Caesar and Cleopatra" opens in New York

1907: Boy Scouts and Mother's Day begun

1908: Jack Johnson becomes first black heavyweight boxing champ

1909: Robert Peary reaches the North Pole

men at the front lines. The priest's lungs were destroyed by the after-effects of being gassed, and he died while serving at Sacred Heart Church in Cairo in the 1930s.

Bishop Cusack offered the federal government the use of the recently acquired Helderberg Inn in Altamont for possible use as a convalescent hospital for wounded soldiers. He had already placed diocesan institutions at their disposal, including the five hospitals. He also gave a truck to Company C of the Albany Battalion, Tenth Infantry.

On October 14, 1917, Bishop Cusack reviewed a patriotic Catholic demonstration of 10,000 Catholic men and boys of every nationality, who paraded from State Street to Eagle Street and Madison Avenue to national airs played on the Cathedral bells. At the church, the festivities ended with Benediction, celebrated from a temporary altar set up in front. After singing the Te Deum, the crowd dispersed. This nationalistic fervor — and also the Catholic Women's Service League, which worked along with the Red Cross and the Patriotic League — was designed to show the patriotism of Catholics, in spite of the doubts cast by Woodrow Wilson.

Coincident with World War I was the Mexican Revolution, during which an archbishop and a bishop were thrown into prison. Bishop Cusack organized a campaign to urge Wilson's administration to pressure Mexico for their release. When it came about, the Archbishop of Guadalajara and the Bishop of Zacatecas traveled to Albany to thank Bishop Cusack personally.

When Bishop Cusack died at 56 of cancer, he was thought so highly of that many lobbied for his canonization. Before he died, he gave $10,000 for the proposed Samaritan Hospital in Troy. He also designated $20,000 to defray the expenses he had incurred in adding electricity and the marble floors in the sanctuary and nave of the Cathedral.

In the three years of his episcopacy, 35 priests, 11 churches, 4 chapels and 5 parochial schools were added to the Diocese. What is more impressive is that an additional 3,000 Catholic young people were listed under Catholic care, yet the total Catholic population remained around 210,000. The most significant increase had come at the high school level, which was being accepted more and more as the normal level of education — for girls as well as boys. During World War I, many high school graduation pictures showed many more girls than boys; the latter were in the war effort.

Many different styles of church architecture dot the Albany Diocese. At right: Our Lady of Good Counsel, Roxbury. Additional examples appear on the following page.

Through the years . . .

1910: Japan annexes Korea: China abolishes slavery

1911: Marie Curie wins Nobel Prize for chemistry

1912: Arizona becomes 48th state of the United States

1913: Cather, Lawrence, Proust and Wharton publish works

The only newly arrived religious order was the Franciscan Fathers, the Friars Minor of the Italian Province in Catskill. They came to set up St. Anthony's College and had four students of theology, two of philosophy, four novices, two brothers professed, a tertiary and 16 postulants.

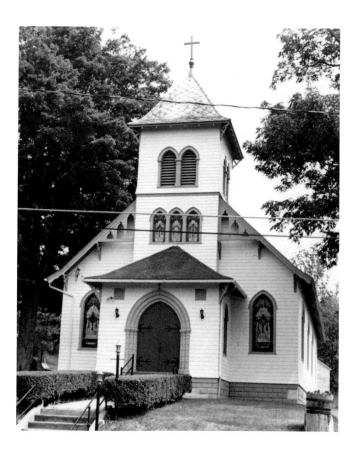

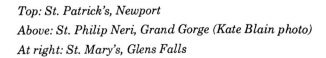

Top: St. Patrick's, Newport
Above: St. Philip Neri, Grand Gorge (Kate Blain photo)
At right: St. Mary's, Glens Falls

Chapter Six
OUR OWN TIMES

*'Every kid there was afraid to die,
and I was afraid, too.'*

The anti-German legacy of World War I, coupled with legislation restricting immigration, signaled a change in people's attitudes toward immigrants in the 1920s. But while the KKK burned crosses, Bishop Edmund F. Gibbons was implementing his motto (at right): "Ut Omnes Unum Sint" — "That All May Be One" — as a means of unifying differences.

One of the ways he promoted that unity was through his emphasis on vocations to the priesthood and religious life. As the 20th century wore on, his motto would bear fruit in men and women serving the Church. By mid-century, people representing many different ethnic groups would join the religious life. Hundreds of sisters taught in schools and nursed in hospitals. There were so many extra priestly vocations inspired by Bishop Gibbons that he ended up loaning 40 priests to other dioceses.

That unusual situation was one of the crowning glories of the Albany Diocese. But it did not occur without great effort on Gibbons' part. It started six months after Bishop Cusack's death in July 1918, when Father Gibbons, pastor of St. Teresa's Church in Buffalo, was appointed the sixth Bishop of Albany. While not a native of the Diocese — he had been born in White Plains — he had spent his youth in Albany attending St. Mary's Church and Christian Brothers Academy. (His father was a stonecutter who came

Page 154: Bishop Gibbons, center, at 1919 ceremonies inducting the bishop of Buffalo.
Opposite: Father Gibbons' ordination photo

to Albany to work on the State Capitol. Eight-year-old Edmund was especially proud to be an altar boy at the cornerstone blessing, since his dad had cut the stone.) After graduating from Niagara University, he spent four years at the American College in Rome, where he was ordained.

His early years as a priest alternated between administrative and pastoral work for the Diocese of Buffalo. One of his first appointments was as superintendent of the Parochial Schools in 1900. It is telling, then, that among his first mandates as bishop of Albany was blessing The College of Saint Rose for women at its founding in 1920 by the Sisters of St. Joseph of Carondelet. Over the course of the 20th century, the college would expand and change with the times while continuing to provide solid liberal arts and professional degree programs. In 1969, it went co-ed; in 1970, it became a private, independent college while still maintaining its religious tradition; in 1974, in the now separate graduate school, new master's degree offerings in non-traditional programs specifically designed by the student supplemented more traditional programs.

In his efforts to educate the young, Bishop Gibbons added 26 parish schools, all with sisters as teachers. The largest number of schools to start in one year — five — began in 1926. The Sisters of St. Joseph and of Mercy each staffed nine schools, while the Italian Venerini Sisters worked at the Mount Carmel schools in Gloversville and Watervliet. The Polish Sisters of the Resurrection staffed Immaculate Conception in Watervliet, while the Sisters of the Holy Names taught at St. John the Evangelist in Schenectady.

Within a very few years of his appoint-

ment, Gibbons would cement the foundation for the Diocese's modern secondary school system, one that would endure until the end of the century. Under Bishop Burke, 15 new academies associated with specific parishes had been founded. During the 1920s, under Gibbons, it became popular to centralize school districts; the tendency was to consolidate smaller schools into larger high schools that were city-wide and offered a variety of courses. Such schools were now possible because trains, trolleys, buses and automobiles were available to deliver students from around the city. These schools were not only more efficient, but also formed a large, cohesive unit that brought together different parts of the small cities and became a rallying source of great Catholic pride — and a breeding ground for the religious vocations Gibbons fostered.

The first such city-wide school was Catholic Central High School in Troy, founded in 1923 under principal Father Edmund J. Burns in the abandoned Troy Hospital. The

Above: The first graduating class from Catholic Central High School in Troy.

faculty consisted of a combination of priests and the Sisters of Mercy and of St. Joseph. Six parish academies closed in Troy and Watervliet to form Catholic Central. Three years later, two other academies closed in Troy and Cohoes, leaving 16 high-school-level academies affiliated with parishes and five private ones during Bishop Gibbons' tenure.

Religious Orders

With schools to staff, along with burgeoning healthcare agencies, many new religious groups were brought into the Diocese by Bishop Gibbons. As was always true before the Second Vatican Council, the largest num-

bers of women religious were involved in education. The new sisters in the parochial schools, as well as those teaching religious education to children in public schools, included: Capuchin Sisters of the Infant Jesus at St. Mary's in Frankfort and St. Anthony's in Herkimer...Franciscan Sisters of the Atonement in Athens, at Ss. Peter and Paul in Canajoharie, at Immaculate Conception in Palmer, at St. Luke's and St. Thomas' in Schenectady, at St. Mary's in Glens Falls, at St. Joseph's in Scotia, at Assumption in Schuylerville, and at St. Peter's in Stillwater...the Sisters of St. Francis of the Providence of God at St. Casimir's in Amsterdam...the Third Order Regular of St. Francis of Allegany, N.Y., at Catskill...the Sister-Servants of the Holy Ghost and Mary

Immaculate at St. Philip's Mission School in Albany...the Religious Teachers Filippini at Mt. Carmel in Schenectady...the Religious of the Holy Union of the Sacred Hearts at St. Anne's in Cohoes...the Venerini Sisters at St. Anthony's in Schenectady, Mt. Carmel in Gloversville and Mt. Carmel in Watervliet...and the Vincentian Sisters of Charity at St. Anthony's in Johnstown.

The only new teaching order of men in the Diocese was the Brothers of the Holy Cross at Vincentian Institute in Albany, who had a junior novitiate in Valatie. The Irish Christian Brothers also had a novitiate, at South Kortright. In Middleburgh, the Franciscan Order of Friars Minor Conventual — O.F.M., Conv. (originally the German and Polish Franciscans, by now all-around American) — also had a novitiate. Meanwhile, the Franciscan Order of the Friars Minor — O.F.M. (of Italian background) — had closed their seminary in Catskill but opened a novitiate in Troy.

An even larger number of novitiates existed for newly arrived women religious. The Carmelite Sisters for the Aged and Infirm, a group that cares for the elderly, founded St. Teresa of Avila novitiate in Germantown. The Missionary Canonesses of St. Augustine located St. Augustine's Novitiate in Menands. The Convent of the Sacred Heart now functioned as the general novitiate for the United States at Kenwood, and the Sisters of the Resurrection opened a novitiate in Castleton.

New institutions for education at the sec-

ondary level included Mater Christi, the diocesan junior seminary. The Missionary Fathers of La Salette started a junior college seminary at Altamont. At Auriesville, the Jesuits established Our Lady of Martyrs Tertianship, a third year in the educational training of members of their order. In Rensselaer, at St. Anthony-on-Hudson, the Immaculate Conception Province of the Friars Minor Conventual out of Syracuse had a major seminary. There were two additional religious communities for men: the Mill Hill Fathers from London in Slingerlands, and the Blessed Sacrament Fathers, who had a summer home at Diamond Point.

Bishop Gibbons, determined to counteract a perceived lack of religious atmosphere in Schenectady, asked the Discalced Carmelites to set up a monastery there to pray for conversions. The cloistered Nuns of the Sacred Order of Preachers, who professed solemn vows and perpetual exposition of the Blessed Sacrament, had a monastery in Albany. The Franciscan Sisters of Allegany came to teach at St. Patrick's in Catskill and also started

Villa Mary Immaculate, a nursing home in Albany. (Currently, they have St. Joseph's Villa in Catskill, a long-term residential care institution for retired men and women.) The Parish Visitors of Mary Immaculate, who visited people in their homes, were also in Al-

Above: Bishop Gibbons lays the cornerstone for a new chapel at the Convent of Mercy in Albany in 1949 (Harry McKenna photo)

Next page: He officiates at the laying of the cornerstone of a new chapel for St. Teresa's Motherhouse and Novitiate of the Carmelite Sisters of the Aged and Infirm in Germantown in 1951 (Gibson photo)

bany. Finally, there was a new hospital: St. Clare's in Schenectady, founded by Bishop Gibbons and co-sponsored by the Sisters of the Poor of St. Francis. That increased the total number of general hospitals to four, with the A.N. Brady Maternity Hospital in Albany and Mt. Loretto Convalescent and Rest Home in Amsterdam adding two more health-related institutions.

Although education involved the largest number of religious, they were also active in other ministries. Two men's communities were new to the Diocese. From 1924-35, the

Salesian Fathers were at St. John's in Albany. In 1934, the Resurrection Fathers opened a mission house in Castleton. Beginning in 1923, Bishop Gibbons also brought in several additional women's communities to serve in areas other than teaching. Three of the communities took care of domestic services and prayed: The Sisters of St. Joan of Arc at LaSalette worked at the bishop's residence; the sisters of the Holy Infancy of the Child Jesus, a Franciscan Third Order, took care of the domestic services at St. Anthony-on-Hudson; and the Franciscan Missionary Sisters of St. Joseph, the women's branch of the Mill Hill, performed domestic services for them.

The Glass School

The only high school started in Albany under Bishop Gibbons was Vincentian Institute. VI was founded in 1917 by Father William Richard Charles, the charming pastor of St. Vincent de Paul Church in Albany. The high school, founded in 1921, became the largest parochial high school in the Diocese as well as a great source of pride for its alumni. The Sisters of Mercy taught there. Later, in 1935, the Brothers of the Holy Cross instructed the boys. This was the first appearance of that order on the East Coast, far removed from their base in Indiana at the University of Notre Dame. It was also

their first time teaching in a parochial school anywhere. Among their numbers was a priest who would become world-famous in the 1940s and '50s: Father Patrick Peyton.

Father Charles, who had been the first director of Diocesan Schools under Bishop Burke, had some idiosyncratic ideas, such as housing the lower grades in greenhouses that he had salvaged from the Hawley estate. As a result, students had to wear sunglasses and treat sunburns in the winter. As enrollment increased and waiting lists grew longer, the priest acquired several properties near his church to enlarge the school and to house the faculty. When it be-

Above: A VI student in his Glass School uniform, complete with sunglasses, 1936

Opposite: The girls orchestra in the 1940s (Frumkin Studio), and the VI library with Mary McNeilly, librarian (The Evangelist archives)

came apparent that he could not conveniently add contingent property, he purchased more than 40 acres on New Scotland Avenue to use as an athletic and social center for the parish. It was named Karlsfeld, German for "Charles' Field." When Father Charles died in 1944, the property, which belonged to him personally, was valued at $3 million. It was sold to the Diocese and in 1952, became the site of Mater Christi Seminary, a diocesan junior seminary. (Following the graduation of the last class in 1969, it was leased to New York State and eventually became the New York State Police Academy. The property was sold to the State in 1986.)

Many of Father Charles' projects were financed, at least in part, by Mrs. Margaret Ruth Brady Farrell, the widow of James C. Farrell, the editor of the Argus, an Albany newspaper, who was also in construction. He died at 48 in the influenza epidemic of 1918. Earlier, in 1915, he and his wife had agreed to give the odd amount of $211,500 out of the $361,500 needed for a school and convent at St. Vincent's; that left the parish with the round number of $150,000 to worry about. Their generous gift was in addition to the property that had been donated primarily by the Farrells. (Such was the prestige of the family that when her brother, Nicholas Brady, died in 1930, Bishop Gibbons and six diocesan priests, including Father Charles, went to his services in New York City. Also in attendance was former Gov. Al Smith. The Evangelist described him as "a close personal friend of Pope Pius XI," "one of the leading Catholic laymen of the United

States" and perhaps "the first layman in the United States to receive the title of Papal Chamberlain.")

After her husband died and until her own death in 1944, Mrs. Farrell continued giving millions of dollars to many Catholic causes. In addition to her husband's money, she was wealthy in her own right; she and her siblings, her mother, and a grandchild had inherited between $70 million and $100 million. Many churches in different parts of the Diocese sport altars, front steps and baptismal fonts donated by her. Because of the order's presence at VI, Mrs. Farrell gave the Brothers of the Holy Cross a family dairy farm in Valatie that had been operated by her son. The site became the order's postulate house, St. Joseph Juniorate. (It later evolved into St. Joseph Spiritual Life Center, hosting workshops, retreats and confer-

ences.) Mrs. Farrell particularly endowed Father Charles, who in turn passed many of the gifts on to the Diocese, making him, in Bishop Gibbons' eyes, virtually a rival. The Bishop did thank her indirectly, though, when he named the mission chapel (later church) of St. Margaret Mary in Albany for her youngest daughter.

Although Father Charles was born in Albany, his father hailed from Ireland and his mother, from Germany. He attended Albany public schools, Christian Brothers Academy, St. Charles College in Maryland and the American College in Rome, until he became too ill and returned to the U.S. to finish his studies at St. Joseph's Seminary in Dunwoodie. Throughout his life, Father Charles fought against corollary problems associated with his diabetes. After ordination, he was assigned to the Cathedral, becoming pastor of St. Vincent's in 1913. Known for his boundless energy, he influenced all aspects of parish life. Father James Pritchard remembered Father Charles as an excellent orator; more importantly, he made no distinction between rich and poor, and could be approached by all.

When he was eight, Father Pritchard lost his father, and his mother had held several political appointee positions in the civil service: in a bakery, in the maintenance department of a hotel and in the State Education Building as a cleaning woman. When their house burned down near their home parish of St. Patrick's and they relocated to St. Vincent's, Mrs. Farrell gave them furniture, groceries, blankets and other necessities. She

Through the years . . .

1918: Armistice ends World War I; Red Sox win World Series

1919: Austria abolishes the death penalty

1920: Joan of Arc canonized by Pope Benedict XV

1921: Faisal I becomes King of Iraq

handed young Jim an ebony and ivory crucifix with this note attached: "Heaven is your true home." When he decided to become a priest, in his naivete he approached a local bank for a student loan. When the bank turned him down because he had no collateral, he went to Father Charles, who told him: "Jim, you're going through [the seminary] anyway."

Father Charles often gave advice to graduating classes via some unique aphorisms that showed his sense of humor. Favorites included: "How is your soul?" and "You don't go through VI; VI goes through you." One of his best was: "The world will praise you, never condemn you, until you cut in on the profits. Profit is its god. We praise you singly or in a group as it is needed. But anyone who knows anything realizes that life is always improvable. Our best successes have come from facing our faults and correcting them. Michelangelo cut, chipped, carved the marble which became the lifelike horse. He could not have done it with a marshmallow."

In spite of his quirks, or perhaps in some

cases because of them, Father Charles was beloved by his parishioners; many of them told tales of his generosity years after his death. He was inclined to use his relative financial independence as a means of implementing innovations by setting his own conditions. After buying property on Madison Avenue, for example, he wrote Bishop Gibbons that he would be willing to give it to St. Vincent de Paul's if he would be "permitted to bring the Brothers of the Holy Cross...to begin teaching in the Vincentian Institute High School dept." He got his wish, but the Bishop placed the priest under a watchful eye and objected to certain practices, such as interchanging the use of a particular space between religious ceremonies and secular dramatic productions. Father Charles stopped doing it but got his own way in the end by purchasing Karlsfeld and using it partially as a space for plays.

Bishop Gibbons at St. Joseph's in Cohoes with 32 of his priests.

Priests of Prestige

In addition to Father Charles at St. Vincent, there were other strong pastors in the Diocese during the early part of the 20th century, especially at St. Mary's and St. Joseph's in Albany; St. Peter's, St. Mary's and St. Joseph's in Troy; St. Bernard's in Cohoes; St. Mary's in Amsterdam; and both of the St. John the Evangelists — in Rensselaer and Schenectady. Those priests created in their communities a strong Catholic ambiance that came to be associated with their parishes, often with their own unique flavor added.

One example is Monsignor John Ligouri Reilly, pastor of St. John the Evangelist Church in Schenectady, who attended Bishop Gibbons at his installation in 1919. Born in Albany in 1853, John Reilly attended CBA, Niagara University and St. Joseph's Seminary in Troy. For the first nine years after his ordination, his assignments were split between administration at the Chancery under Bishop McNeirny and pastoral assignments, particularly in the Adirondacks and in what would become the Syracuse Diocese, as well as in Albany. But Father Reilly eventually became known as the major Catholic force in Schenectady, a role he filled for almost 40 years. In 1890, while still the pastor of St. John the Baptist in Schenectady, he deliberately located the church of St. John the Evangelist with a view of Union College to indicate his openness for contact with the wider world — which he received.

Inspired by the cathedrals of Europe, Father Reilly designed the new church in a semi-circle with no pillars and with rising pews so that each of the 1,700 communicants would have an unobstructed view of the altar. The interior was of white marble and plaster with many angels adorning the columns and ceiling. The main spire was 230 feet high with a glass roof that catches the light, especially at dawn and sunset. Father Reilly asked each parishioner to contribute one week's wages to defray the cost of the $300,000 church. John McDermott and John McEncroe headed the masons, while Edward Hannigan was the chief carpenter. The architect was Edward W. Loth of Connecticut, whose family had moved to Troy when he was a boy. At 13, he left to be educated in Germany, returning to Troy in 1889. He had to compensate for the stream bed and quicksand on the site when the church was constructed between 1900 and 1904. In addition to St. John's, Loth designed nine French-influenced churches, all Catholic except for a Presbyterian church in Troy (since de-

stroyed): St. Patrick's in Watervliet (based on the basilica in Lourdes), St. John's in Rensselaer, St. Mary's in Ballston Spa, St. Paul the Apostle in both Mechanicville and Troy, St. Stanislaus in Amsterdam, the Chapel of St. Margaret Mary in Albany and St. Patrick's in Utica.

Town of atheists

Schenectady had been labeled as an atheistic town because of the large numbers of General Electric scientists who disavowed religion, but Father Reilly — a Lincoln scholar who gave lectures at Union on the Civil War era (the priest was 11 when Lincoln was assassinated) — was equal to taking them on at their own level. Accompanied by educated, professional Catholic Schenectadians, he attended funerals and other events, such as lectures, at non-Catholic churches, including the Unitarian Universalist Church. He was criticized for such activities in the Chancery, but his "liberal" views did much to elevate Catholic presence amid atheism, agnosticism and skepticism. Non-Catholics came to him for advice in myriad areas, including vegetarianism, which he avidly championed. In 1930, Governor Franklin Roosevelt appointed Reilly to the board of visitors at the state training school in Albion.

Such was the reputation of Father Reilly that in both 1894, when Bishop Burke was installed, and in 1919, when Gibbons was appointed, many believed Reilly should have been made bishop. Indeed, in 1915, during the half-year interim between Burke and Cusack, Reilly was appointed administrator of the Diocese. He was often asked to be a speaker at such non-religious events as the graduation of the Schenectady Hospital Association Training School for Nurses. He was also approached to take part in an ecumenical memorial service for those who died in World War I, but Bishop Gibbons blocked his participation. Priests are forbidden, the Bishop wrote, "to join with our esteemed Protestant and Jewish fellow citizens" to take part "in religious functions or services and in my opinion such a memorial service, even though not strictly liturgical, comes under the spirit, if not the letter, of the prohibition."

Bishops from the Albany Diocese

Although Monsignor Reilly never became a bishop, several other priests of the Albany Diocese did. In 1922, for example, Bishop Gibbons traveled to Sioux Falls, South Dakota, to attend the installation of Bernard J. Mahoney as that diocese's bishop. Father Mahoney had been born in Albany but spent his early childhood in Rensselaer. As a young man, he worked at Western Union Telegraph Company, saving enough money to go to Mount St. Mary's. After receiving his M.A. degree, he was assistant pastor at St. Peter's in Troy and then spiritual director of the American College of Rome. From there, he went to South Dakota.

The Albany Diocese has always been famous for exporting priests and bishops. In the 20th century, there have been at least 11 bishops in addition to Mahoney. The later ones received their education under Bishop Gibbons. For example, Father William J. Kenny, who was born in Delhi and worked in

Through the years . . .

1922: Sinclair Lewis writes "Babbitt"

1923: Gershwin composes "Rhapsody in Blue"

1924: Coolidge elected president; Britain recognizes USSR

1925: Chaplin's "The Gold Rush" premieres

the newspaper business for many years in Scranton, Pennsylvania, became the first American-born bishop of St. Augustine, Florida, serving there from 1902 until his death in 1913. As bishop of St. Augustine, he was able to bring back the early records for historic St. Augustine church from Cuba. Because Florida was sparsely populated in general and with Catholics in particular, his efforts were primarily missionary. He was particularly sensitive to the plight of African-Americans, establishing the first church for Blacks in Florida and building seven schools to educate their children. (In 1928 in Albany, two thousand people turned out to watch Bishop Gibbons lay the cornerstone for St. Philip's Church to serve African-Americans. Using the language of the day, The Evangelist noted that "several hundred colored folk were scattered among the big audience and Williams' colored band furnished the music for the occasion." The newspaper estimated that there were between four thousand and five thousand African-Americans in Albany, "the vast majority of whom are not associated with any church." An editorial called the parish "a noble venture" and urged "generous and zealous Catholics" to support St. Philip's until it could develop its own congregation. A school would later be added to the complex to educate Black children.)

Immediately following the Spanish-American War, Father William Ambrose Jones, an Augustinian from Cambridge in Washington County, was assigned a parish in Havana, Cuba. In 1907, after a nine-year stint there, he was made bishop of San Juan, Puerto Rico. As a young priest in Philadelphia, he wrote books on St. Rita of Cascia and Our Lady of Good Counsel, as well as the Augustinian Mission Manual. He also had his translation of "The Life of Blessed Alphonsus Rozco, OSA," published. He died in 1921.

Not only was Syracuse's first bishop, Patrick Ludden, from Albany, but so was his successor: Father John Grimes. He emigrated from Ireland to Albany where he was influenced by then-Father Thomas M.A. Burke at St. Joseph's. After his preparatory studies, he was ordained by Bishop McNeirny and sent to what became the Syracuse Diocese. Father Grimes was made coadjutor bishop of Syracuse in 1909, succeeding Ludden upon his death.

Although Father Frederick Zadok Rooker was born in New York City, his parents moved to Albany when he was a child be-

Above: Bishop Mahoney
Next page, left to right: Bishop Kenny, Bishop Ludden and Bishop Grimes

cause his father was hired as the editor of The Press and Knickerbocker. After three years at Union College studying civil engineering — but minoring in Latin — Frederick decided to become a priest and was sent to the North American College at Rome, where Edmund Gibbons would soon join him. He was so brilliant that shortly after his ordination for the Diocese of Albany, he was appointed vice-rector of his alma mater in Rome, followed by a stint as secretary to the Apostolic Delegation in Washington in 1895. While there, he also taught theology at the newly founded Catholic University. In 1903, he was elected bishop of Caceres and then of Jaro in the Philippines to help in the transition from Spanish to American hands.

Because that involved solving various major problems and intricacies in a foreign culture, he became known as "The Fighting Yankee Bishop."

Another "fighting Yankee bishop" was literally under fire during World War II in the Pacific as a chaplain in the Navy. Archbishop Joseph T. Ryan, born in Albany and a graduate of Christian Brothers Academy, started his higher education at Manhattan College. After various diocesan positions and his stint as a Navy chaplain, he became director of vocations for the Diocese and the first diocesan director of radio and television. After an appointment as the vice-chancellor of the Military Ordinariate in New York City, he was appointed to the Pontifical Mission for Palestine and the Catholic Near East Welfare Association, eventually becoming director of the former. In 1965, he was ordained a bishop; in 1966, he was appointed

the first archbishop of Anchorage, Alaska, where he served for 10 years until he became the coadjutor archbishop of the Military Ordinariate. By tradition, the ordinariate was under the Archdiocese of New York. When it was separated and redefined in 1985, he became the first head of the newly formed Archdiocese for Military Services, with headquarters in Silver Spring, Maryland. The archdiocese is responsible for two million military people and their dependents around the world as well as for civilians employed by the U.S. government and based overseas. The latter group includes some 125,000 Catholics who work for the State Department and other agencies.

Another native of the Albany Diocese — Bishop John G. Nolan of Mechanicville — would follow in Archbishop Ryan's footsteps. After pastoral and teaching experience, particularly at Mater Christi Seminary, The Col-

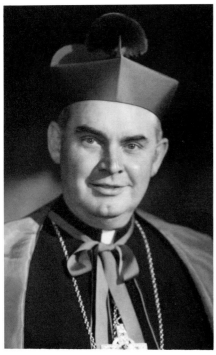

lege of Saint Rose and Maria College, Bishop Nolan was named to the Catholic Near East Welfare Association and president of the Pontifical Mission for Palestine. In 1988, he was ordained auxiliary bishop for the Military Archdiocese. During his time in the Near East, he was honored with the Gold Cross of the Council of Rhodes by the Orthodox Ecumenical Patriarch Athenagoras, the first Catholic to be so decorated.

Currently, two other "Yankees" are bishops in Brazil. Bishop Elias (née James) Manning, OFM Conv., of Troy, attended LaSalle Institute in Troy in the same class with Bishop Hubbard and decided early on that he wanted to become a priest. Now, he is stationed in rural Valenca, about two-and-a-half hours from Rio de Janeiro. The Chancery is a house on a farm, and his see includes nine counties. The people are of mixed race, many of them descendants of

slaves. While he has witnessed liberation theology in motion, under the current democracy in Brazil, he has been involved in social justice, upholding the rights of the landless, as do other bishops in Brazil. At this writing, Bishop Manning is the only American Conventual Franciscan bishop and the only English-speaking one able to travel. (There is a bishop in Kent, England, who cannot.) Hence, he is called on to go to places like Australia to ordain Conventual priests.

Bishop Capistrano F. Heim, OFM, of Catskill, did not decide to become a priest until he had been out of high school for six years — and after working as a meat cutter and being drafted into the Army. At present, he is in Itaituba, Brazil, a remote prelacy (similar to a diocese) assigned to the Franciscans in the center of the Amazon rain forest, a region roughly the size of New York and New England combined. The population is 750 miles from the nearest roads, so they travel "by anything." One time, Bishop Heim traveled in a small plane along with eight recently quartered head of beef. In spite of the

Above, left: Archbishop Ryan; right: Bishop Nolan
Opposite, clockwise from upper left: Bishop Manning, Bishop Heim, Bishop Clark and Archbishop Flynn

relative isolation, many of the problems he faces are urban ones, brought on by prospectors migrating to and congregating in one area within a comparatively short period of time. While he has a number of seminarians, it is a constant struggle to find the money to send them to school, because they have to travel out of the area.

In addition to Bishop Hubbard, two more

archdiocese that includes Minnesota and the Dakotas. Bishop Clark was educated at Catholic Central High in Troy, Holy Cross College in Worcester, Mass., Mater Christi Seminary in Albany, St. Bernard's Seminary in Rochester and the North American College in Rome, Italy, a year ahead of Bishop Hubbard. Both were ordained by then-Archbishop Martin J. O'Connor in Rome. After pastoral duties in Albany,

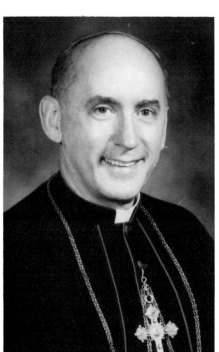

Albany-area bishops are located stateside: Matthew Harvey Clark from Waterford, who is bishop of Rochester, and Harry Joseph Flynn from Schenectady, who is archbishop of St. Paul-Minneapolis, an

he was appointed the spiritual director at the North American College at Rome in 1972, where he stayed until his ordination as bishop of Rochester by Pope John Paul II in 1979.

Archbishop Flynn has said that if he had 100 lives to live, he would still be a priest. He wanted to become one while a freshman at St. Columba's High School in Schenectady. After receiving a B.A. at Siena (he later added an M.A. in English), he went to Mount St. Mary's in Emmitsburg, a favorite choice of Bishop Scully. After ordination, he was assigned pastoral duties at local churches and served on the faculty of Catholic Central High in Troy until 1965 when he was tapped to be the Dean of Men at Mount St. Mary's Seminary and then rector. Returning to the Albany Diocese in 1979, he served as director of Continuing Education for Clergy and as pastor of St. Ambrose Church in Latham. He was appointed coadjutor bishop of LaFayette, Louisiana, in 1986.

Beatification and Canonization

In 1925, the Diocese harkened back to its origins when Bishop Gibbons presided at a celebration marking the beatification in Rome of the North American martyrs who died near Auriesville, including Father Isaac Jogues, René Goupil and John Lalande. At that time, they were the only saints-to-be from North America, so the Diocese of Albany felt justifiably honored. (The Diocese is still the only one in the U.S. with saints who were martyrs.) Their road to sainthood was completed on August 17, 1930, when the trio was canonized in Rome by Pope Pius XI, along with five other Jesuit missionaries. Jesuit Father Peter Cusick, director of the Auriesville shrine, attended the ceremonies along with other priests from the Diocese, including Msgrs. John Reilly and John Slattery.

Through the years . . .

1926: Hirohito becomes emperor of Japan; The Evangelist debuts

1927: Henri Bergson wins Nobel Prize for literature

1928: Al Smith loses bid for U.S. presidency to Hoover

1929: Presbyterian churches in Scotland unite into Church of Scotland

That August, at the Auriesville shrine, 50,000 people turned out for what The Evangelist labeled "the greatest outpouring of religious fervor and devotion ever witnessed on any occasion in the Albany Diocese" — a Mass honoring the newly canonized martyrs. Special trains were arranged to bring pilgrims to the shrine while some of those who drove cars ended up abandoning them in massive traffic jams and walked to the ceremony. The Mass was celebrated by Bishop Gibbons; also on hand for the occasion were Bishop Pietro Fumasoni-Biondi, apostolic delegate to the United States; Father John Wynne, the Jesuit postulator for the martyrs' sainthood cause; and several members of the Onondagas. (It was the apostolic delegate's second trip to the Diocese; a year earlier, he had attended the blessing of the renovated St. Anthony's Church in Albany.) Other bishops came from Charleston, South Carolina; Richmond, Virginia; Scranton, Pennsylvania; Davenport, Iowa; Syracuse; Covington, Kentucky; and even Honduras. In October, the celebrations concluded with a civic observance at the shrine that attracted 3,000 people. Among those paying tribute to the martyrs in person were Albany Mayor Thacher and Dr. John Huston Finley, an associate editor of The New York Times. Written tributes were sent by President Herbert Hoover and Gov. Franklin Roosevelt. (An in-

teresting sidenote: Although neither was a Catholic, the marriage of Hoover and his wife was witnessed, by special dispensation, by a priest who was their friend.)

Shortly after the canonization, Bishop Gibbons was appointed to the Tribunal to start the process for the beatification and canoni-

zation of Kateri Tekakwitha. Personally devoted to her, he promoted her beatification throughout his episcopacy. (She was finally beatified in 1980.)

Newspapers

In 1926, Bishop Gibbons created the diocesan newspaper, The Evangelist, which evolved from a monthly parish publication with the same name at St. John the Evangelist Church in Rensselaer, hence its name. As head of the Propagation of the Faith for the Diocese, Msgr. John F. Glavin, who was also pastor of St. John's, had converted his parish publication into a mission magazine of some 100 pages. When Bishop Gibbons wanted a diocesan newspaper, he went to Glavin, who had the expertise, history and publishing connections. His mission magazine became the official newspaper of the Diocese with its first issue on March 19, 1926, edited by Father Joseph Dunney.

The Evangelist was not the first Catholic

Previous page: Bishop Gibbons, right, at the celebration in Auriesville of the canonization of the North American Martyrs

Above: The Bishop with the winners of the 1938 Evangelist speech contest (The Evangelist archives)

newspaper in the Diocese, however. Earlier weeklies devoted to covering Catholic news could be found in many parts of the Diocese and in many languages, including French, German and Polish. Most of them were independently owned by publishers seeking to meet the needs of a specific readership. Among the names of those papers were The Catholic Pioneer (1853-?), The Catholic Chronicle (1868-69), The Catholic Reflector (1872-75) and The Vatican (1894-99). The Katholisches Volkblatt (Catholic People's Voice) was a German-language paper started in 1885. The Swiat Polsko-Amerykanski (Polish-American World) was published in Polish in 1894. The Catholic Telegraph, started in 1869 out of Little Falls under the direction of Rev. James Ludden, was one of the earlier

Catholic newspapers in the Diocese. After the Syracuse Diocese was founded in 1886, the editor of the Telegraph went there to found its Catholic paper, The Syracuse Sentinel.

Although the Catholic presence in a diocesan newspaper did not happen on a consistent basis until the 20th century, at various times there were secular journals with editors and owners sympathetic to the Catholic cause. One example was the Troy Times, owned by John Francis; in the mid-19th century, it published columns by the Jesuit, Father Thebaud.

The Glavin Family

Another prominent priest of this era was Msgr. Glavin, who was stationed at St. John's in Rensselaer for 65 years. He anticipated the late stages of the devotional church by insisting on the primacy of the Mass. Early in his term, he opposed adamantly the recitation of the Rosary during Mass and placed missals in the pews for people to use.

He came from a family long associated with Bishop Gibbons and the Diocese. His brother, James, taught math and was the assistant principal of Albany High School. He was also the treasurer of St. Peter's Hospital, a real estate agent who operated for Bishop Gibbons in buying diocesan property and a founder of the Community Chest in 1926. By getting in at the ground floor as an originator of the Community Chest, Prof. Glavin assured that diocesan charities would get its fair share of the monies collected. For years, even before the Diocese was formed, Catholic institutions had catered to the entire community, not just Catholics, and had received funding from various governmental agencies, particularly in social services, so the Diocese felt justified in receiving its due.

As a real estate agent acting for Gibbons, Prof. Glavin purchased the plot for what became St. James Church in Albany (hence the parish's name) and the land in Newtonville on which sits the College of St. Bernardine of Siena, better known as Siena College. Many in the local higher education and business communities said that he chose the most desirable site possible in obtaining that property. The college was established by the Franciscan Fathers of the Order of Friars Minor of the Holy Name Province, out of St. Bonaventure. The site consisted of the old brick Garrett house, a smaller frame house to the rear, and several barns and outhouses — all on 38 acres. It was acquired in April 1937 for $35,000. Pushed by Bishop Gibbons, the Franciscans opened that September because of the pressing need for a men's college in the Diocese. Although only 40 students were expected to enroll as freshmen, nearly 100 signed up. Only the two houses had been adapted as classrooms, so every space had to be utilized. Siena has since evolved into a well-respected four-year and masters' level college offering degrees in liberal arts, science and business. It has both day and evening divisions, and its enrollment stands at over 3,100. A friary is also located on campus.

As a friend of Bishop Gibbons, Prof. Glavin

received many phone calls from him seeking advice. One time, he received a long-distance call from the Mohawk valley where the Bishop was confirming children at three services. He had finished earlier than expected and wanted to call the sisters who made his meals to tell them that he was returning in time for supper, even though he had told them otherwise earlier. Just recently, however, the telephone number at his residence had been changed to unlisted. Gibbons had forgotten his own phone number and was incensed when the operator would not put him through to his house. Prof. Glavin, who knew the number, had to relay the information to the sisters.

National and Natural

Because World War I was the first major conflict that had involved America since the Civil War, it served to unify the nation, which had just recently recognized its last contiguous western states (New Mexico and Arizona, in 1912). After the war, many national agencies became pro-active, recognizing that many of the needs in Tacoma were the same as those in Albany. This was also true of the Church. One such group, the National Catholic War Council, changed its name to National Catholic Welfare Conference and in 1919 became a national, collegial, voluntary organization of bishops that represented their combined thinking on issues that affected the Church nationally. The first instance occurred during Prohibi-

tion in the 1920s, when the federal government proposed regulations affecting the procurement of altar wine for sacramental purposes. After hundreds of telegrams poured into Washington from individual priests, many with contradictory messages, the NCWC representatives met with government officials to work out a suitable procedure. This contact established a way of working for the bishops and the state that has proved useful over the years.

In its early years, Bishop Gibbons was the chairman of the NCWC's legal department, which tracked legislative and judicial developments affecting the Church. An outgrowth of the NCWC was the National Catholic Rural Life Conference, formed in 1923. Although it consisted primarily of midwestern and western bishops, Gibbons was active in it because the Albany Diocese was (and still

Girls sing around the piano at Marian Lodge (The Evangelist archives)

is) primarily a rural diocese with a few small cities sprinkled throughout it. He was concerned about the many Catholics who had no nearby church, no access to the sacraments and not enough resources to build a parish. He made a special effort to find money for the rural ministry to build missions, particularly in the mountain areas near and in the Catskills and Adirondacks. Almost without exception, the churches and missions Gibbons established were in the suburbs or rural areas (for example, St. Anna's in Summit, near Cobleskill, which was named for his sister). In 1922, nine churches were built, the largest number in any single year of his tenure.

The Adirondack area appealed to the Bishop's soul. On a property at Lake Luzerne, acquired by Bishop Burke earlier in the century, Gibbons built summer camps. He firmly believed that students should spend their summers outdoors, playing sports and hiking in the woods, a very American idea that was promoted by such national icons as Theodore Roosevelt. Although he himself did not participate in sports, Gibbons spent summers away from the city. Until World War II, when antibiotics were developed to slow the spread of disease under unhealthy conditions, tuberculosis was a common illness (in fact, Father Peyton was inspired to take up his Marian promotion during a bout with TB). At that time, it was believed that TB patients benefitted from exposure to the air of the woods, and several sanitoria were built in the Adirondacks, including large ones at Saranac Lake and

Through the years . . .

1930: Constantinople becomes Istanbul

1931: Football coach Knute Rockne dies

1932: Gandhi arrested in India; FDR elected president

1933: Adolph Hitler named chancellor of Germany

Mount McGregor.

When Father Charles was an assistant at the Cathedral, he had started Camp Tekakwitha at Lake Luzerne in 1909. It continued as a summer camp for boys; Marian Lodge was added for girls and then moved to Pyramid Lake. In 1931, Camp Gibbons was added as a boys' camp with seminarians as counselors. It was called "the most modern and best equipped summer camp in the United States." Boys between 7 and 16 had to submit endorsements from "two persons competent to testify regarding the applicant's high character." Camp Jogues for seminarians is still fondly remembered by many priests, both for the humorous events that happened and for the positive camaraderie developed during their stays there. The priests-to-be spent part of their time instructing children from surrounding parishes for their First Communions and Confirmations. While the children received communion in their parish churches, Confirmation was administered by Bishop Gibbons as part of a festival day that also included games and sports. In East Schodack, the St. Vincent's Child Care Society had Camp St. Vincent for orphans, and Camp Scully on Snyder's Lake in Rensselaer County was started by Catholic Charities. The Franciscan Missionaries of Mary had Camp St. Helene at Palenville.

The Happy Warrior

As governor of New York, Al Smith, "the happy warrior," reorganized state government in a businesslike manner. But the Catholic politician will be remembered for legislation that paved the way for Franklin Roosevelt's welfare legislation of the 1930s. Smith concentrated on items of social concern: improved factory conditions, adequate housing, child welfare, proper care of the mentally ill and the creation of state parks.

The Cathedral was Smith's parish, and the neighborhood people were his friends, including the orphans at St. Vincent's, whom he treated regularly to parties. When his daughter Catherine married Francis Quillinan, deputy attorney general of the state (and a Republican), at the Cathedral, Smith delayed the wedding for more than an hour, waiting for the arrival of a train carrying a man who was bearing a papal blessing. Bishop Gibbons regularly communicated with him and backed his efforts to improve working conditions.

Upon his nomination for president in

This page: Al Smith in his Knights of Columbus regalia with Bishop Gibbons and Cardinal Spellman of New York City

Opposite: St. Mary's Church in Hudson is dedicated in 1929

1928, an editorial in The Evangelist congratulated Smith, adding, with copious praise: "Those who know him love him, as a real man, a good friend, a devoted public servant....His integrity of life, his whole-hearted devotion to duty, his untiring service to the people of the State have been an inspiration and an encouragement to both young and old. The world has been the better for having known and possessed him. We wish him well."

When Smith lost the presidential election to Herbert Hoover, many people believed it was because Smith was a Catholic. There were many anti-Smith cartoons — at least one published by the KKK — and hostile, bigoted articles written by such organizations as the temperance movement and anti-immigrant groups. Certainly, The Evangelist laid

Smith's defeat at the door of bigotry. Before the election, an editorial said that "it is nothing new for the Church to be hailed before the court of a public opinion that does not or will not understand her. From Caiphas to Calles, from Herod to Heflin, the religion of Christ has been the target of attack." After the election, the newspaper blamed "the black murkiness of a tidal wave of religious intolerance" that swept Hoover back into the White House. "Anti-Catholicism had its day," the editorial concluded.

Since then, however, many historians have recognized that other factors also played a role in his defeat. Smith was "wet," meaning he favored repealing Prohibition; and his big-city, urban, Northeast background and lack of education (he had gone to work when his father died) precluded acceptance by a mainstream America that wanted someone with more stature to grace the office. Despite the prejudice against and suspicion of Catholics, Smith drew six million more votes than any previous Democratic candidate; and in an era of Republican presidents, it is doubtful any Democratic candidate could have prevailed. By the time well-educated, sophisticated, handsome John

Kennedy was elected president in 1960, his wealthy family had already been accepted as part of at least an arm of the establishment. In spite of Smith's defeat, as governor of New York, he repeatedly demonstrated his leadership by forcing Republican legislatures to accept his platforms.

Depression

In 1929, the Depression hit the Diocese as hard as it slammed into the rest of America. It is difficult for people born after 1930 to comprehend the hopelessness and utter despair of those years. There was no bank deposit insurance, no unemployment insurance, no welfare, no Medicare or Medicaid, and few places for people to turn to for help. Although the socialist ideas of the Catholic Worker movement nd its members, like Dorothy Day and Peter Maurin, were initiated in 1933, the only effect they seemed to have in the Albany Diocese was intellectual; a group met in Green Island and included some of the priests who taught at Catholic Central in Troy.

Church organizations tried to ease the pain. Within weeks of the Stock Market collapse in 1929, for example, Catholic Charities provided Christmas dinners for 71 families, while "homes that were chilled for want of fuel were made warm by donations of coal." Father William Keane, director of Catholic Charities for the Diocese, reported

St. Vincent de Paul Thrift Store in Schenectady

Next page: Parishioners rode a bus to church at St. John the Baptist in Newport (1940 photo, Zintsmaster Studio, Herkimer)

that his office provided family relief through vacation camps, foster parenting and adoption, and work with those who were disabled. The St. Vincent de Paul societies in various parishes were additional sources of solace. At Christmas in 1929, for example, 250 families were fed by the societies. The St. Vincent de Paul Societies in Troy and Green Island distributed $13,500 to the needy in that city during 1929. Childcare in-

stitutions were aided by the Knights of Columbus, who threw a Christmas party for 500 children at the St. Vincent's Orphan Asylum, LaSalle School and Infants' Home in Albany, and at St. Vincent's Female Orphan Asylum in Troy. The Catholic Daughters of America entertained children from Masterson Day Nursery the day after Christmas, presenting "a delightful little operetta" and handing out gifts.

As the Depression deepened, there were few jobs until the federal Works Progress Administration provided them. In a 1931 editorial, The Evangelist called for government jobs that would not take "the head of the family" to "a place far distant from his home....Such a program instead of being a

help only increases the burden of living....Living costs are increased...[and] families are separated." Other editorials stirred workers to stick by their labor unions. "We feel that it can reasonably be stated," a series of editorials stated, "that capital, in cutting wages, is simply following the line of least resistance. Attacking payrolls may be the quickest but not the most Christian solution of reducing costs and stabilizing profits. On the toiling masses is thereby placed the heaviest burden of slackened business....Protracted idleness and the pangs of hunger may make men willing to work even for a pittance....But there is no doubt that the experience is going

to hasten the day when labor will begin to unravel the riddle why our economic system is such that only by the restriction of the working class can the wealth of the nation be expanded....The workingman of America must look more to organization. Their right to collective bargaining must gain a stronger backing in their own ranks....If labor is to become articulate against injustice and unfairness, it must be organized."

Other than rallying workers and providing stopgap assistance, there was little the Diocese, parishes or Catholic organizations could do to fight the Depression because they, too, were trapped in it. Since they depended on their members for support and those members themselves were caught in the effects of the Depression, Church institutions had nothing to hand on to others. In the 1930s, only two churches were built, which provided a few jobs: St. John the Baptist in Greenville and St. Margaret Mary in Albany. Only two elementary schools were started, St. Philip's for the Black children in Albany and St. Mary's in Gloversville. Only two high schools were changed: St. Columba's in Schenectady added a ninth grade as an extension of their elementary program; and Our Lady of the Star, a private, select boarding school in Saratoga Springs, initiated an academic program.

Issues other than economic ones also confronted the Church during the 1930s, issues that would linger throughout the century. Birth control, sterilization and euthanasia were debated; anti-Catholicism was sniffed out; and public education was still seen as a threat to Catholic children. At St. Mary's Church in Little Falls, for example, Father Edmund O'Connor, the pastor and principal of the parish academy, gave a series of sermons in 1931 railing against the public school district for "the abolition of the study of Latin [and] failure to require home work." The sermons, published in the Little Falls Times, attempted to lure Catholic students to St. Mary's Academy. "Be assured, parents," the priest said, "that St. Mary's will continue to be a cooperating agency with you in the moral well-being of your children;...St. Mary's will require of our students observance of our traditional school and parish

Through the years . . .

1934: Eugene O'Neill, John O'Hara and Sean O'Casey publish works

1935: Gershwin's "Porgy and Bess" opens in New York

1936: China's Chiang Kai-shek declares war on Japan

1937: Insulin used for the first time to control diabetes

regulation: viz., home chores, odd jobs, play in God's fresh air and sunshine after school until 6 o'clock — but after 6 o'clock...studies till the class work of the day is made their own."

World War II

Among the first Americans killed in World War II was Edward Sullivan Jr., a parishioner of Our Lady of Angels Church in Albany. The 21-year-old soldier died at his gun post at Pearl Harbor during the Japanese attack on December 7, 1941.

Within days of the attack, Father John J. Powers, an Oneonta native who was assistant pastor of St. Helen's Church in Schenectady, signed up to become an Army chaplain. Stationed at Fort Jackson, South Carolina, three days before Christmas, he was the first priest of the Albany Diocese to join the military in the wake of the declaration that the United States had entered World War II. But seven other priests were already serving as chaplains when the attack came: Fathers Lawrence Ryan, Wilfred Bouchey, Edward Konisky, Joseph O'Brien, Peter Dunn, Vincent Gorski and Edward Tanski.

Some Catholics in the Albany Diocese had very personal reasons to worry in the wake of the Pearl Harbor attack: They had relatives in the Orient. Two religious sisters from the Kenwood convent were serving in Tokyo; Sisters of the Holy Names had only recently withdrawn members from their mission school in Katoshima, Japan. Father Timothy Daley, a native of Corinth, and Father Maurice Feeney, of Albany, were Maryknoll missionaries in China. Feeney, who had been anticipating a visit home, was captured in Hong Kong by the Japanese and held, along with 60 other American priests and nuns, in a prison camp. Three Maryknoll sisters — Redempta Coffey from Glens Falls, Alicia Shader of Troy and Marie Jogues Coffey of Schenectady — were stationed in Hawaii and the Philippines, putting them in harm's way. But the superior general of the Maryknolls announced that the order's members would remain in their posts. Meanwhile, aboard American naval vessels in the Pacific were young men from such diocesan cities as Schenectady and Rensselaer.

The editor of The Evangelist, in a front-page editorial in the December 12, 1941 issue, opined that "the mad, treacherous fury of a heathen power destroyed" any hope of peace. "We are committed to war — the most

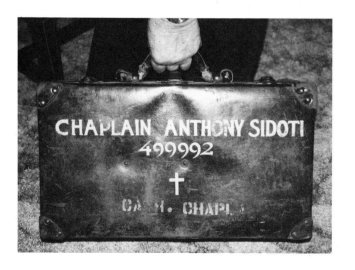

Top: *Father Glavin with missionary nuns who fled from the Japanese*

Middle: *Father Ryan talks with a soldier (RNS photo)*

Bottom: *Father Sidoti's chaplain's case*

Christian Brothers Academy students, in uniform, flank a procession in Albany (The Evangelist archives)

justifiable kind of war — a war of defense and retribution for an unprovoked attack. No Christian need have the slightest qualm of conscience in having part in it."

A second editorial inside the newspaper urged readers to obey "civic and military authorities...in air raid threats. The effectiveness of the 'blackout' is in its completeness. Any serious infraction of prescribed regulations...is a grave moral offense." In the city of Rensselaer, clergy of all denominations were appointed air raid wardens. The designation allowed them to be outdoors when an alert was called and able to minister to people.

By December 19, 1941, The Evangelist had already picked up the newborn slogan,

"Remember Pearl Harbor," encouraging Catholics to remember also "the loss in men....Our hearts go out in compassion to the bereft families." But an unusual war-related issue arose for the Church: Should priests be exempt from the ban on the purchase of automobile tires? Conserving rubber for the war effort was essential, but priests — especially those in rural areas — had to travel to celebrate Mass, visit the sick and perform other religious duties. "We consider the issue one of vital concern," The Evangelist editorialized. "More and more in the conduct of the war, our lives will be regulated by Federal restrictions. If, in the first instance, religious worship is to be brushed aside as non-essential, where will it end?" Clergy were later exempted from the restriction by the Office of Price Administration in Washington.

Although World War II broke up homes as men were drafted and died, tremendous patriotism accompanied the war effort. A star on a flag hung outside a house meant that someone had died in the effort, and churches listed their names, as they also had in World War I when tabulations of the war dead were inscribed on plaques and hung in church entries or printed in parish histories.

The war effort meant jobs for those men who were not drafted — at the arsenal in Watervliet (as it has always been locally known), in Schenectady at General Electric and at American Locomotive. Many smaller area industries, such as the machine shops in Menands, also contributed to the war effort. There were also the small stories that had large meaning about family and faith. For example, Edwin Bylancik, a Marine from

Albany who was stationed in the South Pacific, fashioned a seashell rosary for his mother back home as a gift for his parents' 30th wedding anniversary. They used the gift to pray the daily Rosary; and when his mother died in 1973, Edwin placed it around her neck so she could be buried with it.

Fathers Joseph Ciulek, Tony Sidoti, Joseph Konisky, Bill Turner, Walter Baniak, Arnold English, Edward Glavin and Joseph Ryan were other priests from the Albany Diocese who served in the Army, Navy, Marines and Merchant Marines during the war. Their numbers represented the largest group of chaplains per capita from any diocese in the nation. "Why did we go?" asks Ryan. "Because those were the days of patriotism. We saw all these young men going off, so we figured we should do something to be with them. That is really what moved all of us priests who served as chaplains. Young priests were needed to take care of those young men."

Father Sidoti followed the D-Day troops into Europe in 1944. Aboard a small landing craft, as shells landed around him, he prayed: "God, I'm trying to do your job, so you worry about it now." Serving in the European Theater, he was wounded twice and given the Silver Star. Father Glavin was assigned to a long-range penetration infantry group in China, Burma and India, storied as Merrill's Marauders.

Father Ryan, a Navy chaplain assigned to the Marines, earned a citation for "exceptional zeal and courage under fire" with a Marine regiment on the islands of Okinawa, Shima and Ryukyu. During one heavy bombardment on Peleliu, he crawled from foxhole to foxhole, sometimes celebrating Mass while lying down to get out of the line of fire. "Every kid there was afraid to die," he reported, "and I was afraid, too." At night, "I found myself with a gas mask, a knife and the Blessed Sacrament, surrounded by all these kids. They wanted to sleep near Our Lord." At one gun post, he heard the confessions of three soldiers and gave them communion. Just minutes after leaving them, he heard an explosion and turned to find that two of them had been killed instantly while the third lay dying. When Father Ryan told the young man that his comrades were dead, the Marine said: "They had Jesus with them. He took them straight to heaven. How good God has been to us today!" The teenager

Through the years . . .

1938: Pearl S. Buck wins Nobel Prize for literature

1939: "Gone With the Wind" wins best picture Oscar

1940: FDR elected president for unprecedented third time

1941: Japanese attack Pearl Harbor; U.S. enters World War II

then died in the priest's arms. "I used to write letters to the parents" to tell them how and when their sons had died, Father Ryan said. "I could surely tell them that their sons were in heaven."

On Okinawa on Easter Sunday 1944, three priests from the Albany Diocese found themselves together in a cemetery, performing funeral services at the massed graves: Fathers Ryan, Konisky and Joseph Varden. "The stench of dead bodies was everywhere," recalled Father Konisky. A Marine from the Diocese had spotted Varden on Okinawa during the heat of the fighting, "all alone, Mass kit and pack on his back, looking for wounded Marines to minister to."

After the war, Father Richard O'Connor of Siena College, who spoke German, was asked to be the chaplain to the accused at the Nuremburg trials. He was to give "religious solace to the eleven Nazi war criminals as they meet their death," according to the Albany Knickerbocker News. The report added that he also "converted Hans Frank, former Nazi Governor of Poland, to the

Catholic Faith."

Since World War II, other priests from the Diocese have been assigned military chaplaincy as an optional ministry. Father Frank Gilchrist, for example, spent 26 years as a chaplain in the Air Force, rising to the rank of colonel. Among his assignments, he was

Father Joseph Varden preaches at a Veterans' Memorial Service in St. Henry's Church, Averill Park, 1948. Also shown, Father John O'Connor, pastor of St. Henry's, and Father Edward Reilly, pastor of Sacred Heart, Troy (Joseph F. Connors photo)

chaplain at the Air Force Academy in Colorado Springs, spent a tour of duty in Vietnam and was Archbishop Ryan's secretary in the Military Ordinariate. Most recently, three priests from the Diocese served in the Persian Gulf War.

Home from the Front

After World War II, the GI bill increased the numbers of laymen who went to college, often while holding jobs at the same time. Men who before the war never would have dreamed of going to college were able to do

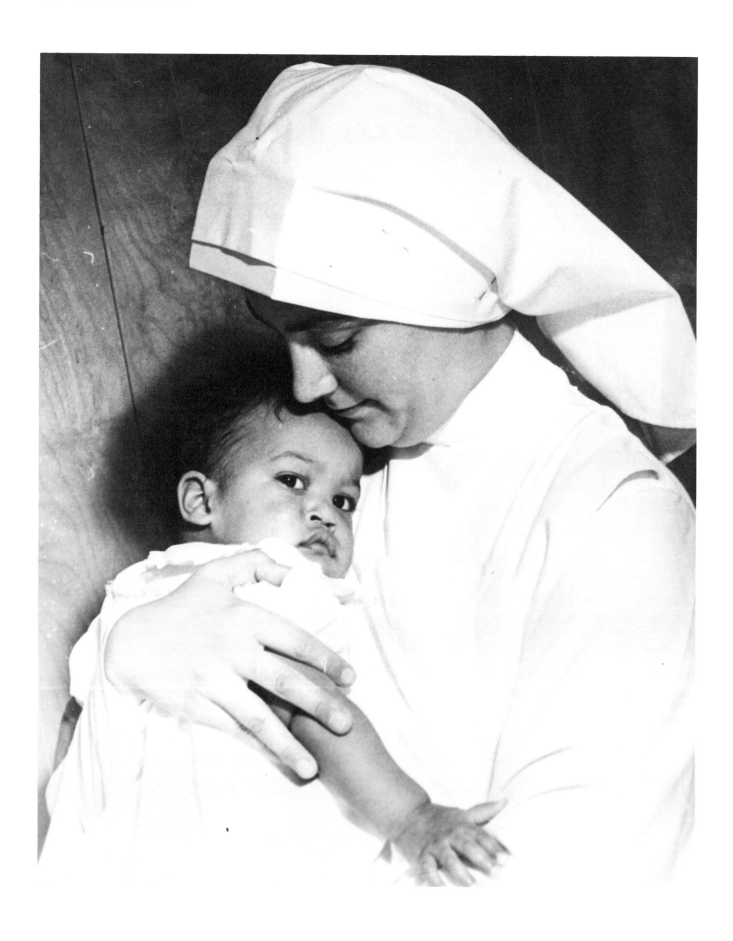

so with the generous financial incentives of the government. Siena College, swamped with applicants, had to turn away some of them because their campus was just too small. As a result, the college expanded considerably, becoming well-known for producing quality education by the 1960s.

Of those who took advantage of the GI bill, many were of Southern and Eastern European background. They had been able to prove themselves in World War II as being just as American as the next guy in spite of being Catholic, much as the Irish had done during the Civil War. (Earlier, the American involvement in World War I was so brief that these groups did not have sufficient time to prove themselves in the field, and thus universal acceptance of them at that time was negligible.)

The Fifties

For 11 years, starting in 1949, one of James Glavin's sons, Father Edward R. Glavin (later a monsignor) was the chaplain at The College of Saint Rose. While he was there, May Day was organized on a diocesan-wide basis as a procession of thousands to the steps of the State Capitol. The march was put together by the students at Saint Rose and Siena as a rally during the Cold War to show their solidarity against Russian oppression of the peoples and religion of

Facing page: A woman religious with one of the orphans at St. Catherine's Infant Home in Albany (John J. Keller photo)

Above: The laying of the cornerstone of a dormitory at The College of Saint Rose in Albany, 1958 (Pinto Photo Service)

Eastern Europe. In 1948, 4,000 people marched. Within three years, 70,000 Catholics were taking part in the prayers and speeches, described in one newspaper account as "the greatest anti-communist demonstration ever held in upstate New York."

Traditionally, May Day has been an international labor holiday. In the wake of the Russian Revolution, May 1 had been promoted by the Communists, who commended the proletariat — especially the industrial working class — via long parades that primarily demonstrated machines of war. Since May 1 is the Feast of St. Joseph the Worker, the Church had a reason to honor working people in a religious way. Since May is also a month to honor Mary and she was married to Joseph, Catholics began connecting her to

May Day celebrations that protested communism. Thousands throughout the United States responded positively to this emotional appeal, which was intertwined with the nationalism held over from World War II.

Father Patrick Peyton

Marian devotion blossomed in the 20th century, fostered by her apparitions at Lourdes in 1858 and at Fatima in 1917, and culminating in the definition of the Assumption by Pope Pius XII in 1950. In that decade, one of the popular ways to express devotion to her was public and private recitation of the

---

Pictured here: Father Peyton prays with the Woods family of Canton, New York (CNS photo)

Opposite: With the Brockley family at the College of Saint Rose in 1951 (George Burns photo). With Bing Crosby in 1949 (CNS photo)

Rosary, a popularity that arose through the diligent efforts of an Irish-born Holy Cross priest who lived in Albany and took his ministry world-wide. Father Patrick Peyton promoted his Family Rosary Crusade from the residence of the Holy Cross Brothers at Vincentian Institute (Family Rosary still has its world-wide corporate headquarters in Albany). With the help of business students at VI and college students from Saint Rose, the Irish priest who credited his recovery from tuberculosis to the intercession of the Blessed Mother began his promised efforts to bring devotion to her to the world.

After successfully airing a weekly recitation of the Rosary on a program known as "The Voice of the College of St. Rose" on WABY, Father Peyton went national. He

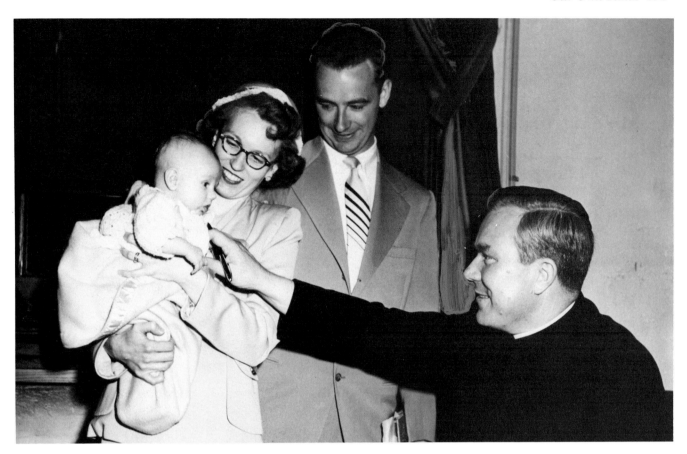

was so successful with a VE Day program in 1945 that he was able to interest major Catholic Hollywood stars — Bing Crosby and Loretta Young, Irene Dunne and Charles Boyer — in performing on his radio show and in the religious films made by the Family Theater Productions in Hollywood. His efforts, along with those of the renowned Bishop Fulton J. Sheen, were among the first Catholic uses of the national mass media. By promoting family prayer via radio and film (and, later, TV), Father Peyton created international Rosary Crusades that attracted hundreds of thousands of people to hear him. His slogans — "The family that prays together stays together" and "A world at prayer is a world at peace" — captured the world's imagination.

Bishop William Scully

Bishop Gibbons was the longest tenured bishop of the Albany Diocese, lasting the 35 years between 1919 and 1954. In 1954, there were 195 parishes with 81 schools served by a burgeoning population of sisters, totaling 1,636. He might have gone on longer, but ill health forced his resignation. (Ironically, he then lived almost as long as his successor.) Bishop Gibbons will be remembered as the last of the old-style, formal, authoritarian bishops who lived out the 19th-century mandate of devotional Catholicism, expressed in the codification of Canon Law completed in 1917. He died in 1964 as the Second Vatican Council was being played out, an event that would forever change the Roman Catholic Church.

Bishop William A. Scully automatically succeeded Bishop Gibbons. He had been co-adjutor with the right of succession since 1945 because of Gibbons' various bouts with throat cancer. (He was a smoker who used a cigarette holder in the belief it would filter the bad effects out.) Due to the population jump experienced when men returned from World War II, the 1950s witnessed a geometric increase in school-age children. That fostered a proportional boom in building Catholic schools, which had been stifled during the Depression. Bishop Scully was involved with this expansion.

Born in New York City in 1894, Scully attended St. Joseph's Seminary in Yonkers, popularly known to this day as Dunwoodie. After his ordination, he was sent to The

Through the years . . .

1942: George M. Cohan dies; Irving Berlin writes "White Christmas"

1943: Supreme Court rules children need not salute flag in school

1944: Allied forces land in Europe on D-Day

1945: Nobel Prize for medicine honors discovery of penicillin

Catholic University of America in Washington, D.C., for further studies. Upon his return to New York, he performed pastoral work before being tapped to head various areas, particularly religious education and schools, for the New York Archdiocese. Well versed in administration, he was ordained a bishop in 1945 and came to Albany to assist Bishop Gibbons while serving as pastor of St. Mary's in Troy. He was not unknown in the Diocese; his cousins, Fathers Joseph and Peter Scully, were diocesan priests, and he often visited relatives in Albany, Kinderhook and Coxsackie. As a seminarian, he had even been a counselor at Camp Tekakwitha in Lake Luzerne.

Because of the post-war economic expansion that fueled the 1950s, Bishop Scully was able to inaugurate the Bishop's Fund in 1955. The monies realized from the campaign supported a program of improvement and expansion of the schools, which involved considerable construction, necessitated by the phenomenal baby boom generation of children that followed the end of World War

Tibi Servire Regnare

II. Cardinal McCloskey Memorial High School in Albany; Notre Dame High School for Girls and Bishop Gibbons High for Boys, both in Schenectady; Bishop Scully High in Amsterdam; Bishop Burke High in Gloversville; and St. Patrick's High in Catskill were added to the parish high schools already in existence. At the same time, schools like St. John's Academy in Rensselaer and Catholic Central in Troy were expanded. Thirteen new parishes and 21 new elementary schools were built in less than 20 years. In addition, construction occurred in many other facili-

Bishop Scully, right, with his coat of arms and motto, "To Serve Is To Reign"

ties, such as Villa Mary Immaculate Nursing Home in Albany and the summer camps, as they were enlarged, modernized or added on to. (The Bishop's Fund would change its name twice — first, to the Diocesan Development Program and then to the Bishop's Appeal, its current designation. The collection now funds diocesan programs in education, charity, administration, service and prayer that support parish efforts.)

In 1958, Maria College contributed to this expansion of facilities by developing as an outgrowth of the Sisters of Mercy formation college when the order began offering an associate's degree program in early childhood

THE CONTINUITY OF BISHOPS

Bishops Scully and Gibbons in 1945...

...Maginn and Gibbons in 1953...

*...Maginn, Gibbons and Scully in 1949
(with Father Raymond Rooney and
Father J. Norbert Kelly)...*

...Maginn and Hubbard...

...Hubbard, Clark, Maginn and Ryan...

...Broderick and Hubbard.

education. Ten years later, it affiliated with St. Peter's Hospital to offer a degree in nursing. The college then expanded into programs in physical and occupational therapy. It now also offers degrees in secretarial sciences, office management, accounting and paralegal work.

In a related area, Bishop Scully's association with Catholic University and connections in the Maryland area opened the way for more priests from the Albany Diocese to study out of state, effectively broadening their exposure to other viewpoints. Three other areas in which Scully was active primarily involved the family, especially the welfare of women and children. For many

Through the years . . .

1946: United Nations General Assembly holds first session

1947: Dead Sea scrolls found in Middle East

1948: Israel founded; Gandhi assassination; Truman elected

1949: Soviet Union tests first nuclear weapon

years, he was chairman of the National Catholic Welfare Conference's Motion Picture Department, better known as the Legion of Decency. Through it, movies were rated according to their moral content, Catholics were warned away from films that were objectionable and parishioners took an annual pledge not to patronize offensive movies. He also recommended the establishment of lay-led clubs to discuss films and promote better movies.

As often happens with bishops of the state's capital, Scully was chairman of the New York State Catholic Welfare Committee and was involved with legislation that affected Christian rights and privileges. At that time, some of these bills affected adoption, divorce, Sunday "blue laws," school bus transportation for children in Catholic schools and pornography. He was also active in improving race relations, advocating better housing and working conditions for minorities.

The 1960s also witnessed the beginnings of federal legislation to fund grants to groups

at the grassroots level. Diocesan Catholic
Charities was founded in 1917 by Bishop
Cusack, who asked Mary L. Farrell to come
from the Archdiocese of New York to Albany
to organize the agency. Rev. Vincent de Paul
Archambeau was its first director. At first,
Catholic Charities was primarily concerned
with orphanages, adoption, hospitals and related matters, such as employing foster mothers and working with the Society of St.
Vincent de Paul to organize clothing drives
and provide Christmas baskets. The office

*Opposite: The construction of St. Clare's Hospital in
Schenectady, 1947*

*Above: Bishop Scully after his first Mass as Bishop at St.
Patrick's Cathedral in New York City, 1945. With him is
his brother, Father Edwin Scully*

consisted primarily of volunteer women and
sisters whose ministry was care for the poor.
When Father Richard Downs became director of Catholic Charities in 1957, it was centralized in Albany, with programs based
primarily there, in Troy and in Schenectady.
This placement was partly because social
work began in urban areas where problems
were more readily visible than in rural areas. In addition to child welfare, an emphasis of Charities was nursing home care. Villa
Mary Immaculate and Teresian House in Albany were built during Father Downs' tenure.

In the mid-1960s, President Johnson's
Great Society program provided tremendous
amounts of federal money for myriad pro-

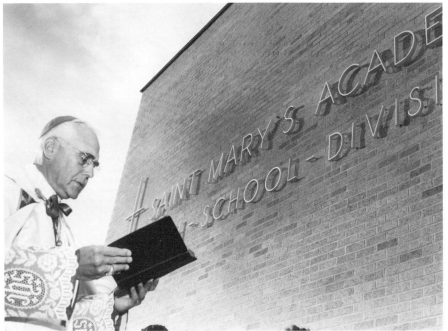

grams. Since the original function of Catholic Charities was for child welfare (in particular, orphanages), the St. Vincent's Child Care Society became the vehicle for accepting public monies. This initiated a partnership between the government and Catholic Charities that would lead to care for people throughout the 14 counties of the Albany Diocese through such programs as substance abuse treatment, domestic abuse prevention, care for unwed mothers and counseling for families.

Meanwhile, the Diocese continued its heavy construction on urgently needed institutions: nursing homes, schools and, especially, churches. The population growth in general and in the suburbs in particular led to crammed churches with people sitting on folding chairs in the center aisles and standing against the walls. To accommodate such

large numbers, Masses were added to parish schedules. Some priests became known for their ability to celebrate half-hour liturgies with five-minute homilies so that enough Masses could be squeezed into Sunday morning to serve all the laity who wanted to participate.

Above: Bishop Scully blesses St. Mary's High School, Hoosick Falls, 1960 (Andrick Studio)

Right: The Bishop's throne in the Cathedral (J.A. Glenn photo)

Through the years . . .
The 50s

1950: U.S. recognizes Vietnam

1951: 22nd Amendment to Constitution restricts presidential terms

1952: Revised Standard version of Bible published for Protestants

1953: Stalin dies; Queen Elizabeth II crowned

1954: Arnold Palmer wins Amateur Championship of U.S. Golf Association

1955: AFL and CIO merge; Blacks boycott Montgomery, Alabama, buses

1956: Don Larson hurls only perfect game in World Series history

1957: Olaf V becomes king of Norway ,

1958: Pope John XXIII succeeds Pius XII; first satellites launched

1959: "Ben Hur" wins 11 Academy Awards, the most ever

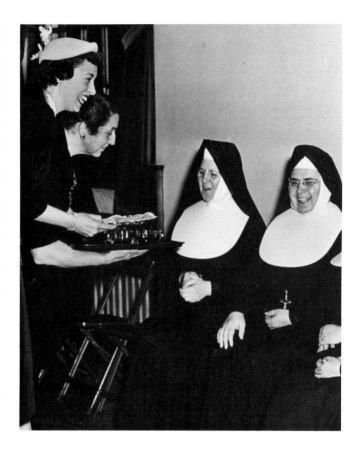

Page 201: Bishop Scully blesses the new chapel and novitiate of the Sisters of the Resurrection in Castleton (Pinto Photo Service)

Page 202, top: Sister Catherine Francis, president of The College of Saint Rose, and Sister Louise are served by alumnae, 1953 (A.J. O'Keefe photo)

Bottom: The dedication of Bishop Gibbons High School, Schenectady, 1957 (Burns Photography)

This page, above: Sisters of Mercy about to take their vows, 1956 (A.J. O'Keefe photo)

Right: Bishop Gibbons in his later years

Bishop Edward J. Maginn

Due to the activities involved with major construction and the resultant increase in the bishop's duties, Edward Joseph Maginn, a local priest, was made auxiliary bishop in 1957. By the early 1960s, it became apparent that Scully had developed health problems of his own. While he was never diagnosed with it at the time, since it was not a commonly recognized disorder, priests who knew him suspect he had Alzheimer's disease. It was not until 1966, however (two years after Gibbons' death), that Bishop Maginn was appointed administrator of the Diocese, a post he held until Scully died in 1969.

Bishop Maginn was born in Glasgow, Scotland, but his family emigrated to America when he was seven. By the time he was 14, they had lived in Mechanicville, Stillwater, Fort Edward and Glens Falls. He completed his undergraduate studies at Holy Cross College in Worcester, then went to St. Joseph's at Dunwoodie for seminary studies. Upon his return to the Diocese, he was made assistant chancellor and later chancellor, hand-chosen by Bishop Gibbons for promotion. He succeeded Father Charles at St. Vincent de Paul as pastor and principal of VI, not an easy task.

Bishop Maginn seemed destined to face difficult tasks but, because of his positions as

vicar general and auxiliary, often did not receive credit for his successful handling of those responsibilities. He was the man-behind-the-bishops who oversaw developments during a large part of Bishop Gibbons' tenure as well as Bishop Scully's. One issue on which he gained recognition was civil rights, particularly for the way in which he averted problems in the turbulent 1960s by allowing

This page: Monsignor Maginn when he was Vicar General
Opposite: Children surround Bishop Maginn and Father Peter Young at St. John the Baptist, Albany, 1966 (Acme Photograph)

such priests as Fathers Thomas Tooher, Nellis Tremblay and Peter Young to deal with the politically charged, inner-city tensions. Father Young admired Bishop Maginn for being "a man of absolute total integrity, of total commitment, totally open." Because he had those qualities, Albany was one of the few cities in New York that did not experience riots.

Under Bishop's Maginn's guidance, the Church was the main white stabilizing influence in the inner city; for that reason, the Diocese became a source of energy and attempted to correct some of the injustices in such basic ways as allowing church buildings to be used for meetings and social service activities. Bishop Maginn also directed $100,000 of the annual Diocesan Development Program for the poor, an act of Christian generosity and economic justice for which he received considerable flak — and a flagging in donations from some disgruntled Catholics. By such actions, sometimes in spite of his personal views, Bishop Maginn laid the background for the modern Church in which social justice and Catholic charities play major roles.

He remained auxiliary bishop under Bishops Edwin B. Broderick and Howard J. Hubbard, dying in 1984.

Vatican II

Bishop Maginn represented the Albany Diocese at the Second Vatican Council, held in four sessions at St. Peter's Basilica in Rome during the autumns from 1962-1965. Because of the radical changes that followed in so many areas of Church life, the Council's effects are still being felt more than 30 years later. While most Catholics adjusted to using English instead of Latin during Mass, many felt that parts of the new official translation were awkward and sometimes too vernacular. At the same time, they applauded some of the newer translations — "Holy Spirit" for "Holy Ghost," for example — when the meanings of words had wandered afar of their original meaning in Middle English.

When the changes were put into place, it was left to parish priests to implement them — from the minor, such as the addition of St. Joseph to the canon; to the more radical, such as the celebration of the liturgy in the vernacular; to the very significant, such as having the altar face the people and receiving the Eucharist under both species. At the same time, the educational level among American Catholics was rising so that many parishioners no longer were satisfied with the explanation of "Rome says so" as a response to their asking, "Why should we change?" The laity wanted solid reasons for the changes, such as an effort to return to early Church customs and teachings, particularly as they were being asked to assume more responsibility in the Church, one of the Council's main emphases. Among the ways the Diocese tried to explain the changes were a massive, 50-part series in The Evangelist, guided by its editor, Father William Jillisky; and a traveling "road show" spearheaded by the vice chancellors, Fathers Howard Russell and Leo O'Brien.

Part of the confusion came also from priests who were being asked to delegate segments of their authority. Some of them felt that they were also being required to relinquish traditional roles and authority, changes that could not be accepted immediately, by either many of the clergy or laity.

When Pope John XXIII voiced his rationale for the changes needed — that the Holy Spirit speaks to others, not just to "us," the pope — two things happened: He opened the study of theology to the laity and stressed the recognition of the Holy Spirit as a guiding light for the Church. Currently, the numbers of laity studying theology are much higher than ever before. With the encouragement of Bishop Hubbard, St. Bernard's Institute of Rochester established a site in Albany, becoming the only graduate school of theology in the area. It has witnessed an enrollment increase of 62 percent since 1990. Since 1989, 200 students have taken courses and 40 have obtained graduate degrees.

Another major change in the wake of the Council was the restoration of the permanent diaconate. In June 1976, the first class of 23 deacons was ordained by Bishop Broderick, creating a cadre of married, widowed and single men — many with children, most working and some retired — who were ordained for service to the Church in such areas as hospital, nursing home and prison ministry. Assigned to parishes, they preach, witness marriages, perform funeral rites and assist in other liturgical activities. By mid-1997, the Diocese boasted nearly 100 deacons serving in diverse ministries.

Previous page: The bishops of the world assembled in St. Peter's in Rome for the Second Vatican Council

Through the years . . .
The 60s

1960: Belgian Congo granted independence

1961: Farthings are no longer legal tender in England

1962: James Baldwin publishes "Another Country"

1963: John F. Kennedy assassinated; C.S. Lewis dies the same day

1964: "Hello Dolly" and "Fiddler on the Roof" open on Broadway

1965: Martin Luther King leads protestors to Selma, Alabama

1966: United Brethren and Methodists vote to merge as United Methodists

1967: Langston Hughes, Cardinal Spellman and Jimmy Foxx die

1968: Martin Luther King assassinated; LBJ withdraws candidacy

1969: Neil Armstrong walks on the moon

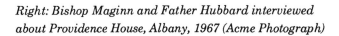

Opposite page: A teacher and student at St. Joseph's in Albany, 1966

Above: Four Sisters of St. Joseph, Sisters Anne Martin, Carmela Ann, Celine John and Mary Ethna, in Anchorage, Alaska, 1967. They were there to conduct a census of the Archdiocese, headed by Archbishop Ryan, an Albany native.

Right: Bishop Maginn and Father Hubbard interviewed about Providence House, Albany, 1967 (Acme Photograph)

Bishop Edwin B. Broderick

At the time of Bishop Scully's death in 1969, the numbers of priests, brothers and sisters were at their peak. Since his accession in 1954, priests totaled 764, up 190; there were 154 brothers, up 53; and 1,903 sisters, up 267. Those statistics were out of a Catholic population of 422,067, up almost 100,000, a number that represented one-third of the population of the area. Approximately 55 percent of the children attended

Catholic schools.

Bishop Scully's successor, Bishop Edwin Bernard Broderick, an auxiliary bishop of New York City, was born in the Bronx to Irish immigrant parents. After training at Dunwoodie and his ordination, he held pastoral and teaching positions in the New York Archdiocese while, at the same time, getting a master's and then a doctorate in English literature at Fordham. He became the first full-time director of radio and television for the Archdiocese, producing shows for Bishop Sheen as well as "Chapel of the Air" and "Frontiers of Faith." Before he was named to Albany, Bishop Broderick held various other positions, including secretary to Cardinal Spellman and rector of St. Joseph's at Dunwoodie.

Broderick, the first Albany bishop under

the more relaxed atmosphere after Vatican II, brought a personableness to the position and a clarity to the changes by creating a series of open sessions called "Listen to the Spirit," held at locations throughout the Diocese. At those gatherings, he heard firsthand the concerns and proposed solutions of Catholics. He also kept alive the Diocese's historic interest in ecumenism, helping to found Christians United in Mission, an interdenominational social action network; and welcoming to Albany in 1974 the Archbishop of Canterbury, Michael Ramsey, and hosting a clergy day at the Cathedral with him.

During the seven years of his tenure, he also brought to the fore the temporal needs of people, making such services as Catholic Charities more available in the Diocese in order to respond to people more holistically. When Sister Serena Branson, D.C., became director of Catholic Charities in 1974, decentralization occurred, and separate corporations were set up in different counties as needed. Supplementing the already existing ones in Troy, Albany and Schenectady, nine additional county centers were designed to confront the problems in each of the regions. Otsego County, for example, needed a rural dentist, so funding was acquired for a dental van.

The appointment of Sister Serena — who continued as director under Bishop Hubbard until 1990 when she became head of special

Opposite: Bishop Broderick (Joseph Merante photo)
Left: Bishop Broderick ordains a priest, 1974 (Mark Haight photo)

projects, including working with the elderly — marked a significant change: the designation of a woman to direct one of the largest departments of the Diocese. Previously, these departments, such as Catholic schools and religious education, had been headed by priests. But as the winds of change from Vatican II blew through the Diocese, both Bishop Broderick and Bishop Hubbard began extending authority to women religious and to lay people: Sister Serena and later Sister Maureen Joyce, RSM, in charge of Catholic Charities; Amato ("Matty") Semenza as superintendent of schools; and Sister Danielle Bonetti, CSJ, and Jeanne Schrempf leading the Office of Religious Education. Eventually, laity and women religious would be in charge of the liturgy office, The Evangelist, the Bishop's Appeal and other departments. (This trend would culminate in 1996 when Bishop Hubbard named

Left to right: Sister Serena, Sister Maureen, Mr. Semenza and Sister Danielle

Next page: Bishop Broderick greets Michael Ramsey, the Archbishop of Canterbury, at the Cathedral of the Immaculate Conception in 1974

as co-chancellors a priest, a woman religious and a layman: Father Geoffrey Burke, Sister Kathleen Turley and John Feeney.) And while Irish clergy had dominated the Diocese for many years, reflecting the immigrants from Ireland who were so plentiful, recent years saw changes so that, in 1997, the list of deans included not only priests named Jeremiah Nunan and James Daley but also Joseph Benintende, Thomas Berardi, Donald Ophals and John Provost. Similarly, the 1997 Presbyteral Council, a group of clergy who advise the bishop, numbered Fathers Donald Czelusniak, Dominic Ingemie and Michael Farano alongside Kenneth Doyle and James Donlon.

Serving the Whole Person

The Diocese also originated services that addressed emotional and psychological problems. In 1969, Bishop Broderick appointed Father John Malecki director of the Consultation Services Center for priests and religious, one of the first psychological consulting centers in the nation designed to serve the needs of clergy and vowed religious. It would expand to serve laity, as does the diocesan

Counseling for Laity office.

Inner-city churches also became centers for social services, serving a population that often was not necessarily Catholic but definitely needy. Often, those individuals would appear at churches wanting to find out how to approach governmental programs designed to help them, but which were too impersonal to care. A sister/social worker was assigned to inner-city parishes, such as the Cathedral, St. Mary's and St. John's, in Albany. She helped people find the services they needed, and organized clothing drives, collected food and found housing.

A prime example of governmental impersonality being tempered by Church presence occurred in the wake of the 1971 Attica Prison uprising in western New York. In its aftermath, the state needed the assistance of people with solutions. Bishop Broderick was

the only clergyman named to a state committee of nine chosen by state judges to review what happened there and to recommend policies to prevent similar occurrences.

With such a background, Bishop Broderick was approached to serve a far wider audience and in 1976 resigned as bishop of the Diocese to become director of Catholic Relief Services, the U.S. Catholic Church's overseas aid agency.

As he left, the fallout from the Second Vatican Council was starting to take its toll around the world and in the Diocese with priests and sisters leaving their vocations, and fewer replacements for them entering

Previous page, top: Suburban population growth leads to a new parish center at Corpus Christi, Ushers, in 1977 and a new church (bottom), Our Lady of the Annunciation, Queensbury, in 1970

Above: The interior of St. Edward the Confessor, Clifton Park

seminaries and novitiates. Those losses specifically affected the schools where lay teachers had to be hired to fill open spots as the 1970s progressed. Some parents with children in parochial schools often chose to send them there because the sisters were the teachers. But with fewer and fewer nuns in the schools, more and more lay teachers had to be paid more than the stipends nuns received; as a result, tuitions rose. Parents unable or unwilling to pay the tuitions withdrew their children. The almost empty school buildings that resulted in some areas became a liability that forced Bishop Broderick to close them. When Bishop Broderick left in 1976, seven years after coming to the Albany Diocese, there were 63 fewer priests in the Diocese. The losses among the sisters were proportionally much greater. There were 65 percent fewer sisters, which meant 658 fewer women religious, most of whom had been teachers.

Through the years . . . The 70s

1970: 231 million TV sets estimated to be in use around world

1971: 26th Amendment permits 18-year-olds to vote in U.S.

1972: Five men arrested in Watergate complex in Washington, D.C.

1973: Supreme Court legalizes abortion nationwide in U.S.

1974: Richard Nixon resigns presidency; Miami Dolphins win Super Bowl

1975: Haile Selassie, Thornton Wilder and Casey Stengel die

1976: U.S. celebrates its bicentennial

1977: Orthodox Church in America selects first U.S.-born prelate

1978: Year of three popes: Paul VI, John Paul I and John Paul II

1979: Mother Teresa wins the Nobel Peace Prize

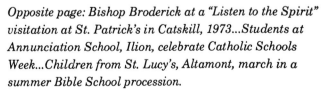

Opposite page: Bishop Broderick at a "Listen to the Spirit" visitation at St. Patrick's in Catskill, 1973...Students at Annunciation School, Ilion, celebrate Catholic Schools Week...Children from St. Lucy's, Altamont, march in a summer Bible School procession.

This page: Retired priests are welcomed to Sacred Heart, Cohoes, 1972...Twenty-five men are ordained to the subdiaconate in Our Lady of Angels Seminary, Glenmont, 1971...Sister Maria De Monte presents religious education licenses to teachers at Our Lady of the Assumption, Latham, 1978

Bishop Howard J. Hubbard

The search for Bishop Broderick's successor ended on the downtown streets of Albany where Father Howard James Hubbard, a native of Troy, was ministering to the needy. Upon his installation in 1977, he became the first native-born son of the Diocese to be its bishop.

After graduating from Mater Christi and St. Joseph's Seminary at Dunwoodie, Hubbard went to Rome to study at the Gregorian University. Following ordination in 1963 and early pastoral positions, he was sent to Catholic University to do graduate studies in social service. When he returned, Bishop Maginn asked him to establish Providence House, a crisis intervention and prevention center in Albany's South End. From then on, he became involved in various capacities in the administration of the Diocese, culminating in his appointment as bishop of Albany in 1977.

Bishop Hubbard began to meet the daunting tasks he faced when installed by writing a pastoral letter to the Diocese; in it, he outlined his philosophy and goals. He would emphasize shared responsibility, collaboration and collegiality; encourage new ministries among the laity; bolster priests; and stress religious education for all ages.

Under Hubbard, Catholic Charities dramatically increased its services and outreach into the Diocese; currently, among the more than 30 divisions in Charities are senior citizen housing development, developmental disabilities programs, caregiver guidance, help for dysfunctional families, healthcare serv-

Opposite: Father Hubbard with Hope House residents, 1977

Right: Preparing with WTEN's staff for his televised retreat, 1979

ices, counseling for individuals, aid for the homeless and victims of domestic abuse, a tenants' association for the poor and disadvantaged, and maternity services. Church-related programs now function in areas where few others want to work, such as Farano Center, one of the first programs in the nation to house infants with AIDS-related problems. (The center was named for Father Michael Farano, long-time chancellor and current vicar general of the Diocese along with Father Leo O'Brien.)

Where necessary, Hubbard has enlarged or established diocesan-wide commissions on peace and justice, on aging, and on alcohol and other substance abuse, as well as Hispanic Outreach Services. He has also been a strong voice in the pro-life movement. His regular columns in The Evangelist have focused on abortion more often than any other single issue. He also became the first and only bishop in the nation to sue Planned Parenthood when it attempted to open an abortion clinic in Albany, a suit the Diocese won

Through the years . . . The 80s

1980: John Lennon shot to death; Israel inaugurates the shekel

1981: John Paul II and Ronald Reagan victims of assassination attempts

1982: Vietnam Veterans' war Memorial dedicated in Washington, D.C.

1983: Ethiopia appeals for aid to help millions of drought victims

1984: Apple Macintosh computer, with mouse, introduced

1985: Mexico City earthquake kills thousands

1986: Red Sox Bill Buckner's error helps give New York Mets the World Series

1987: Terry Waite, Archbishop of Canterbury's envoy, kidnaped in Beirut

1988: Nobel Prize for literature goes to Naguib Mahfouz of Egypt

1989: TV preacher Jim Bakker sentenced to 45 years in prison for fraud

Opposite, top: Sister Joan Curley, CSJ, pastoral administrator of St. Joseph's Church, Schoharie, meets with parishioners, 1986

Bottom: Bishop Hubbard digs a hole for a time capsule at St. Agnes Cemetery, Menands, 1981 (Maryrose Robilatto photo)

Upper left: Father Michael Farano, chancellor, meets with Victor Riley, Jr. of KeyCorp and Peter Pryor, president of the Urban League, to plan its 20th anniversary dinner, 1986. Father Farano was past president of the Urban League. (Maryrose Robilatto photo)

Upper right: A computer in the classroom fascinates students, Father Paul Bondi, pastor, and Sister Mary Albertus, math teacher, at St. Mary's, Ballston Spa, 1982

Middle: Mary Reed Newland from the diocesan Office of Religious Education speaks at a ministry fair at St. Mary's, Oneonta, 1983

Bottom: Organist Bob Brown inspects a restored organ at St. James, Albany, 1984 (Maryrose Robilatto photo)

in the first two courts but ultimately lost before the state's highest court.

Because these programs help all people regardless of race, creed or sex, much of their funding comes from various governmental agencies, as well as grants and private sources. Since the Church operates with a very low administrative budget, if it were to withdraw its social services, in many areas the government would have to scramble to fill in the loss at a much greater cost.

In 1995, the most recent year for which statistics are available, the total population of the area was 1,315,414. Catholics numbered 403,403, or 31 percent, about the same

Above: Addressing a Martin Luther King, Jr. Memorial at Missionary Baptist Church, Albany, 1996 (Dave Oxford photo)

Opposite: Meeting with Pope John Paul II (Foto felici)

as 20 years previously, although the proportional number of Catholics has declined to some extent. More significantly, the general population of the area has declined since 1976 by 11 percent, while the Catholic population has dropped by only 5 percent. With the decline and with shifts in populations to the suburbs, some churches have had to close or consolidate, an emotionally wrenching experience for many lifelong parishioners. From a high of 207 parishes in 1976, there are now 187. To compensate somewhat, there are more missions now — 62 — than 20 years ago.

At the end of October 1996, there were 327 diocesan priests, 128 religious order priests, 91 deacons, 980 sisters and 86 brothers to staff those churches and missions in addition to filling other positions, such as in the schools. Diocesan Catholic schools are, per-

haps, one of the best-kept secrets in that their success has been measured by consistently producing students who perform up to their individual capacities. These schools provide a nurturing atmosphere while teaching values, but are famous particularly for maintaining test scores above the public school levels. There are 40 elementary schools, two of which are private, and seven high schools, of which three are private, serving a total of

Lay ministers being commissioned at St. Anthony's Church in Herkimer, 1994 (John R. Dillon photo)

Bishop Hubbard greets those joining the Catholic Church during a Rite of Christian Initiation of Adults ceremony at the Cathedral, 1988

Page 225: Lee Niemietz of Amsterdam prays before the Pope arrives in Queens in 1995; she was part of a delegation from the Diocese (Dave Oxford photo)

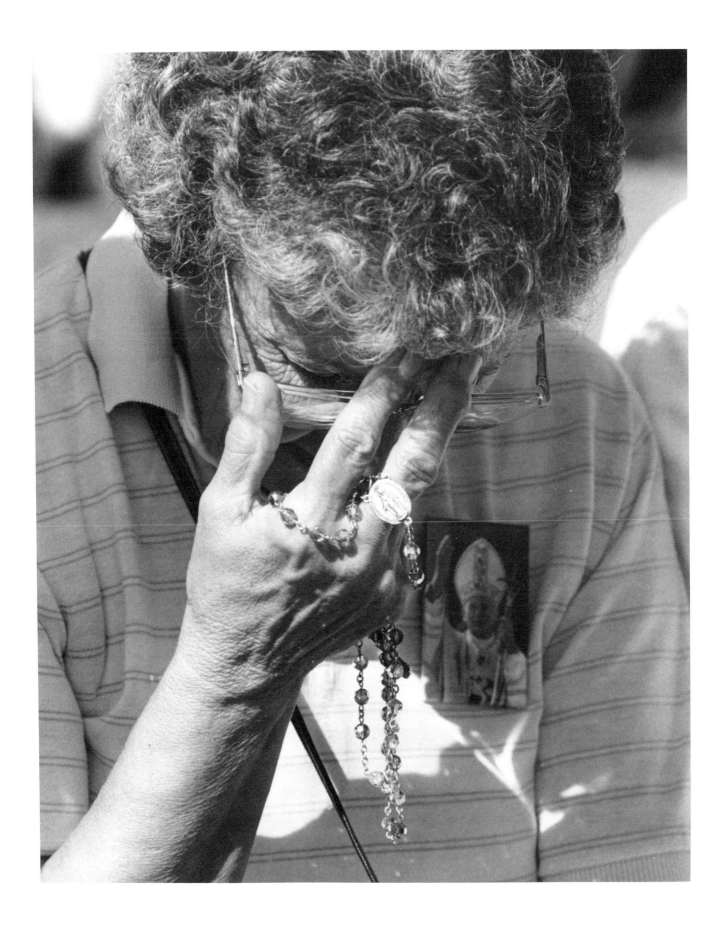

Through the years . . . The 90s

1990: First female priests in England ordained for Anglican Church

1991: Persian Gulf War waged in Middle East against Iraq

1992: Arkansas Gov. Bill Clinton elected president in three-way race

1993: "Schindler's List," story of Holocaust, wins Best Picture Oscar

1994: Oksana Baiul of Ukraine wins figure skating gold at Olympics

1995: Bombing of Oklahoma federal building kills scores

1996: N.Y. Yankees win World Series as manager's brother receives heart transplant

1997: Diocese of Albany celebrates its Sesquicentennial

Opposite, top: Bishop Hubbard confirms Amelia Michaela Walag at St. Joseph's Church, Broadalbin, 1995... bottom: Catholics at St. John the Baptist, Greenville, at a Eucharistic Day of Devotion, 1995

Above: Bishop Hubbard on an ecumenical Good Friday walk in Troy, 1995...right: breaking ground for a new church building at St. John Francis Regis parish, Grafton, 1995 (Dave Oxford photos)

almost 13,000 students. Significantly, only 12 percent of the teachers in these schools are sisters, priests and brothers. Meanwhile, lay administrators and teachers, who have proven they can effectively carry out the mission of Catholic education, have been well accepted by pastors, parents and pupils.

Beyond the children served by Catholic

schools, there are almost 37,000 children attending public schools who are served through religious education classes. They are generally instructed by the laity, of which there are more than 4,000 leaders and catechists and almost 40 youth ministers. On 17 college campuses, there are 20 chaplains.

The Albany Diocese always has been an area in which several religious communities have had regional headquarters. Currently, there are seven motherhouses, novitiates and scholasticates — college-level schools of

Above: Students from St. Stanislaus School, Amsterdam, visit the official Sesquicentennial Exhibition in Albany, 1997

Opposite: The bishop and clergy at an ordination in the Cathedral, 1995 (Dave Oxford photos)

general studies — for women religious, while there are 32 different orders represented in the Diocese. Among the men religious, there are half that number — 16. Some of these men and women are leaders in the Diocese's 12 retreat houses, such as the Dominican Retreat House in Schenectady, and houses of prayer, such as Abba House of Prayer in Albany.

Bishop Hubbard fits well within the modern Church. His selection as bishop of the state capital was well-thought out because he has proven equal to the task of challenging state leaders on moral issues, such as the death penalty, abortion, and health and welfare reform, among others. He has done so in testimony before hearings by the State Legislature, in open letters to political leaders and through his columns in The Evangelist.

To directly counteract economic problems at the grassroots level, innovative programs have been initiated. The sphere of activities of diocesan Catholic Charities has become focused on areas lacking funding, such as seed money to help budding low-income neighborhood entrepreneurs start businesses. His approach to such problems has revealed imagination in finding and backing others with solutions.

His approach has also bolstered a constant theme in the Diocese since its earliest days: interreligious cooperation. He has spoken from the pulpits of other Christian churches;

he has joined with Muslims, Jews and Protestants to oppose legislation that harms the poor; he has traveled to the Holy Land on a Catholic-Jewish pilgrimage; he has been honored by those of other faiths for his leadership in the community. He also signed, with the Episcopal bishop, a covenant that linked the Cathedral of the Immaculate Conception and the Episcopal Cathedral of All Saints.

Arguably the most significant example of this spirit of interfaith cooperation occurred in 1986, when Bishop Hubbard took part in what is believed to be the first Jewish/Catholic Reconciliation Service held anywhere in the world. At the Cathedral on Palm Sunday of that year, more than 1,000 Catholics and Jews gathered to pray together and to reconcile themselves after centuries of anti-Semitism. Three years later, when a sculpture titled "Portal" was installed behind the Cathedral to commemorate the event, Bishop Hubbard and Rabbi Martin Silverman walked through it, hand-in-hand, in a gesture of friendship that echoed back three centuries to the cooperative spirit of Father Jogues and Domine Megapolensis.

Pictured here: Bishop Hubbard and Rabbi Silverman walk through "The Portal," 1986

Facing page: Children from St. Clare's parish, Colonie, with the motto of the Sesquicentennial (1970s photo by Gene Tobler)

Honoring Tradition . . .

. . . Discovering Tomorrow

Afterword

ON DECEMBER 8, 1996, ONLY HOURS after the second nor'easter of the week had dumped a heavy load of snow on the region, thousands of Catholics trekked from every corner of the Albany Diocese to the Cathedral of the Immaculate Conception in Albany. The occasion was the prayer service marking the opening of the Diocesan Sesquicentennial, and both the site and date were entirely appropriate: at a Cathedral named for Our Lady and on the Feast of the Immaculate Conception, the title under which the both the Diocese and the U.S. are dedicated to her.

It's not unusual for meteorological omens to threaten diocesan celebrations without disrupting them. As readers of this book know, on April 23, 1847, the date the Diocese was officially established, a spring storm brought so much rain to the area that the Hudson River flooded Albany streets along its banks. A year later, when the cornerstone of the Cathedral itself was laid, a cloudburst scattered the crowd moments after the ceremony concluded. As a contemporary reflection of those historic near-misses, by the time the 3 p.m. prayer service began on December 8, 1996, the snow had been cleared, the sun was peeking through light clouds and the temperature stood around 40.

It was easy for those in attendance at the Cathedral to imagine themselves back 150 years at the founding of the Diocese as an outdoor procession (below) of nearly 500 priests, religious and laity marched along Eagle Street, bearing banners and candles. Behind them came four bishops connected to the Diocese: Archbishop Joseph Ryan, an Albany native who is now retired; Bishop Howard J. Hubbard, the current ordinary; Bishop Edwin B. Broderick, his immediate predecessor; and Bishop Matthew Clark, a native of Waterford who is ordinary of the Rochester Diocese (next page).

As the line wended its way toward the Cathedral, those inside were listening to classical music, composed by Bach and Beethoven, and performed by a massed choir and instrumentalists, another touch of the past. But there were signs of the modern Church, too, reminders that this is 1997, not 1847: Permanent deacons dotted the line of marchers and attended the bishops...women religious and laywomen played prominent roles in the readings and prayers...the Episcopal bishop and a

rabbi delivered greetings from the Cathedral's pulpit...and videocameras recorded the event for future Catholics to examine at the diocesan Bicentennial and Tricentennial.

After the two-hour-plus service concluded, many in the congregation lingered, sharing favorite moments, complimenting those in charge, savoring what had happened and guarding their candles from the evening breeze. The candles' flames, lit from the Sesquicentennial candle during the service, are now housed in parishes throughout the 14 counties of the Diocese as a way of connecting everyone to the opening service.

That opening inaugurated not only the Sesquicentennial observance but also the next 150 years of Catholics in the Albany Diocese. It is always fun but ever futile to imagine what those 15 decades will bring. To the Catholics of 2147, therefore, we offer our warm greetings from the past, our hopeful appeal for their prayers in the future and our deeply felt wishes that their Tricentennial will be as charged with spiritual exhilaration, historic memories and diocesan-wide unity as is our Sesquicentennial.

James Breig

Opening Homily

Here is the full text of Bishop Howard J. Hubbard's homily, delivered at the Cathedral of the Immaculate Conception in Albany on the occasion of the opening prayer service of the Diocesan Sesquicentennial Celebration, December 8, 1996.

IT IS FITTING ON THIS FEAST of the Immaculate Conception, the patroness of our Diocese, that we gather — from the Vermont border to the Pennsylvania border; from the foothills of the Berkshires and the Green Mountains to the threshold of the Appalachian mountain range; from the Adirondacks to the Catskills; from the Hudson Valley through the Mohawk Valley; from Hoosick Falls to Little Falls; from the Sacandaga Reservoir to the Delaware River Basin; from the Naval Museum in Whitehall to the Baseball Museum in Cooperstown; from Glens Falls to Copake Falls and Haines Falls; from Fort Ann to Fort Plain; and from all the various villages, towns and cities that dot our fourteen-county Diocese. We gather for this spirit-filled prayer service in which we commence the year-long celebration of our Sesquicentennial Anniversary, that anniversary which commemorates the founding in 1847 of this local Church we call the Diocese of Albany.

We have chosen as our sesquicentennial theme: "Honoring Tradition, Discovering Tomorrow." From this gathering this afternoon to the closing ceremony on the Vigil of the Immaculate Conception a year from now, in our parishes, schools, religious education programs; in our families, diocesan offices and agencies; on our college campuses and in our religious communities, we will be looking for ways to honor our faith heritage, imbedded as it is in the soil made rich by the blood of the North American martyrs, and to discover how the Lord's Spirit is truly leading us to advance the reign of God into the new millennium.

Ours indeed is a rich faith tradition: a heritage of saints and scholars; a heritage of sinners and scoundrels; a heritage of wave after wave of immigrants, with each wave making its own indispensable contribution to our cultural, social and spiritual fabric; a heritage of priests, deacons, religious and lay persons, like all of us gathered here today, who have built up and maintained the magnificent network of churches, schools, hospitals, nursing homes and human service agencies that grace our Diocese — a Diocese which currently consists of 403,000 Catholics, 187 parishes, 38 mission churches, 3 colleges and one graduate school of theology, 47 high schools and grammar schools serving an academic total of 17,400 students, with another 37,000 young people under instruction in our religious education programs; 17 campus ministry chapters; 4 hospitals ministering to 560,000 patients annually, 9 extended-care facilities caring for 1,500 aged and infirm persons, 2 Diocesan Counseling Centers; 25 diocesan departments; 27 persons serving in prison or jail ministry; 12 retreat centers and houses of prayer, 8 residences for senior citizens; and 31 social service agencies attending to the social, emotional and psychological needs of those who are poor, homeless, refugees, addicted, incarcerated, deaf, developmentally disabled, experiencing problem pregnancies, in need of adoption, foster care or day care or coping with AIDS or family dysfunction, just to mention a few of the multi-faceted social services that are rendered annually by our Catholic Charities agencies to over 154,000 people in our Diocese, regardless of their racial, religious, ethnic or socio-economic background.

This does not include the countless number of services provided by fraternal and sororal organizations like the St. Vincent de Paul Societies, the Ladies of Charity, the Legion of Mary, the Knights of Columbus, Malta, St. John and Lithuania, and the Catholic Daughters of the Americas; or the contributions of Catholic lay people in their neighborhoods and communities and through their activities in the workplace and marketplace.

The sterling heritage, which we celebrate in this Sesquicentennial observance, precedes the founding of our local Church in 1847. It is a heritage illumined by Saints Isaac Jogues, John Lalande and Rene Goupil, the 17th-century Jesuit missionaries who traversed the trails from Canada to Lake George, from the mighty Hudson to the majestic Mohawk Rivers in a valiant venture to bring the Good News to our native Americans, and by Blessed Kateri Tekakwitha who became the premier respondent to the message proclaimed by the French missionaries; a heritage of Sir William Johnson, a Catholic sympathizer, if not an underground Catholic, who fostered Catholic colonization in that area of the Mohawk Valley that now bears his name, despite the anti-priest laws that were in effect in his day; a heritage of Thomas Dongan, the Irish Catholic who served as the first English Governor of New York State and who penned the historic Dongan Charter with its religious freedom clause, which charter was to become the basis for the future New York State Constitution.

It is a heritage of Catholic patriots like France's Lafayette and Poland's Kosciuszko, who fought so courageously for freedom on our diocesan soil during the American Revolution; a heritage of circuit-riding priests out of historic St. Mary's in Albany, the first Catholic church in upstate New York and the second oldest in our state; and of pioneering parishes in New-

port, Troy, Hudson Falls, Schenectady, Hoosick Falls, Saratoga Springs, Amsterdam, Little Falls, Schaghticoke, Hunter, Watervliet, Waterford, Hudson, Gilboa, Whitehall, Cohoes, Schuylerville and Ballston Spa, all of which were in existence before the establishment of our Diocese.

It is a heritage of French-Canadian, German and Irish Catholics, who in the late 18th and early 19th centuries, came to this area, settled originally by the Dutch and the English, in search of work and a better life: building the roadways, the canals and the mills that made our region both the gateway to the West and an economic powerhouse in our nation's first half-century.

The first Roman Catholic Diocese in the New World was the Diocese of Baltimore, established in 1789 with John Carroll as its bishop and the entire 13 colonies as its territory. In 1809, the Diocese of New York was erected, which embraced all of New York State. The growing presence of Catholicism in northeastern New York State led to the establishment of our Diocese in 1847, under Bishop John McCloskey, who held a series of firsts: the first priest ordained for the Diocese of New York, the first Bishop of Albany and who later, as Archbishop of New York, was to become the first American cardinal.

On the same day, April 23, 1847, the Diocese of Buffalo was also established. Buffalo embraced what is now the Diocese of Rochester, which was severed in 1868; and our Diocese of Albany included what are now the Dioceses of Ogdensburg and Syracuse, which were established in 1872 and 1886 respectively. The visionary and energetic Bishop McCloskey enabled the fledgling Diocese to grow and flourish organizationally. Many of the aforementioned immigrant groups brought with them their priests and religious communities to help meet their pastoral, educational, social and spiritual needs. The Augustinians, Jesuits, Redemptorists, and Franciscan Fathers; the Sisters of St. Joseph of Carondelet, the Daughters of Charity, the Sisters of Mercy, the Religious of the Sacred Heart, the Holy Names and Assumptionist Sisters; and the Christian Brothers established parishes, schools, hospitals and orphanages. This cohort of immigrants was followed at the end of the century by arrivees from Poland, Italy, Lithuania, Slovakia and the Ukraine — all accompanied by their priests and religious: the Resurrection and Felician Sisters for the Poles; the Baptistine, Venerini and Filippini Sisters for the Italians. Also, the Little Sisters of the Poor came to care for the aged in Albany and Troy; the Sisters of the Good Shepherd, to develop reformatory schools for girls in these same communities; and the Sisters of the Presentation, to run an orphanage for boys and girls in Watervliet.

The first half of the 20th century saw the Diocese strongly impacted by its bishops, the pastoral Bishop Thomas Burke, the saintly Bishop Thomas Cusack, and especially Bishop Edmund Gibbons, who guided the Diocese from the waning days of World War I through the Great Depression, World War II, the Korean War and the onset of the Cold War. Bishop Gibbons' great devotion to the Carmelite saints, Teresa of Avila and Therese of Lisieux, moved him to establish the cloistered Carmelite Monastery in Schenectady and to welcome to Germantown the Carmelite Sisters of the Aged and Infirm. His background as superintendent of schools for the Diocese of Buffalo prompted him to become a staunch advocate for Catholic education, involved in the founding of Saint Rose and Siena Colleges, Mater Christi Seminary and our diocesan newspaper, The Evangelist, originally developed as a parish bulletin by the legendary Msgr. John F. Glavin, the pastor of St. John the Evangelist in Rensselaer for 61 years.

Bishop William Scully and Bishop Edward Maginn built upon Bishop Gibbons' legacy, especially in the realm of education, opening 22 new parochial schools and 4 new high schools between 1950 and 1960. They represented the Diocese at that watershed event of 20th-century Catholicism, the Second Vatican Council, continuing in the tradition of Bishop John Conroy, the second Bishop of Albany, who represented the Diocese at the First Vatican Council.

However, it fell to the eighth Bishop of Albany, Bishop Edwin Broderick, who is present with us today, to implement the norms and reforms of the Second Vatican Council, especially in the areas of liturgy, ecumenism, catechetics and the development of collegial bodies like the Priests' Senate, Sisters' Council and Diocesan Pastoral Council. He also saw to the expansion of the Church's social service ministry from its Capital District focus to all fourteen counties of our Diocese.

Throughout the history of our Diocese, there have been towering figures like:

• Father Peter Havermans, the Dutch Jesuit-become-diocesan priest, who founded St. Peter's, St. Mary's and St. Joseph's parishes in Troy; the Troy Hospital (now Seton); LaSalle Institute; two orphan asylums; and St. Joseph's Provincial Seminary;

• Madame Henriette de La Tour du Pin, a French aristocrat and lady-in-waiting to Marie Antoinette who came to America to escape certain death during the French Revolution and upon whose farmhouse cellar was built the historic house, located on the grounds of the current St. Joseph's Provincial House in Latham, which, from structural evidence, may have served as a way station on the Underground Railroad to Canada in mid-19th century;

• Fathers Edward Wadhams and Clarence Walworth, fellow seminarians for orders in the Episcopal church, who as a result of their involvement with the Oxford Movement, spearheaded by John Henry Newman, followed Newman into the Roman Catholic Church. Father Wadhams became the first rector of our Cathedral and the founding bishop of the Diocese of Ogdensburg; and Father Walworth, the pastor of historic St. Mary's.

• They fostered the career of Isaac Hecker, the founder of the Paulist Community, and built upon the groundwork for the positive ecumenical climate that exists in this part of the Lord's vineyard, laid initially by

• Domine Johannes Megapolensis, the pastor of the Dutch Reformed Church in Albany, who harbored Isaac Jogues from his Iroquois tormentors and secured for him safe passage back to France.

• Then there were Peter Cagger, the prominent Catholic layman who was instrumental in the establishment of St. Peter's Hospital, which bears his name, as well as in assisting Bishop Francis McNeirny, the third Bishop of Albany, to complete the construction of our magnificent Cathedral Church in 1892;

• Leandre Alexandre du Mouchel, the great Cathedral organist, whose musical compositions and choral work earned him a world-renowned reputation;

• Lucy Eaton Smith, of Glens Falls, a convert to Catholicism, who became the foundress of the Dominican Sisters of the American Congregation of St. Catherine de Ricci, promoting the retreat movement for the laity within our Diocese and beyond; and

• Margaret Brady Farrell and the members of the Brady/Farrell family, whose largesse was responsible for the development of the Brady Maternity Hospital, St. Catherine's Infant Home, the Grotto at St. Vincent's in Albany, and the Mercy Mother House Chapel, as well as for donating the land that would eventually be used for the new St. Peter's Hospital, Maria College, Mater Christi Seminary, the Dominican Monastery, and the Holy Cross Novitiate and Retreat House in Valatie.

• There were also Martin Glynn of Schenectady, who became the first Catholic governor of New York State and a leading advocate for workers' rights, and

• the Happy Warrior, Governor Al Smith, who along with his family, became such an integral part of the Cathedral parish and the first Roman Catholic to run for the office of President of our United States.

Nor must we forget our native sons and daughters who first heard the Good News proclaimed in the churches, schools and catechetical programs of our Diocese and then went to serve God's people in other parts of the Lord's vineyard. For example, we honor people like:

• Bishop Patrick Ludden, the first Bishop of Syracuse;

• Bishop Henry Gabriels, who succeeded Bishop Edgar Wadhams as the second Bishop of Ogdensburg;

• Bishop William John Kenny of Delhi, third Bishop of Saint Augustine;

- Bishop Bernard Mahoney of Rensselaer, Bishop of Sioux Falls, South Dakota;

- missionary bishops like William Ambrose Jones, of Cambridge in Washington County, who as an Augustinian priest became the second North American Bishop of San Juan, Puerto Rico; the Franciscan Bishops Elias James Manning of Troy, now serving in Valenca, Brazil, and Bishop Capistran Heim of Catskill, now serving in Itaituba, Brazil;

- Archbishop Harry Flynn of Minneapolis-St Paul and Bishop John Nolan of the Military Ordinariate, who regret they cannot be with us today;

- Archbishop Joseph Ryan, the first Archbishop of Anchorage, and Bishop Matthew Clark of Rochester, who honor us with their presence today.

Many other native sons and daughters of our Diocese have brought the Good News to other parts of the vineyard. Some have gone to Maryknoll and from thence to distant places. Many others have exercised their ministries as members of religious congregations of women and of men in missions that they serve abroad. Numerous laypersons have served the mission of Jesus in dedicated ministry in other countries. It is appropriate to remember also the many other laypersons who laid down their lives on foreign battlefields in defense of our freedom. We honor and celebrate them all today.

In addition to the dynamic personalities and movements of people who helped shape this local Church, our Diocese has endured all the isms of the past century-and-a-half: lay trusteeism, know nothingism, nativism, modernism, Americanism, pietism, anti-Semitism and the threat of Fascism, Communism and McCarthyism. As a faith community, we have dealt for better or worse with the Abolitionist Movement, the Labor Movement, the Civil Rights Movement, and the Peace Movement. We've wrestled with and continue to refine our position on the role of religion in society, the place of the Catholic school in a pluralistic democracy and the mission of the laity to be about the transformation of society.

And so for all these splendid facets of our diocesan history and tradition, which I have touched upon, and so many more that could be cited, we give thanks today and hopefully will continue to be inspired by this glorious faith heritage we have been bequeathed.

However, as our sesquicentennial theme suggests, we must not only honor tradition but discover tomorrow. Please God, then, our year-long jubilee observance will not only enable us to reflect with pride on the sterling accomplishments of the past, but also serve to re-energize us to meet the challenges of the present and to prepare us to address the still uncharted spiritual and pastoral opportunities of the third millennium of Christianity.

The words set forth by Bishop John McCloskey in his inaugural homily delivered to the faithful assembled in 1847, which we heard earlier in the service, still remain most appropriate today: "Fortunately for us, the foundations have already been laid....Yet we are called

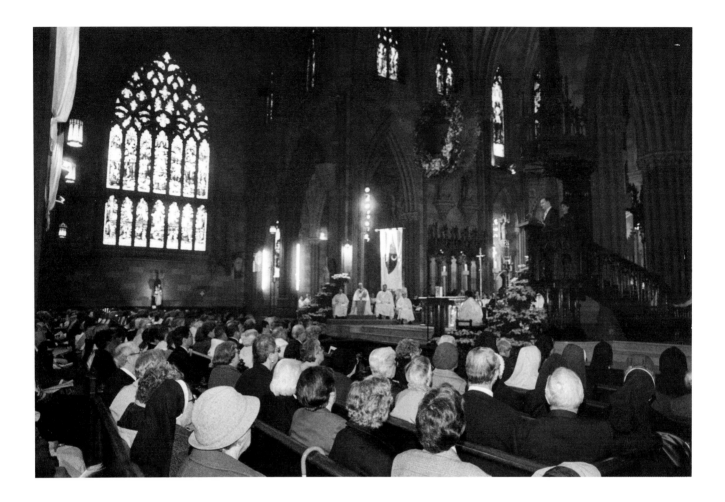

upon not only to continue the work but to enlarge and increase it; to lay new foundations broader and deeper, to erect a structure more spacious and more enduring that the stranger and the wayfarer may enter in and find rest."

And what is the mission that lies ahead and rests upon what has gone before? It is captured beautifully and succinctly in that prophetic vision of Isaiah, which Jesus cites in today's Gospel passage to describe for his hearers his own mission (Luke-4 16:20), namely, "To bring glad tidings to the poor,...to proclaim liberty to captives and recovery of sight to the blind, to let the oppressed go free, and to proclaim a year acceptable to the Lord."

And this, my friends, is still our mission both now and for the future. The mission to show a preferential option for the poor by our service and advocacy, the mission to heal those who are spiritually blind through our programs of lifelong faith formation; the mission to free those who are oppressed by the materialism, consumerism, ageism, sexism, racism and narrow parochialism and regionalism of our day by refreshing and enlivening them with the living word of God and the liturgical and sacramental life of our Church; and the mission to proclaim liberty to those captivated by political correctness and the fickle and fleeting fads and fashions of the moment, by nourishing them with the time-proven and time-tested spiritual tradition of our ancestors in the faith.

More specifically, we must address those six major needs surfaced in our recent pastoral planning process:

1. The need to develop more collaborative models of ministry that enable the laity, in particular, to take their full and rightful place in the life of the Church by providing the formal and informal educational and formational programs that will assist them to recognize, to develop and, then, to utilize their God-given gifts and talents for the service of the Church and our wider society;

2. The need to foster and promote youth ministry so as to involve our young more dynamically in the life of the Church, and to pave the way for them to be active and effective Church leaders in the 21st century;

3. The need to be more innovative and creative in adult education and formation especially using modern means of communications like VCRs, cable programming and the Internet, as well as to offer more experiential forms of learning such as the small faith-sharing groups that the RCIA and the RENEW process provide;

4. The need for evangelization to reconnect with the large number of our fellow Catholics who are alienated from the Church and the rising tide of our fellow Americans totally unchurched, as well as to serve the needs of the growing Hispanic, Black, Vietnamese and Korean communities within our midst;

5. The need, in light of the declining number of ordained priests, to ensure that the Eucharist remains the center and focus of the life of Catholic Christians; and

6. The need to help our people grasp and digest our Church's social teaching about the sacred dignity of the human person, the sanctity of human life, the solidarity that exists among all the members of the human family and the responsibility to promote the common good as we struggle to relate this teaching to the issues of the economy, the environment, welfare and healthcare reform, euthanasia and physician-assisted suicide, abortion, the arms trade and the growing gap between the haves and have nots, both at home and abroad.

Hopefully, the sharing of the stories of our ancestors during this Sesquicentennial observance will remind us powerfully that many of them were the poor and vulnerable of their day who suffered great discrimination, intolerance and injustice, and thus move us to a greater sensitivity to the plight of the poor and immigrants of our day who, unfortunately, are often being made the scapegoats for our current socio-economic woes. And for the clarity of our witness and the effectiveness of our advocacy and service, more and more we must do so on an ecumenical and interfaith basis as the welcome presence of representatives of other faith traditions at our celebration today reminds us so visibly and tangibly.

And it is my hope and prayer that as we refocus on our mission as a Diocese during this Sesquicentennial observance, it will lead us to renew and deepen our relationship with Jesus; to make Him and His plan of life the centerpiece of our lives, and to recommit ourselves to live as His faithful disciples during our sojourn here on earth. For if a deeper bonding with Jesus is not the end result of our anniversary observance, then all of our festivities — successful as they may be from an educational, social, cultural and fiscal point of view — will be as the proverbial sounding brass and tinkling cymbals.

In a moment, it will be my privilege to make the formal proclamation of our Sesquicentennial observance as a year of jubilee. Our reading from the Book of Leviticus today reminds us that during the jubilee year, we must stand in fear before the Lord: not fear in the sense of foreboding, but fear in the sense of awe and wonder at the majesty of God leading to a conversion of heart, that enables us to attune our way of life to God's way of life.

Historically, one of the characteristics of a jubilee year is that of forgiveness of debt so that we might begin the next phase of our journey with a clean slate. In that tradition, then, today I hereby announce a forthcoming plan to forgive the indebtedness for assessments and insurance accrued by our parishes, schools and institutions within the Diocese, which our Chancellor for Finance Jay Feeney informs me amounts to over 3.4 million dollars.

I hope that this gesture on the part of diocesan administration will spur a similar response of healing, forgiveness and reconciliation throughout our Diocese, especially manifest in our care and concern for the poor and vulnerable, and prepare us well to move toward our 200th anniversary and into the new millennium as a people of faith and service; a people sustained by the intercession of Mary our diocesan patroness; a people inspired by the sterling accomplishments of our ancestors in the faith, both those mentioned here this afternoon and all those countless unsung heroes and heroines who have brought us to this happy day; and a people imbued with the spirit of Jesus, symbolized by the Sesquicentennial candle, which we are about to light and whose flame will be transported to each parish of our Diocese to be kept burning brightly throughout our year-long anniversary celebration.

Through our Sesquicentennial observance, then, may we continue to grow in our unity with one another and with Jesus, our light, our life and our salvation so that we can fulfill our diocesan vision statement: "To live as God's priestly people, sharing the responsibility to witness to God's unconditional love and to bring Christ's healing presence to our world."

Opening ceremony photos by Dave Oxford (pages 232, 233, 234, 239, 241 and 245); and Michael P. Farrell (page 236)

Selected Readings

The following four readings were presented during the opening ceremony of the Diocesan Sesquicentennial Celebration at the Cathedral of the Immaculate Conception in Albany on December 8, 1996.

I. From the spiritual diaries by Saint John de Brebeuf, priest and martyr:

Jesus, my Lord and Savior, what can I give you in return for all the favors you have first conferred on me? I will take from your hand the cup of your sufferings and call on your name...my beloved Jesus, and because of the surging joy which moves me, here and now I offer my blood and body and life. May I die only for you, if you will grant me this grace, since you willingly died for me. Let me so live that you may grant me the gift of such a happy death. In this way, my God and Savior, I will take from your hand the cup of your sufferings and call on your name: Jesus, Jesus, Jesus!

My God, it grieves me greatly that you are not known, that in this savage wilderness all have not been converted to you, that sin has not been driven from it. My God, even if all the brutal torture which prisoners in this region must endure should fall on me, I offer myself most willingly to them...

II. From a narrative sent to the Jesuit superior by Saint Isaac Jogues, priest and martyr:

We, Rene Goupil and I, had the consolation en route of being together, and so I was witness to his many virtues.

On the way, Rene was always caught up in God. His words and various conversations reflected submission to the will of divine Providence and a ready acceptance of the death God would send.

After our capture and while we were en route to Mohawk country,...badly wounded though he was, he cared for other wounded both the enemy who had been hurt in the fight and his fellow prisoners.

His humility and the obedience he yielded to his captors confounded me. The Iroquois who were conducting both of us in the same canoe bade me take up a paddle and ply it. I simply refused, being haughty and proud even in the face of death. A little later, they asked Rene the same thing, and he, without demur, began paddling, and, since these Indians because of his example tried to pressure me to do the same, he, noticing this, begged my pardon.

During the trip I raised with him several times the possibility of his escape. The freedom we were allowed presented more than one occasion. However, he never accepted the offer, prefer-

ring to leave everything to the will of our Lord who did not at all suggest that he flee.

It was on the 29th day of September, the feast of Saint Michael, that this angel of innocence gave his life for Jesus Christ who had given him His life.

III. From the official document of Pius IX, Pope:

In spite of Our limited qualifications, having been elevated to the supreme pinnacle of the apostolate, it devolves upon Us to establish, where circumstances render it advisable, new Episcopal Sees, that, by augmenting the number of Shepherds the flock of the Lord may be ably and readily attended and safeguarded.

Since, therefore, the Archbishop of Baltimore and the Bishops of the United States of North America assembled in the Sixth Provincial Council held during the month of May of the year 1846, were convinced that the growth of the Catholic Church will be greatly promoted by the establishment of two new Episcopal Sees and Dioceses in the extensive territory of New York State, distinct from the See of New York, one of which should be centered in the City called Albany, and whereas they have sent Us a formal petition concerning this proposal; Now We, with the advice of our Venerable Brothers, those Cardinals of the Holy Roman Church, charged with the duty of the Propagation of the Faith, have determined to proceed with the establishment of this new Episcopal See.

Wherefore, with the consent of Our Venerable Brother, John Hughes, Bishop of New York, having maturely weighted all the circumstances, acting on Our own initiative, with complete understanding, and with the fullness of Our apostolic power, We hereby found and establish a new Episcopal See in the aforementioned City of Albany and define as its diocesan boundaries those already suggested by the Council of Baltimore, namely, the northern and eastern boundaries of the new Diocese of Albany shall be identical with the northern and eastern boundaries of the State of New York; its southern boundary shall be the forty-second parallel of the north latitude; it shall extend westward to the eastern boundaries of the Counties of Cayuga, Tompkins and Tioga.

Accordingly, We hereby withdraw all of the above delineated territory from the jurisdiction of the Bishop of New York and constitute it a proper Bishopric in its own right. We furthermore confer upon the Bishop destined to rule this new See of Albany each and every power and privilege with which Bishops generally are endowed either by the law or the Church or by legitimate custom.

Thus We ordain and command, willing this present legislation to supersede any and all previous apostolic pronouncements and enactments, whatsoever their tenor or mode of promulgation.

Given at Rome, from the Basilica of Saint Mary Major, under the ring of the Fisherman, this 23rd day of April, in the year of our Lord 1847, the first year of our Pontificate.

IV. From the inaugural homily of John McCloskey, first Bishop of Albany:

The future history of the Diocese of Albany, as such commences with you and me. Whether it shall be a history to relate its blessing or relate its curse, depends upon us. According to the foundations which we lay, will be strength or weakness, the comeliness and unsightliness of the edifice, reared upon them. According as the seed is first carefully planted, and the soil well tilled and watered, will it grow up in fresh and healthy vigor, and the vigor of its maturity, its fitness for bearing fruit, will be in proportion to the early care bestowed on it. Fortunately for us, foundations have already been laid and the edifice is advancing, the soil is already tilled, the seed planted and the tree is producing

IN SPEM VITAE AETERNAE

fruit. Yet we are called upon not only to continue the work, but to enlarge and increase it; to lay new foundations broader and deeper, to erect a structure more spacious and more enduring, that the stranger and the wayfarer may enter in and find rest, to plant seed for a larger growth, that the tree's branches may spread out far and near, that you and your children, and your children's, may sit down beneath its ample shade, and partake abundantly of its refreshing fruits.

This is our task. Let us enter in on it with trust in God. 'Unless the Lord build the house, they labor in vain that build it.' It is ours to plant and to water, but it is His prerogative to give the increase.

V. From the homily of Rev. James Kelly on the occasion of the Centennial of the Diocese:

The Albany Diocese of a hundred years ago, was, of course, vastly different in contour and aspect from the diocese of today. Half the State of New York, twenty-five thousand square miles of untracked and mountainous territory; all of the Adirondacks, most of the Catskills, and the rolling hills that form the outworks of the Berkshires; all in their almost primeval silence and aloofness. The population outside of the Episcopal City of Albany, was thinly scattered over the vast region, with no means of travel inland but by foot or horse. Its cure was a stupendous undertaking for any bishop.

John McCloskey, our first Bishop, was such a soul. Into the most difficult recesses of the mountains, up and down the Hudson and Mohawk, from the Canadian border to the Pennsylvania line, from Massachusetts to the shores of Ontario, the priests journeyed in periodic and tireless visitations, establishing everywhere, like Saint Paul in Asia Minor, the nuclei of Catholic congregations. There are today in all those parts parishes that trace an unbroken history back to the beginning laid down by those men.

In twenty-five years after its founding Albany was able to turn over ten thousand square miles of its northern territory, fully organized into parishes and missions, to the new bishopric of Ogdensburg; and fourteen years later, five thousand square miles of its western territory, likewise fully organized, to the new bishopric of Syracuse. And today, Albany and its offerings, Ogdensburg and Syracuse, with all their multiple works of religion, stand debtors to the groundwork, to the toil and sweat of those pioneers.

But their story is not all told when we have scanned the physical difficulties of the terrain they cultivated. They had with it all a cross to carry that was exceedingly heavy. All the old bigotries of northern Europe were carried to these shores by the earliest immigrants. Laws against Catholics were part of the early legislation of every State in this young Union. They were excluded from public office, they were taxed to support non-Catholic worship, and when the influx of immigrants took a Catholic turn, they became the victims of violence and open persecution. Albany was made a diocese when all this un-Christian furor was at its whitest heat; and Albany suffered with the rest.

Albany has a note of majesty to which every other diocese must yield precedence; it is the majesty of sainthood and martyrdom within its borders. The very soil of this diocese has been wet with the blood of Christian martyrs; Jogues, la Lande, Goupil. Up and down our lakes and rivers, in and out of our hills and valleys, they carried the first Catholic Credo heard in this vast primeval region — until God accepted the bloody consummation of their service on the banks of our own Mohawk.

It will be recalled that Albany, in its hundred years, has been ruled by six Bishops. There was McCloskey, the organizer and scholar of repute; there was Conroy, the bull-dog, who by his tenacious and aggressive Catholicism pulled his people out of the bog of an inferiority complex and set them on their way to self-respect; there was McNeirny, the courtly, the administrator; there was Burke, who to the day of his death remained the parish priest; there was Cusack, cut down untimely, but vigorous and full of promise; there is our present Bishop (Gibbons), the embodiment of the highest expression of the priestly life.

And the future? That no man knoweth save God alone. But, under God, the future may often be seen partially reflected in a view of the past.

Previous page: Bishop McCloskey's coat of arms with his motto: "In Hope Of Eternal Life."

Bibliography

Amsterdam Daily Democrat.

Albany City Directory 1756-1763. ms. Compilation of several ms., primarily *The Loudon Survey of 1756.*

"Albany Affairs," *New York Freeman's Journal,* 1/12/1856.

"The Albany Cathedral," *Catholic Mirror.* 2/7/1891.

Alexander, Robert S. *Albany's First Church and It's [sic] Role in the Growth of the City.* Delmar, NY: Newsgraphics Printers, 1988.

Alexander, Robert S. Interviews, 1994-1996.

Allen,Vernell. Interview, 4/27/95.

Anderson, Robert. Interview re origins of Troy, NY, 1/23/96.

Andreoli, Sister Mary of St. Victoria. "Good Shepherd, Sisters of Our Lady of Charity of the," *New Catholic Encyclopedia.* 6. New York: McGraw Hill Book Company, 1967.

"Anthony, Susan B(rownell)," *The New Encyclopaedia Britannica.* 1. 15th ed. Chicago: Encyclopaedia Inc., 1992.

Apel, Willi. *Harvard Dictionary of Music.* Cambridge, MA: Harvard University Press, 1958.

"Archbishop Ryan retires," *The Evangelist,* 5/16/91.

"Arendt Van Curler, Founder of Schenectady." *Address Delivered at the Erection of a Commemorative Tablet by The Netherlands Society and the Schenectady County Historical Society, September 29, 1909.*

Bailey, Dorothy J. Interviews, 3/15/96, 4/4/96.

Barford, Burns. Interview, 12/16/95.

Barron, William Stanton. "Church, History of, III (Early Modern: 1500-1789)," 3. *New Catholic Encyclopedia.* New York: McGraw Hill Book Company, 1967.

Bayley, Rev. J.R. *A Brief Sketch of the Early History of The Catholic Church on the Island of New York.* 2d ed., rev. and enl. Rep[rinted] from the 1870 edition. New York: United States Catholic Historical Society, 1973.

Becker, Martin Joseph. *A History of Catholic Life in the Diocese of Albany, 1609-1864.* Yonkers, NY: United States Catholic Historical Society, 1975.

Benintende, Rev. Joseph A. Interview, 7/18/95.

Berberian, Rev. David. Consultations, 11/96.

Bielinski, Stefan. Various interviews, Winter, 1996.

"Boston at the Century's End," *New England, A Collection From Harper's Magazine.* New York: W.H. Smith Publishers, Inc., 1990.

Bowers, Virginia B. *"The Texture of a Neighborhood."* Albany, NY: South End Historical Society, 1991.

Branson, Sister Serena, DC. Interviews, 5/2 & 7/11/95.

Brigham, Clarence S. *History and Bibliography of American Newspapers, 1690-1820.* 1. Worcester, MA: American Antiquarian Society, 1947.

Broderick, Bishop Edwin. Interview, 4/6/95.

Broderick, Robert C. *The Catholic Encyclopedia.* Nashville, TN: Thomas Nelson Inc., Publishers, 1976.

Broderick, John Francis, SJ, "Church, History of, III (Early Modern: 1500-1789), *New Catholic Encyclopedia.* 3. New York: McGraw Hill Book Company, 1967.

Broyles, Bro. B. Paul, FSC. *Brothers and Friends.* Albany, NY: CBA, 1990.

Broyles, Bro. B. Paul, FSC. *A Journey in History in Time.* Albany, NY: La Salle School, 1987.

Brunner, Sister Nola, CSJ. Interview, 1/12/95.

Bryson, Bill. *Made in America.* New York: William Morrow and Co., Inc., 1994.

Buckley, Sister Mary J., RSM. Interview, 4/20/95.

Bunson, Margaret R. *Kateri Tekakwitha, Mystic of the Wilderness.* Huntington, IN: Our Sunday Visitor Publishing Division, 1992.

Carroll, Eamon Richard, O.Carm. "Mariology," *New Catholic Encyclopedia.* 9. New York: McGraw Hill Book Company, 1967.

Carmody, Denise Lardner and Tully, John. *Roman Catholicism, An Introduction.* New York: Macmillan Publishing Company, 1990.

Casey, Daniel J. and Larkin, F. Daniel. "From Dromore to the Middle Sprite: Irish Rural Settlement in the Mohawk Valley," *Clogher Record 1986.* (12:2).

"The Cathedral," *The Evening Union.* 6/18/1891.

Casey, Jack. *The Trial of Bat Shea.* Troy, NY: Diamond Rock Publishing Company, 1994.

Cathedral, Albany, New York, 1852-1952. Albany, NY: Roman Catholic Diocese of Albany, 1952.

"Cathedral Extension," *The Evening Union.* 3/13/1891.

The Catholic Almanac for 1848. Baltimore, MD: F. Lucas, Jr., 1848.

Catholic Charities, Roman Catholic Diocese of Albany. "Directory of Human Services." 1995.

Catholic Mirror. 7/31/1886.

The Catholic Weekly. 1/31/1891.

A Centennial Remembrance, Church of Saint Patrick, Watervliet, New York 1840-1990. [n.p.] [n.d.]

Centennial Souvenir of St. Mary's Church, Hudson, New York, 1848-1948.

Certificate of Incorporation of St. Colman's Industrial School and Orphan Asylum of Watervliet. 7/22/1884.

Champlain, Samuel de. *The Voyages and Explorations of Samuel de Champlain.* Edward Gaylord Bourne, Trans. New York: A.S. Barnes & Co., 1906.

Charles, John Patrick and Lewis, Richard J. "'Red Menace in Albany,' Catholic May Day Fete at Capitol Upset Red Plans," *Times-Union.* May 1950.

Chauvin, Sister Mary John of Carmel, SSA, "Sisters, of St. Anne," *New Catholic Encyclopedia.* 12. New York: McGraw Hill Book Company, 1967.

Christoph, Florence. *Upstate New York in the 1760s. Tax Lists and Selected Militia Rolls of Old Albany County 1760-1768.* Camden, ME: Picton Press, 1992.

Christoph, Peter R. "The Time and Place of Jan van Loon: A Roman Catholic in Colonial Albany: Part I," *de Halve* Maen 60 (2).

Christoph, Peter R. "The Time and Place of Jan van Loon: A Roman Catholic in Colonial Albany: Part II," *de Halve* Maen 60.

Church of St. Adalbert, 1903-1978. Crane Street Hill, 550 Lansing Street, Schenectady, New York 12303. Hudson, NY: Park Publishing Company, [n.d.]

"Church Repairs," *Albany Times.* 3/30/1891.

Clark, Bishop Matthew J. Interview, 12/94.

Cobb, Sanford H. *The Story of the Palatines, An Episode in Colonial History.* Reprint: Bowie, MD, Heritage Books, Inc. 1988. [New York: G. Putnam's Sons, 1897.]

Cohalan, Rev. Msgr. Florence D. "John McCloskey: America's First Cardinal," *The Catholic News.* Part One, March 6, 1975; Part Two, March 13, 1975.

Cohalan, Rev. Msgr. Florence D. *A Popular History of the Archdiocese of New York.* Yonkers, NY: United States Catholic Historical Society, 1983.

Collections of the New-York Historical Society for the Year 1891. Muster Rolls of New York Provincial Troops. 1755-1764.

New York: New-York Historical Society, 1892.

Collections on the History of Albany from its Discovery to the Present Time. 1. Albany, NY: J. Munsell, 1865. [2, 1867; 3, 1870; 4, 1871]

Collins, Denis B. Letter to Bishop Thomas M.A. Burke, 5/30/1892.

"Colonial New England," *New England, A Collection From Harper's Magazine.* New York: W.H. Smith, Publishers, Inc., 1990.

"Completing the Cathedral," *The Argus.* 3/31/1891.

Connell, Nancy. "Famed Sch'dy church goes back a long way," *Times-Union.* 5/21/1978.

Conway, Rev. Joseph P. Interviews, 12/13/94 & 2/28/95.

Coon, Lewis. Letter to parents. October 27, 1856. File No. 1-57. Cooperstown, Library, New York State Historical Association.

"Contract for the Cathedral." *The Argus.* 6/19/1891.

Cooney, Rev. Romaeus, O.Carm, Interview. 1995.

Cooper, J.C. *An Illustrated Encyclopaedia of Traditional Symbols.* London: Thames and Hudson, Ltd., 1978.

Corrigan, Archbishop Michael Augustine. Letter to Bishop McNeirny, 1/30/1886.

Corwin, Edward Tanjore, ed. *Ecclesiastical Records, State of New York.* 2, 3, 7. Albany, NY: 2: James B. Lyon, State Printer, 1901; 3: J.B. Lyon Company, State Printers, 1902; 7: The University of the State of New York, 1916.

Costello, Michael, Interview, 2/14/96.

Craib, Stephanie (Hicks) and Craib, Roderick Hull. *Our Yesterdays, A History of Rensselaer County.* ms. [n.p.]: Roderick Hull Craib, 1948.

Crewell, Patricia. Interview re Eastern Rites, 10/18/96.

Crews, Clyde F. *American and Catholic, A Popular History of Catholicism in the United States.* Cincinnati, OH: St. Anthony Messenger Press, 1994.

Croteau, Hank. Interview and consultation, 1995.

Cunningham, Ruth, RSCJ. *Life Through 125 Years, 1852-1978.* Albany, NY: Society of the Sacred Heart, 1978.

Curran, Francis X. *Ossernenon Mohawk Castle 1642-1660. Martyrs' Shrine 1885-1985.* Auriesville, NY: National Shrine of the North American Martyrs, 1985.

Day, Edmond 1. Letters re ethnic rivalry, 1/18/1996 & 1/27/1996.

Delello, Martha. Interview, 1995.

de Lourdes, Mother M. Bernadette, O.Carm. *Women of Faith Mother M. Angelilne Teresa, O. Carm.* Germantown, NY, 1984.

de Ricci, Sister Maria, OP. Letter to Bishop McNeirny, 1/27/1893.

de Sales, Sister Mary, RGS. Letter to Bishop McNeirny, 8/15/1884.

de Tocqueville, Alexis. *Democracy in America.* ed. J.P. Mayer. Trans. George Lawrence. Garden City, NY: Doubleday & Company, Inc., 1969.

"Decade of Bishop's Episcopate. Vast Accomplishments," *The Evangelist,* 11/12/64.

Decker, Lewis G., "Catholic Immigrants from Scotland May Have Shared Church in 1773-74," *The Leader-Herald.* 20:12.

Decker, Lewis G., "First Catholic Priest, Flock in Tryon Safe Under Sir William's Influence," *The Leader-Herald.* 21:247.

Decker, Lewis G., "Scottish Immigrants, in 1774, Find Friend, Benefactor in Person of Sir William Johnson," *The Leader-Herald.* 20:44.

Decker, Lewis G., "600 Scots, Irish Emigrate to U.S., Headed for Sir William Johnson Land," *The Leader-Herald.* 19:307.

Decker, Lewis G., "200th Anniversary of County's First Catholic Congregation, Priest Is Noted," *The Leader-Herald.* 19:284.

Delaney, Joseph A. Letter to Rev., J. F. Mullaney, Syracuse, N.Y., 11/4/1911.

Dewey, Melvil. Letter to Bishop McNeirny, 5/4/1893.

DiGiovanni, Stephen Michael. *Archbishop Corrigan and the Italian Immigrants.* Huntington, IN: Our Sunday Visitor Publishing Division, 1994.

Diller, George, Bishop of Limerick. Letter to Bishop McNeirny, 3/10/1880.

Dillon, Rev. John J. *The Historic Story of St. Mary's, Albany, N.Y. First-Second-Third Church.* New York: P.J. Kenedy & Sons, 1933.

The Diocese of Albany—Erected April 23, 1847. ms. n.p., 1909.

Dolan, Jay P. *The American Catholic Experience.* Garden City, NY: Image Books, 1985.

Dolan, Louise. Interview, 1995.

Dollen, Msgr. Charles. "Catholic joy topic of study," *The Evangelist,* 5/2/96.

Doman, Sister Mary Tullia. "Felician Sisters (CSSF)," *New Catholic Encyclopedia.* 6. New York: McGraw Hill Company.

Downs, Rev. Richard J. Interviews, 1996.

Doyle, Rev. Kenneth J. Interview, 4/4/95.

Drown, Mary. Interview re Italians, 8/27/96.

Dugan, Rev. Edwin A. "Bishops of See Add Glory to Epoch," *The Evangelist Centennial Edition,* 5/16/47.

Duggan, Patrick, Bishop of Clonfert. Letter to Bishop McNeirny, 3/10/1880.

Dunigan's American Catholic Almanac and List of the Clergy, for the Year of Our Lord 1858, the 83rd of the Independence of the United States. New York: Edward Dunigan & Brother, James B. Kirker, 1858.

Dunn, Shirley W. *The Mohicans and Their Land 1609-1730.* Fleischmanns, NY: Purple Mountain Press, 1994.

"The Dutch Influence in New England," *New England, A Collection From Harper's Magazine.* New York: W. H. Smith Publishers, Inc., 1990.

Eagan, Arthur. Interview, 10/25/95.

"The English in New England," *New England, A Collection From Harper's Magazine.* New York: W.H. Smith Publishers, Inc., 1990.

Eustace, Sister Frances Regis, CSJ. Interview, 1995.

Exercises in Commemoration of the Seventy-Fifth Anniversary of the Hunter Presbyterian Church, Held at Hunter, N.Y., February 13th and 14th, 1897. Albany, NY: Brandow Printing Company, 1897.

Farley, John Cardinal Murphy. *History of St. Patrick's Cathedral.* New York: Society for the Propagation of the Faith. 1908.

Farley, John Cardinal Murphy. *The Life of John Cardinal McCloskey, First Prince of the Church in America, 1810-1885.* New York: Longmans, Green and Co., 1918.

Farano, Rev. Michael A. Interview, 12/27/94.

Ferguson, George. *Signs & Symbols in Christian Art.* New York: Oxford University Press, 1955.

"First Flag Over a Catholic Church," *Catholic American Historical Notes. The American Catholic Historical Researches.* 5, 4. October, 1901.

Fitzsimmons, Sister Susan, O.Carm. Interview, 1995.

Flannery, Austin, OP. *Vatican Concil II, The Conciliar and Post Conciliar Documents.* Northport, NY: Costello Publishing Company, 1975.

Flexner, James Thomas. *Mohawk Baronet: Sir William Johnson of New York.* New York: Harper & Brothers, Publishers, 1959.

Flick, Alexander C. *The Papers of Sir William Johnson.* 4. Albany, NY: The University of the State of New York, 1925.

Flynn, Archbishop Harry Joseph. Interview, 5/6/95.

Fogarty, Rev. Gerald P., SJ. "The American Catholic Tradition of Dialogue," *America.* October 26, 1996.

Foy, Felician A., OFM, editor and Avato, Rose M., assoc. editor. *1994 Catholic Almanac.* Huntington, IN: Our Sunday Visitor, Inc. 1994.

Frazier, Patrick, *The Mohicans of Stockridge.* Lincoln, NB: University of Nebraska Press, 1992.

"French Canadians in New England," *New England, A Collection From Harper's Magazine.* New York: W. H. Smith Publishers, Inc., 1990.

Fry, J. *Albany Directory.* Albany, NY: Websters and Skinners, 1813.

Fry, J. *Albany Directory.* Albany, NY: H.C. Southwick, and Packard & Van Benthuysen, 1814.

Gabriel, Bro. Angelus, FSC. *The Christian Brothers in the United States 1848-1948.* New York: The Declan X. McMullen Co., Inc., 1948.

Gabriels, Henry, Bishop of Ogdensburg. *Historical Sketch of St. Joseph's Provincial Seminary, Troy, N.Y.* New York: United States Catholic Historical Society, 1905.

Gallo, Sister Adolfo, CSJB. "St. John the Baptist, Sisters of" *New Catholic Encyclopedia.* 12. New York: McGraw Hill Book Company, 1967.

Garnett, Edna Bailey. *West Stockbridge, Massachusetts, 1774-1974.* Great Barrington, MA: The Berkshire Courier, 1974.

Gibbons, Bishop Edmund F. Letter to Msgr. John L. Reilly, December 11, 1919.

Gilchrist, Rev. Francis J. Interview, 3/16/95.

Girzone, Rev. Joseph F. Interview, 2/13/96.

Gilmore, Jon P. Letter to Rev. J. Collins, 6/6/1881.

Glavin, Msgr. Edward R. Interviews, 1/7/95 & 3/28/95.

Grassi, Giovanni Antonio. *Notizie varie sullo stato presente della repubblica degli Stati uniti dell'America Settentrionale, scritte al principio del 1818.* Rome: Presso L.P. Selvionio, 1818.

Griffin, Martin I.J., ed. *The American Catholic Historical Researches.* 7. Philadelphia, PA: Martin I.J. Griffin, 1890, Vol. 8:4. Vol. 9:1, 1892. Vol. 13:4, 1896. Vol. 17:4, 1900. Vol. 18:1, 1901. Vol. 20:4, 1903. New series: Vol. 2:4, 1906; Vol. 3:3, 1907; Vol. 5:4, 1909.

Griffin, Martin I.J., ed. *Documents Relating to the History of the Catholic Church in the United States.* 1. Philadelphia, PA: Martin I.J. Griffin, [n.d.] Same as Vol. 5 of *The American Catholic Historical Researches.* Vol. 2, [n.d.]

Gruber, Sebastian Bartholomew. Letter to Bishop McCloskey, May 31, 1849.

Halpin, Sister Margery. Interviews, 1996.

Halsey, Francis Whiting. *The Old New York Frontier; Its Wars With Indians and Tories, Its Missionary Schools, Pioneers and Land Titles, 1614-1800.* New York: Charles Scribner's Sons, 1901.

Hannefin, Sister Daniel, DC. *Daughters of the Church: A Popular History of the Daughters of Charity in the United States 1809-1987.* Brooklyn, NY: New City Press, 1989.

Hans, Janet. Interview, 1995.

Hans, Mary B. "History of the Infant Home of Albany," *An Evaluation of the Program of the Maternity Hospital and Infant Home of Albany, Albany, New York, August, 1950.* ms. Saint Louis, MO: Saint Louis University, 1951.

Harcourt, Felice, ed. & trans. *Memoirs of Madame de La Tour de Pin.* New York: The McCall Publishing Co., 1971.

Hart, Msgr. James G. Inverview, 1/31/95.

Hart, Simon Hart and Hart-Runeman, Sibrandina Geertruid. *The Albany Protocol, Wilhelm Christoph Berkenmeyer's Chronicle Of Lutheran Affairs in New York Colony, 1731-1750.* Ann Arbor, MI: John P. Dern, 1971.

Hastings, Helen Prescott. *A Little History of New York's North Country.* Syracuse, NY: Advanced Color Techologies, 1995.

Hauley, Barbara. "Lizzi biography brings Glynn's life to the light," *Courier.* 170. 24. 11/10/94.

Hauprich, Audrey Bopp. Letter, 1/26/95.

Havermans, Rev. Peter. Letter to Bishop McNeirny, 1/30/1885.

Havermans, Rev. Peter. Letter to Bishop McNeirny, 2/7/1885.

Havermans, Rev. Peter. Letter to Bishop McNeirny, 2/28/1886.

Hayner, Rutherford. *Troy and Rensselaer County, New York. A History.* New York: Lewis Historical Publishing Co., Inc., 1925.

Hays, Diana. Interview, 5/24/96.

Heads of Families, New York. Baltimore, MD: Genealogical Publishing Co., 1966.

Hedrick, Ulysses Prentiss. *A History of Agriculture in the State of New York.* Orig. Pub. 1933. New York: Hill and Wang, 1966.

Heim, Bishop Capistrano F. OFM. Interview, 6/27/96.

Hennepin, Rev. Louis. *A New Discover of a Vast Country in America.* Reuben Gold Thwaites, ed. 2 vol. Chicago: A.C. McClurg & Co., 1903.

Hewig, Kay. Interview, 1995.

Higgins, A., Bishop of Killarney. Letter to Bishop McNeirny. n.d. [prob. 1880]

Higgins, William, Bishop of Newark. Letter to Bishop McNeirny, 1/14/1886.

The Historical Records Survey, Service Division, Work Projects Administration. *Guide to Vital Statistics Records of Churches in New York State (Exclusive of New York City).* I. Albany, NY Works Projects Administration, 1942.

History of Greene County, New York. New York: J.B. Beers & Co., 1884.

History of St. Ann's Parish, 1866-1966.

History of St. John the Baptist Church, Schenectady, N.Y. ms [n.d.]

History of St. Joseph's Church, Albany, New York, 1856-1981.

"History of St. Peter's Hospital, Part One: Beginnings" *Mercycare Corporation Magazine.* Spring/Summer 1994.

History of St. Peter's Hospital, Part Two: Growing toward a Vision," *Mercycare Corporation Magazine.* Winter 1995.

Hoban, Virginia. *St. Peter's and Paul's Church, 1862-1987, 125th Anniversary.* Canajoharie, NY, 1987.

Hoffmanns' Catholic Directory, Almanac and Clergy List—Quarterly, For the Year of Our Lord 1895. Containing Complete Reports of the Dioceses in the United States, Canada and Newfoundland, Ireland, The Vicariate-Apostolic of the Sandwich Islands and the Hierarchies in Austria-Hungary, Belgium, Germany, Great Britain and Oceania. 1, 1. Milwaukee: Hoffmann Brothers Co. 1895.

Hohenstein, Robert J. Interview, 3/4/96.

Howell, George Rogers. *Bi-Centennial History of Albany. History of the County of Albany from 1609-1886.* New York: W.W. Munsell and Co., Publishers, 1886.

Hoye, Sister Elizabeth, RSCJ. Interview, 1995.

Hubbard, Bishop Howard J. Interview, 4/18/95. Consultations, 1995-1996.

Hubbard, Bishop Howard J. Statement on the appointment of Msgr. John Nolan as Titular Bishop of Natchez and Auxiliary Bishop of the Archdiocese for Military Services, 12/14/87.

Hudson, Boyd R. Diaries: 1855, 1864, 1866, 1868, 1878, 1886. Auriesville.

Hunt, James C. Interview re German emigration. 3/4/96. Consultations, 1996.

Hurley, Francis T. "National Catholic Welfare Conference (NCWC)," *New Catholic Encyclopedia.* 10. New York: McGraw Hill Book Company, 1967.

Hyde, Louis Fiske. *History of Glens Falls, New York and Its Settlement.* Glens Falls, NY: Glens Falls Post Company, 1936.

"Improving the Cathedral," *Albany Evening Journal.* 3/30/1891.

"Improving the Cathedral," *Albany Express.* 3/31/1891.

"In Catholic Churches," *Press & Knickerbocker.* 3/30/1891.

Information Please Almanac, Atlas & Yearbook. 1995. Boston: Houghton Mifflin Co., 1995.

Ireland, John, Archbishop of St. Paul. Letter to Bishop McNeirny, 12/1/1890.

"The Irish Relief Movement," *The Argus.* 1/22/1880.

Department of the Interior. *Compendium of the Tenth Census (June 1, 1880), Compiled Pursuant to an Act of Congress Approved August 7, 1882.* Parts I and II. Washington: Government Printing Office, 1883.

Jameson, J. Franklin, ed. *Narratives of New Netherland, 1609-1664.* New York: C. Scribner's Sons, 1909.

Janson, H.W., *History of Art.* Englewood Cliffs, NJ: Prentice-Hall, Inc., 1966.

Jenks, Bro. Christopher Stephen, BSG. "The Akron Plan Sunday School." *American Religious Buildings.* 11:3. [December 1995.]

Jillisky, Rev. William F. Interview, 1995.

Jones, Msgr. John L. Interview, 2/27/95.

Joyce, Sister Maureen, RSM. Interview and consultations, 1995-96.

"Joyous Welcome Home. Reception to Bishop M'Neirny," *Knickerbocker.* [No.] 15,531. 10/6/1886.

Juet, Robert Cf. New York Historical Collections.

Kalm, Pehr. *Peter Kalm's Travels in North America.* Adolph B. Benson, ed. New York: Dover Publications, Inc., 1987.

Kane, Sr. Mary Fidelis. *The Sisters of Mercy in the Diocese of Albany 1863-1942.* Albany, NY: Sisters of Mercy, [n.d.]

Kane, Thomas P. "A History of the Church of Saint Patrick," *A Centennial Remembrance Church of Saint Patrick, Watervliet, New York, 1840-1990.* [n.p., n.d.]

Kauffman, Bill. *Country Towns of New York.* Castine, ME: Country Roads Press, 1994.

Kavanaugh, Kathy. Interviews, 1996.

Kendricks, Sophia. Interview, 1995.

Kennedy, John Harold. *Thomas Dongan, Governor of New York (1682-1688).* Washington: Catholic University of America, 1930. Reprint New York: AMS Press, 1974.

Kennedy, Roger G. *Greek Revival America,* New York: Stewart, Tabori & Chang, 1989.

Kennedy, William. *O Albany!* New York: Viking Penguin, Inc., 1983.

Kephart, Horace, ed. "The Narrative of Francisco Giuseppe Bressani, SJ, Relating His Captivity Among the Iroquois, in 1644." *Captives Among the Indians.* Oyster Bay, NY: Nelson Doubleday, 1915.

Kerns, John. Interview, 2/2/1995.

Kim, Sung Bok. *Landlord and Tenant in Colonial New York. Manorial Society 1664-1775.* Chapel Hill, NC: The University of North Carolina Press, 1978.

Kloster, Anthony. Letter to Bishop McNeirny, 9/14/1884.

Krause, Kyle. Interview, 1995.

Lefebvre, Rev. James. Interviews, 1995.

Lambert, Rev. James Henry, SM. "Venerini Sisters (MPV)," *New Catholic Encyclopedia.* 14. New York: McGraw Hill Book Company, 1967.

Lamb, Brother Andrew, FSC. Interview and consultations, 1995.

Langley, Harold David. "Temperance Movements," *New Catholic Encyclopedia.* 13. New York: McGraw Hill Book Company, 1967.

Lavin, Mother Mary of Our Lady of Sorrows, SMR. "Mary Reparatrix, Society of (SMR)," *New Catholic Encyclopedia.* 9. New York: McGraw Hill Book Company, 1967.

Leary, Sr. Mary Ancilla. *The History of Catholic Education in the Diocese of Albany.* Washington, DC: The Catholic University of America Press, 1957.

Leo XIII, Pope. "Slavery in Africa."

Light, Sally. *House Histories, A Guide to Tracing the Genealogy of Your Home.* Spencertown, NY: Golden Hill Press, 1989.

"Little Sisters mark 150th anniversary," *The Evangelist,* 9/22/90.

Littlefield, Henry W. *History of Europe 1500-1848.* New York: Barnes & Noble Inc., 1959.

Lizzi, Dominick C. *Governor Martin H. Glynn, Forgotten Hero.* Valatie, NY: Valatie Press, 1994.

Lodge, Henry Cabot, ed. *The Works of Alexander Hamilton.* 8. New York: G.P. Putnam's Sons, [n.d.]

Loding, Paul. Interview, 2/26/96, re Hudson Falls/Sandy Hook/Town of Kingsbury area.

Lomasney, Sister Eileen, CSJ. Interview, 1995.

Lord, Phil. Interview re Little Falls, Rome and German Flatts Canals. Also some on Erie Canal, 1/30/96.

Louden, M.J. *Catholic Albany, An Illustrated History of the Catholic Churches and Catholic Religious, Benevolent and Educational Institutions of the City of Albany.* Albany, NY: Peter Donnelly, 1895.

Sister M. Loyola of Jesus, OP. "Summary of the Spirit and Works of the Dominican Sisters of the American Congregation of St. Catherine de Ricci, O.P." ms. 9/5/1901.

Ludden, Rev. Patrick. Letter to Bishop McNeirny, 9/28/1885.

Mackay, Charles. *Life and Liberty in America: Sketches of a Tour in the Uniited States and Canada in 1857-8.* London: Smith, Elder and Co., 1859.

Mahoney, Sister Mary Berchmans, RSM. Many interviews, 1995-1996.

Mahoney, Neva. Interview, 1995.

Manning, Bishop Elias (née James). Interview, 5/28/96.

Manning, James H., editor. *New York State Men.* Albany, NY: The Albany Argus Art Press, 1914.

Manny, Msgr. Howard. Interview, 1995.

Marchione, Sister Margherita Frances, MPF. "Filippini, Lucy, St.," *New Catholic Encyclopedia.* 5. New York: McGraw Hill Book Company, 1967.

Martin, Michael and Gelber, Leonard. *Dictionary of American History.* Ames, IA: Littlefield, Adams & Co., 1956.

Martos, Joseph. *Doors to the Sacred, A Historical Introduction to Sacraments in the Catholic Church.* Garden City, NY: Doubleday & Company, Inc., 1982.

Marty, Martin E. *A Short History of American Catholicism.* Allen, TX: Tabor Publishing, 1995.

"May Day an Act of Faith and Patriotism." ms. ca. 1951.

Maynard, Theodore. *The Catholic Church and the American Idea.* New York: Appleton-Century-Crofts, Inc., 1953.

Maynard, Theodore. *The Story of American Catholicism.* New York: The Macmillan Co., 1941.

McAlester, Virginia & Lee. *A Field Guide to American Houses.* New York: Alfred A. Knopf, 1986.

McAvoy, Thomas T., CSC. "Americanism," *New Catholic Encyclopedia.* 1. New York: McGraw Hill Book Company, 1967.

McCaffrey, Sister Catherine, CSJ. Interview, 1995.

McCarthy, D., Bishop of Killarney. Letter to Bishop McNeirny, 3/9/1880.

McCarty, R. Paul, Taylor, Jo Ann, Turner, Pat. *History of St. Joseph's Church, Fort Edward, New York, 1869-1994.* [n.p., 1994].

McCloskey, John, Bishop of Albany. Letters to the Propagation de la Foi.

McCloskey, Cardinal John. Letter to Bishop McNeirny, 7/11/1881.

McDonough, John T. Letter to Bishop McNeirny, 6/29/1889.

McEneny, John J. *Albany, Capital City of the Hudson.* Albany, NY: Albany Institute of History and Art, 1981.

McEneny, John J. Interview and consultations, 1995-1996.

McHenry, Robert, ed. *The New Encyclopaedia Britannica.* 15th ed. Chicago, Encyclopaedia Inc., 1992.

McIncrow, J.P. [sic] Letter to Bishop McNeirny, 5/10/1883.

McGuire, Rev. Ken[neth.] Interviews, 1996.

McMartin, Barbara. "Fulton County—Tanners of World Renown." ms. Gloversville, NY: Fulton County Museum, 1982.

McMartin, Barbara. "Fulton County's Glove Industry Tells the Story of Our Country's Role in the Industrial Revolution." ms. Gloversville, NY: Fulton County Museum, 1982.

McMullen, Jane T. Interviews, 1996.

McNamara, Jo Ann Kay. *Sisters in Arms. Catholic Nuns through Two Millennia.* Cambridge, MA: Harvard University Press, 1996.

McNamara, Robert F. *The Diocese of Rochester 1868-1968.* Rochester, NY: The Diocese of Rochester, 1968.

McNamara, Robert F. *Historic St. Mary's Church, Albany, New York.* Lowell, MA: Sullivan Bros., Printers, 1973.

McNamara, Robert F. Interview and consultations, 12/94-12/96.

McNamara, Robert F. "Trusteeism," *New Catholic Encyclopedia.* 14. New York: McGraw Hill Book Company, 1967.

McNeirny, Bishop Francis, 1888 Passport.

McNeirny, Bishop Francis. Pastoral Letter.

McNeirny, Bishop Francis. Letter to Bishop Conroy, 10/4/1875.

Mendel, Mesick, Cohen, Waite Architects. *A Master Plan for the Renovation of the Cathedral of the Immaculate Conception, Albany, New York.* ms 1984.

The Merriam-Webster New Book of Word Histories. Springfield, MA: Merriam-Webster Inc., Publishers, 1991.

Mettler, Elinor. Interview, 1995.

The Metropolitan Catholic Almanac, and Laity's Directory, for the Year 1844. Baltimore, MD: Fielding Lucas, Jr., 1844.

The Metropolitan Catholic Almanac and Laity's Directory, for the Year of Our Lord 1854. Baltimore, MD: Fielding Lucas, Jr.

Middleton, Thomas. "An Old Time Catholic Pioneer of Lansingburg," *Records of the American Catholic Historical Society of Philadelphia.* VII, 10. Philadelphia, PA: American Catholic Historical Society of Philadelphia, 1896.

Millard, Mary. "St. John the Evangelist Parish, Schenectady," *The Evangelist,* 1/21/1965.

Miller, William, *A History of the United States.* New York: Dell Publishing Co., Inc. 1958.

Miller, Kerby and Wagner, Paul. *Out of Ireland. The Story of Irish Emigration to America.* Washington, DC: Elliott & Clark Publishing, 1994.

Moody, T. W. and Martin, F. X., ed. *The Course of Irish History.* Dublin: The Mercier Press, 1993.

Morris, Richard B. ed. *The Basic Ideas of Alexander Hamilton.* New York: Pocket Books, Inc., 1957.

Morrison, Rev. John A. Interview re Maronite Rite, 10/18/96.

"Mott, Lucretia," *The New Encyclopaedia Britannica.* 15th ed. 8. Chicago, Encyclopaedia Inc., 1992.

Mulcahy, Rev. John H.C. Interviews, 1995.

Mulderry, Benjamin F. Interview, 2/15/95.

Mulhall, Rev. J. Gregory. Letter to the Editor, *Times-Union,* 10/19/96.

Mullany, Rev. John F. *The Pioneer Church of the State of New York.* Syracuse, NY: St. John's Rectory, 1897.

Munsell, Joel. *Annals of Albany.* 1, 3. 4 2nd ed. Albany: J. Munsell, 1871.

Murphy, Jacqueline. Interview and consultations, 1995.

Murphy, John Dunn. Interview, 4/21/95.

Murphy, Sister M.J. Evangelist. Letter to Bishop McNeirny, 4/1/1884.

Nabozny, Rev. Peter. Interview, 1995.

Naramore, Sally B. "From the Land of Eagles: Eastern Europeans in Columbia County 1890-1990," *The Columbian Repository,* Summer 1996.

Neufeldt, Victoria and Guralnik, David B., ed. *Webster's New World Dictionary of American English.* 3rd college ed. New York: Prentice Hall, 1994.

Nevins, Albert J., MM. *The Maryknoll Catholic Dictionary*. New York: Grosset & Dunlap, 1965.

New York Landmarks Conservancy. "American Religious Buildings: The Wren-Gibbs Church," *Common Bond*. 10:3. Dec. 1994.

The New York Evangelist. 19; 12, Whole No. 939, March 23, 1848. New York. W.H. Bidwell, Editor and Proprietor. pp. 45-48.

New York State. *Laws of New York*. Book 17. Election Law. Section 8-102 & 300. Subsect. 2.

New York State. *Laws of New York. Twenty-Second Session. Chapter 72. An Act for the assessment and collection of taxes. Passed the 1st of April, 1799*.

New York in the Revolution as Colony and State. 2. Albany, NY: J.B. Lyon Company, Printers, 1904.

1910-1985, Church of Saint John the Baptist, Amsterdam, New York, Seventy-fifth Anniversary, June 8, 1985.

O'Brien, Rev. Leo. Interview, 2/9/95.

O'Brien, Rosemary. Interview, 1995.

O'Callaghan, Edmund Bailey. *The Documentary History of the State of New-York. Vol. I, II, III, IV*. Albany: Weed, Parsons & Co., Public Printers, 1850.

O'Callaghan, Edmund Bailey. *Lists of Inhabitants of Colonial New York. Excerpted from The Documentary History of the State of New-York*. Indexed by Rosanne Conway. Baltimore, MD: Genealogical Publishing Co., 1979.

O'Callaghan, Sister Mary Rosaria. "Presentation of the Blessed Virgin Mary, Sisters of the," *New Catholic Encyclopedia*. 11. New York: McGraw Hill Book Company, 1967.

O'Connor, John, CSSR. Interview, 1995.

The Official Catholic Directory. New York: P.J. Kenedy & Sons, Publishers.

O'Hare, Michelle. Interview, 1995.

Olton, Jean. Interview, 1995.

O'Mara, Rev. William Anthony. "Marriage, Cannon Law of 3. Impediments to Marriage," *New Catholic Encyclopedia*. 9. New York: McGraw Hill Book Co., 1967.

100 Years of Faith, 1883-1983, St. Mary's Oneonta.

"120th Anniversary of Our Lady Help of Christians Parish 1874-1994." Pamphlet. Albany, NY: 1994.

O'Rourke, Edward William. "National Catholic Rural Life Conference," *New Catholic Encyclopedia*. 10. New York: McGraw Hill Book Company, 1967.

Orth, Herbert W. Consultations, 1995.

Pacini, Rev. Mario and Toma, Roberta J. *Saint Rita's Roman Catholic Church, Cohoes, New York. The History of an Italian-American Parish, 1914-1983*. Troy, NY: Alchar Printing, 1983.

Pape, Rev. William H. Interview and consultations, 10/25/95.

Paret, Rev. John J. Interview, 3/28/95.

Patterson, Rev. Randall. Interview, 5/25/95.

Paul III, Pope. *Sublimis Deus*, 1537.

Pearce, B. ed. *The Albany Directory for the Year 1820*. Albany, NY: E. & E. Hosford, 1820.

Peyton, Rev. Patrick. *All for Her*. Hollywood, C.A.: Family Theater Publications, 1973.

Phelan, Rev. Thomas W. Interview, 2/22/95.

Piwonka, Ruth and Blackburn, Roderic H. *A Visible Heritage*. Kinderhook, NY: The Columbia County Historical Society, 1977.

Plavcan, Rev. James, OFM. Interview, 1995.

Pollock, Onna. Interview, 1995.

Pool, Daniel. *What Jane Austen Ate and Charles Dickens Knew*. New York: Simon & Schuster, 1993.

Powers, Rev. Thomas. Interview, 2/7/95.

"Private Schools and Academies, Albany, N.Y." Pamphlet. ca. 1906.

Pritchard, Rev. James. Interview, 3/3/95.

Provost, Rev. John. Interview, 3/6/95.

Redmond, Rev. Paul V. Interview, 2/28/95.

Reilly, Msgr. John L. Letter to Bishop Edmund F. Gibbons, June 10, 1926.

"Relief for Ireland," *Press & Knickerbocker.* 1/22/1880.

Reynolds, Rev. James A. "McCloskey, John," *New Catholic Encyclopedia.* 9. New York: McGraw Hill Company, 1967.

Rice, Rev. Patrick William. "Marriage, Canon Law of. 2. Preparation for Marriage," *New Catholic Encyclopedia,* 9. New York: McGraw Hill Book Co., 1967.

Roberts, Anne F. and Cockrell, Marcia W., ed. *Historic Albany, Its Churches and Synagogues.* Albany, NY: Library Communications Services, 1986.

Roesch, Carl. Interview, consultations and letters, 1995-1996.

Roos, Rev. John. Interview, 5/23/95.

Roos, Rev. Robert E. Interview, 4/24/95.

Roseberry, C.R. *Flashback, A Fresh Look at Albany's Past.* ed. by Susanne Dumbleton. Albany, NY: Washington Park Press Ltd., 1986.

Rouillard, Philippe, OSB. "Marian Feasts," *New Catholic Encyclopedia.* 9. New York: McGraw Hill Book Company, pp. 210-212.

Rowley, William Esmond. *Albany: A Tale of Two Cities, 1820-1880.* ms. Cambridge, MA: Harvard University, 1967.

"Ruthenian Catholic Church." *The New Encyclopaedia Britannica.* 10. Chicago: Encyclopaedia Britannica, Inc., 1976.

Ryan, Archbishop Joseph. Interview, 3/21/95.

Sacred Heart Church, Castleton, New York, 1887-1987. [n.p., n.d.]

Sadlier's Catholic Almanac and Ordo For the Year of Our Lord 1866: With a Full Report of the Various Dioceses in the United States, British North-America, and Ireland. New-York: D. & J. Sadlier & Co., 1866. [Also, 1871, 1876, 1877, 1878 and 1895.]

Saint Anne Institute, "A Brief History of Saint Anne Institute," ms. Albany: n.d. [ca. 1991]

St. Mary's Church, Little Falls, New York. So. Hackensack, NJ: Custombooks, Inc. 1979.

St. Patrick's Church, Johnstown, NY 1869-1994.

St. Mary's Parish, Hamilton, New York, 1968-1994.

Savage, Sr. Mary Lucida. *The Congregation of Saint Joseph of Carondelet, A Brief Account of Its Origins and Its Work in the United States (1650-1922).* St. Louis, MO: B. Herder Book Co., 1927.

Schlesinger, Arthur M., Jr. *The Age of Jackson.* New York: The New American Library, 1945.

Schrempf, Jeanne. Interview, 1995.

Schweigardt, Rev. Erwin H. Interview, 2/14/95.

Scruton, Bruce. "Architect subject of lecture," *Knickerbocker News.* 12/4/1984.

"Seneca Falls Convention," *The New Encyclopaedia Britannica.* 15th ed. 10. Chicago: Encyclopaedia Inc., 1992.

The Seventh Census. Report of the Superintendent of the Census for December 1, 1852; to which is appended the Report for December 1, 1851. Washington: Robert Armstrong, Printer, 1853.

"Seward, William H(enry)," *The New Encyclopaedia Britannica.* 10. Chicago: Encyclopaedia Inc., 1992.

Shannon, Joseph A. *St. Joseph's Parish, Greenwich, N.Y.,* Greenwich, NY, 1979

Shannon, Thomas Interview, 1995.

Shannon, William H. *Silent Lamp, the Thomas Merton Story.* New York: The Crossroad Publishing Co., 1992.

Shaw, Diane. "Fabricating the House of God: Religious Buildings in North America," *Vernacular Architecture Newsletter.* No. 69, Fall 1996. [Vernacular Architecture Forum]

Shaw, Michael. "Early Post-Medieval Tanning in Northampton, England," *Archaeology.* 40:2. [March/April 1987]

Shaw, Rev. Richard Denis, PhD. *Chaplains to the Imprisoned.* New York: The Haworth Press, Inc., 1995.

Shaw, Rev. Richard. *From Joques to JFK: Eleven Tales of Catholic Albany.* Albany, NY: *The Evangelist,* 1986.

Shaw, Rev. Richard. Interviews and consultations, 1995-1996.

Shaw, Richard. *John DuBois: Founding Father.* United States Catholic Historical Society, Yonkers, NY and Mount Saint Mary's College, Emmitsburg, MD, 1983.

Shea, John Gilmary. *History of the Catholic Church in the United States.* 3. New York: D.H. McBride & Co., 1890.

Shinos, Rev. Robert S. Interview, 7/10/95.

Sidoti, Rev. Anthony R. Interview, 1/31/95.

The Siena Sphere. 8 & 9, Spr. 96. Loudonville, NY: Siena College, 1996.

Sise, Rev. John. Interview, 5/23/95.

"Smith, Alfred E(manuel)," *The New Encyclopaedia Britannica.* 10. 15th ed. Chicago: Encyclopaedia, Inc., 1992.

Smith, Rev. John Talbot. *The Catholic Church in New York; A History of the New York Diocese From its Establishment in 1808 to the Present Time.* 1. New York: Hall & Locke Company, 1905.

Smock, John C. "Building Stone in the State of New York," *Bulletin of the New York State Museum of Natural History.* No. 3, March, 1888. Albany: Charles Van Benthuysen & Sons, 1888.

Smyth, Sister Mary Genevieve, RSCJ. Interview, 1995.

Souvenir-Journal, St. Joseph's Church Fair. 1, 1. January 6, 1902. Troy, NY

"Stanton, Elizabeth Cady, née Elizabeth Cady," *The New Encyclopaedia Britannica.* 15th ed. 11. Chicago: Encyclopaedia Inc., 1992.

Stasiewski, Bernhard Clemens. "Poland," *New Catholic Encyclopedia.* 11. New York: McGraw Hill Book Company.

Stritch, Thomas. *The Catholic Church in Tennessee, The Sesquicentennial Story.* Nashville, TN: The Catholic Center, 1987.

Sullivan, Robert. "The Mystery of Mary," *Life.* December 1996.

Sulzman, Paul. Interview, 1995.

Sylvester, Nathaniel Bartlett. *History of Rensselaer Co., New York.* Philadelphia, PA: Everts & Peck, 1880.

Swastek, Joseph Vincent. "Dabrowski, Joseph," *New Catholic Encyclopedia.* 4. New York: McGraw Hill Book Company, 1967.

Taylor, Sister Mary Christine, SSJ, PhD. *A History of Catholism in the North Country.* Camden, NY: A.M. Farnsworth Sons, Inc., 1972.

Taylor, Sister Mary Christine, SSJ, PhD. *A History of the Foundations of Catholicism in Northern New York.* Yonkers, NY: United States Catholic Historical Society, 1976.

Tessier, Rev. C. Henri. Interview, 2/17/95.

Thacher, John Boyd. Letter to Bishop McNeirny, 5/11/1886.

Thebaud, Rev. Augustus, SJ *Three-Quarters of a Century (1807-1882): A Retrospect.* 3. "Forty Years in the United States of America." New York: The United States Catholic Historical Society, 1904.

Thwaites, Reuben Gold. *The Jesuit Relations. Travels and Explorations of the Jesuit Missionaries in New France 1610-1791. I. Acadia 1610-1613. XXXI. Iroquois, Lower Canada, Abenakis. XXXIX. Hurons 1653.* Cleveland: The Burrows Company, 1896.

Thompson, John H., ed. *New York State.* Syracuse, NY: Syracuse University Press, 1966.

Torrey, Marion. Interview and consultations, 1995.

Tower, John, Bishop of Waterford. Letter to Bishop McNeirny, 3/27/1880.

Traver, Mary Anne. Interview, 1995.

Tremblay, Rev. Nellis. Interview, 12/8/95.

Turbin, Carole. *Working Women in the Collar City.* Urbana, IL: University of Illinois Press, 1994.

Turley, Sister Kathleen, RSM. Interview, 1995.

Turnbull, Rev. William D. Letter, 12/6/96.

Tyrrell, William G. *A Century of Spiritual Service, Church of Saint Vincent de Paul, Albany, New York 1885-1985.* Albany, NY: Church of St. Vincent de Paul, 1985.

Urban, Rev. Carl A. Letter, 12/5/96.

Valden, Diane. "Irish famine remembered; Local landscaper designs memorial," *The Independent.* 23;82, 3/96.

Vadnais, Paul. "Catholic Youths Pray for Russia," *Times-Union.* 5/24/48.

Vail, Rev. Thomas J. Interview, 7/10/95.

Valden, Diane. "The Irish potato famine," *The Independent.* 23;82.

Van Biema, David. "Mary, So Contrary," *Time.* 148. 28. December 23, 1996.

Vierzehnte General-Versammlung des D.R.K. Staats-Verbandes von New York am 30-31 Mai & 1 Juni, 1909, Schenectady, N.Y. [the 14th Assembly of the United States German Roman Catholics of New York, May 30-31 and June 1, 1909, Schenectady, N.Y.]

Visions of New York State, The Historical Paintings of L.F. Tantillo. Wappingers Falls, NY: The Shawangunk Press, 1996.

von Simson, Otto. *The Gothic Cathedral.* Princeton, NJ: Princeton University Press, 1988.

Vosko, Rev. Richard S. Consultations, 1995.

Xavier, Sister Anne, CSJ. Interview, 1995.

Waite, John G. & Waite, Diana S. *Industrial Archeology in Troy, Waterford, Cohoes, Green Island, and Watervliet.* Troy, NY: Hudson-Mohawk Industrial Gateway, 1973.

Walworth, C.A. *Reminiscences of Edgar P. Wadhams, First Bishop of Ogdensburg.* 12d ed. New York: Benziger Brothers, 1893.

Walworth, Clarence E. *The Oxford Movement in America.* Reprint ed. 1895. New York: United States Catholic Historical Society, 1974.

Walworth, Ellen H. *Life Sketches of Father Walworth with Notes and Letters.* Albany, NY: J.B. Lyon Company, Printers, 1907.

Weed, Thurlow. Letter to Bishop McCloskey, 9/2/1850.

Weise, Arthur James. *The City of Troy and Its Vicinity.* Troy, NY: Edward Green, 1886.

Wheeler, Sister Elaine, DC. Interview and consultations, 1995-96.

Wheeler, Sister Mary C., RSCJ. Interview, 1995.

Whitaker, Mrs. Raymond et al. *The St. Pius X... 25th Anniversary as a parish.* [1976]

Weiser, Francis X., SJ. *Kateri Tekakwitha.* Caughnawaga, P.Q., Canada: Kateri Center, 1972.

Williams, Craig. Interviews re eastern terminus of canal. 2/96.

Woodlock, Bartholomew, Bishop of Newtonforbes, Co. Lonagford. Letter to Bishop, 3/10/1880.

Woodworth, John. *Reminiscences of Troy, from Its Settlement in 1790, to 1807.* Albany, NY: Joel Munsell, 1853.

Worth, Gorham A. *Random Recollections of Albany from 1800-1808.* 3rd ed. Albany, NY: J. Munsell, 1866.

"Yale University," *New England, A Collection From Harper's Magazine.* New York: W.H. Smith Publishers, Inc. 1990.

Young, Rev. Peter. Interview, 4/27/95.

Zander, Mary. Interview and consultations, 1995-1996.

"1821-1832, Steps Toward Equalitarianism," *The Annals of America.* 5. Chicago: Encyclopaedia Britannica, Inc. 1976.

NOTES